Colin Dyer has a doctorate in history from the University of Caen in France, and is research adviser in the School of Language and Comparative Cultural Studies at the University of Queensland. He has written several books in French, including *La France revisitée* (1989), as well as a number of works in English — most recently *A Frenchman's Walk across the Nullabor* (2000).

The FRENCH EXPLORERS *and the* ABORIGINAL AUSTRALIANS

1772–1839

Colin Dyer

First published 2005 by University of Queensland Press
Box 6042, St Lucia, Queensland 4067 Australia

www.uqp.uq.edu.au

Typeset by University of Queensland Press
Printed in Australia by McPherson's Printing Group

Distributed in the USA and Canada by
International Specialized Books Services, Inc.,
5824 N.E. Hassalo Street, Portland, Oregon 97213–3640

 This book has been published with the financial support
of the Embassy of France in Australia.
*Ce livre est publié avec
le soutien financier de l'Ambassade
de France en Australie.*

Cataloguing in Publication Data
National Library of Australia

Dyer, Colin L.
 The French Explorers and the Aboriginal
 Australians 1772-1839

 Bibliography.
 Includes index.

 1. Explorers – Australia. 2. French – Australia – History.
 3. Aboriginal Australians. 4. Australia – Discovery and
 Exploration. I. Title

994

ISBN 0 7022 3512 1

Contents

85 12/5/05

Preface

MY aim in this book is to enable readers to make as close an acquaintance as possible directly with the French explorers and the Aboriginal Australians during their encounters. To this end I have endeavoured to absent myself from the text as much as possible, and to allow the participants to speak for themselves.

While the book must necessarily have a certain overall personal analysis to permit an organised plan of presentation, I have no personal axe to grind (of which I am aware), no thesis or argument to prove, no preconceived conclusion to impose. Rather, by presenting what is essentially the evidence, I hope to enable the readers, if they so wish, to draw their own conclusions, to form their own arguments, or indeed perhaps to create their own axe.

As I am of course also myself a reader of this book — the writer reads as he writes — it is not always easy to be indifferent to the subject in hand. Some of the material in fact at times appears quite outrageous and even shocking. Some of the French interpretations can seem too culturally unilateral, or 'blinkered'. My own interpretation of the French interpretations of the Aboriginal Australians, however, if expressed, could be but one among endless others, and could form an obstacle to readers who may wish to form their own opinion.

My aim, to use a culinary image, is to offer the ingredients, and not the prepared recipe. This is doubtless an impossible task in this context, but I have done my best.

A note on vocabulary

THE significance of the words 'sauvage' in French or 'savage' in English (from the Latin 'silvaticus', of the forest) may not be the same today as two centuries ago. Today, according to *Le Petit Larousse illustré*, 2001, the French adjective 'sauvage' means only 'féroce', 'cruel' or 'violent', although the noun still retains the 'old sense' of 'who is not civilised, who has a primitive mode of life'.[1] The English adjective 'savage' also has these meanings of 'fierce', 'ferocious' or 'cruel', and the noun may indicate a 'cruel or fierce person'.[2]

At the end of the eighteenth century, however, the French word 'sauvage' may have had quite different connotations. In 1755 Jean-Jacques Rousseau had proposed that 'civilised' man was inferior to the 'sauvage' in many ways. 'I venture to declare,' he wrote, 'that a state of reflection is contrary to nature, and that a thinking [i.e. 'civilised'] man is a depraved animal.' He also considered that there was 'a greater difference between savage and civilised man than between wild and tame beasts: for ... the several conveniences in which men indulge themselves ... are so many additional causes of their deeper degeneracy'.[3] By 1758 'natural' man had become quite generally superior. 'Everything is good in nature,' proclaimed Denis Diderot; 'it is the miserable conventions which pervert mankind and not human nature which should be accused.'[4] Rousseau also expressed this idea quite firmly in 1762 in his famous remark: 'Everything is good as it comes from the hands of the Maker of the world, but degenerates once it gets into the hands of man'.[5] Some (including Voltaire) suggested rather maliciously that Rousseau (who had never ventured outside Europe) dreamed of becoming a primitive person himself, but he responded that 'human nature does not go backward, and it is never possible to return to the times of innocence ... once they have been left behind'.[6]

These philanthropic outlooks appeared to be supported at the time by reports from the French explorers Wallis (in 1767) and Louis de Bougainville (1768), on the idyllic life-styles of the Tahitians, and would still be reflected by D'Entrecasteaux in 1792–93 regarding the Tasmanians. Already then, however, the 'noble savage' (or *bon sauvage*) image had been rather tarnished by the murder of Marion Dufresne in New Zealand in 1772 and of Captain Cook in Hawaii in 1779, and then by Lapérouse's declaration of disillusionment in 1788 and Baudin's experiences in 1802. By the nineteenth century this ideology received a further blow with the growth of commercial (and perhaps military) interests, combined with the need to find an emplacement for convicts and to 'show the flag' in these distant parts. Finally, at the end of the twentieth century the word *sauvage*, according to the *Dictionnaire historique de la langue française*, 'is felt to be unduly pejorative, and is proscribed'.[7]

The French explorers also called the people they met *les naturels*, meaning 'an inhabitant originating from a country'. This word, however, explains Littré in his *Dictionnaire de la langue française* in 1885, 'is not used when speaking of civilised nations'. Littré quotes Buffon as an example: 'New Holland,' he wrote, 'is a low-lying land without water, without mountains, sparsely inhabited, of which "les naturels" are "sauvages" [used as an adjective here] and not industrious'.[8] This word is now considered *vieilli*[9] (i.e. outdated). I have translated this as 'natives'.

The French also use the word *natifs*, meaning someone born of a country, which I have of course also translated as 'natives'.

The word *Australie* does not appear in these French journals until 1825 (when Hyacinthe de Bougainville spoke of *les naturels de l'Australie*,[10] although the noun 'Australiens' was used in 1824 to indicate the indigenous people.[11] The word 'aborigène' appears only in 1831 (when Cyrille Laplace would write of 'les aborigènes de la Nouvelle-Galles du Sud'.[12]

English usage seems to have been similar. 'The nineteenth century was well within its second quarter,' wrote Ernest Scott in his *Life of Matthew Flinders*, 'before the name New Holland gave place … to the more convenient and euphonious designation: Australia.'[13] The word 'Aborigine' (from the Latin *ab origine*, from the beginning) also seems to have come into use at this time. Both words indeed are seen in the title of a book published in 1830 in London by Robert Dawson, *The Present State of Australia; a Description of the Country … and of Its Aboriginal Inhabitants*. Dawson had been Chief Agent in Sydney since 1825 (and until 1829) of the Australian Agricultural Company.

The French referred to the mainland generally as 'la Nouvelle-Hollande', and to Tasmania (which was confirmed to be an island in 1798) as 'la terre de Van-Diémen'.

Finally, the spelling of people's names may vary here, as they did in the original texts when orthographical homogeneity was much less required than today. D'Entrecasteaux, for example, spelled his name thus in his signature,[14] although his colleague Rossel would spell this 'Dentrecasteaux' in his publication of the explorer's memoirs. Louis Freycinet's name is written thus on the title page to the *Voyage de découvertes* in 1815, but 'Louis de Freycinet' on the title page to his *Voyage autour du monde* in 1839.[15]

The expeditions

French explorers in Australia in the late-eighteenth and early-nineteenth centuries were neither few nor far between. They came and they saw, but they made no attempt to conquer. They did, however, on many an occasion make acquaintance with the indigenous people, and these encounters are the subject of our interest here. The French visited Australia (then called New-Holland) from north to south (including Tasmania, then called Van Diemen's Land) and east to west, and their relations with the indigenous people varied from the most friendly to the extremely hostile.

Ten French expeditions established such relations over the sixty to seventy years examined in this book.

The first, led by Marion Dufresne, arrived in Australia in 1772. He was followed by Lapérouse in 1788, and then Bruny d'Entrecasteaux (searching for Lapérouse) in 1792 and 1793. Nicolas Baudin would stop here in 1801, 1802 and 1803, and then Louis de Freycinet in 1818 and 1819. Louis-Isidore Duperrey arrived in 1824, followed by Hyacinthe de Bougainville one year later. Dumont d'Urville visited in 1826, then Cyrille Laplace in 1831, and then D'Urville once again in 1839. The longest interval between visits was thus sixteen years, and the shortest just one.

Marion Dufresne set out from Mauritius (then called Isle de France) in October 1771, with two ships, *Le Marquis de Castries* and *Le Mascarin*, and arrived in what is now called Marion Bay (some 50 kilometres east of today's Hobart) where he dropped anchor on 6 March 1772. Here he and his colleagues became the first Europeans to see and communicate with the Indigenous inhabitants of Tasmania. Dufresne had in fact landed at almost exactly the same spot as Abel Tasman had in 1642, but Tasman had seen no one, although, he wrote, 'we suspected that some [inhabitants] scrutinized our movements and doings with watchful eyes'.[1] (It was Tasman who, on his map of 1644, gave the name 'New-Holland' to the future Australia). Dufresne stayed here for four days before sailing to the North Island of today's New Zealand, which he named *France Australe*, and where, three months later, with twenty-five of his crew, he was killed and eaten by Maoris.

After Dufresne's death one of his companions, Julien Crozet, took command of his ship. Dufresne's journal having been lost, it is that of Crozet which serves as one of the sources of the information in this book. Other journals still in existence are those of Ambroise Duclesmeur (captain of *Le Marquis de Castries*) and three other crew members: Lieutenant Le Dez, and ensigns Jean Roux and Paul Chevillard de Montesson. A major aim of Dufresne's expedition was to return Aotourou, a Polynesian who had travelled to France in 1768 with Louis de Bougainville's expedition, to his home in Tahiti. Dufresne, however, also took the opportunity to explore the southern seas along the way.

When first anchoring in Tasmania, Crozet had seen 'about 30 men who were assembled on the shore' and, the day before departure, his colleague Jean Roux would conclude: 'I have seen very few children among the women, and ... I have not seen more than 300 men'. Duclesmeur noted that the inhabitants appeared to 'live in troupes of 50 to 60 men and women altogether'.[2]

The next expedition is that of Jean-François de Galaup de Lapérouse (as he signed his name himself)[3] who stayed in Botany Bay in January 1788 — arriving just six days after Captain Phillip and the First Fleet — before sailing north and disappearing without a trace with his two ships *L'Astrolabe* and *La Boussole*. Lapérouse's journal does not mention the Indigenous people, but some of his correspondence makes reference to relations with '*les Indiens de la Nouvelle-Hollande*' as he called them.

Three years later, an expedition led by Bruny d'Entrecasteaux was sent to search for Lapérouse. D'Entrecasteaux had two ships, *La Recherche*, commanded by himself and having on board Lieutenant Paul de Rossel and the naturalist Jacques de Labillardière, and *L'Espérance*, under the command of Huon de Kermadec. These two vessels arrived in Tasmania for the first time in April 1792 then set out for New Caledonia, Vanikoro and New Guinea before circling Australia down its west and south coasts and returning to Tasmania in January 1793. D'Entrecasteaux died in July of that year. His journal, however, was put together and published by his colleague Rossel, who assures us that he took 'every care to put in order and to preserve [the original] in all its simplicity'.[4] Labillardière (thus spelled by himself) published his own journal in 1800.[5] Other members of this expedition also kept records of their encounters, including D'Hesmivy d'Auribeau (lieutenant), Louis Ventenat (chaplain), Louis-Auguste Deschamps and Jean-Louis Féron (fusiliers) on *La Recherche*, and La Motte du Portail on *L'Espérance*. Many places in Australia today recall names from this expedition, including the D'Entrecasteaux Channel, Bruny Island with its Labillardière State Reserve and Ventenat Point, Huonville, the Esperance River and Recherche Bay in Tasmania, and Esperance, Kermadec Island and the Archipelago of the Recherche in Western Australia.

D'Entrecasteaux's official *Instructions*, however, show that much more was expected of him than solely to search for his predecessor. In the first part of Louis XVI's instructions (drawn up by the Comte de Fleurieu, who had also drafted those for Lapérouse), entitled *Mémoire du Roi pour servir d'instruction particulière au sieur Bruny-Dentrecasteaux*, we see that the expedition was to have a keen anthropological interest. The leader, we read, 'will seek to know the ways of life and customs of the natives [*naturels*], their ... manner of making war, weapons, boats, the character of each nation, what it can have in common with other savage nations [*nations sauvages*] and with civilized peoples'.[6] The next four parts of the *Mémoire* are 'the same as those given to Lapérouse' and D'Entrecasteaux is simply instructed to refer to these.

Part IV is entitled *Of the Conduct to be observed with the Natives of the Countries where the two Frigates may make a Landing* and expresses in detail sentiments altogether worthy of the Age of Enlightenment. Exchanges of 'merchandizes of objects', it says, were to be 'invited', but the expedition leader 'will regulate the value of these exchanges, and will never allow any one to surpass the price which shall be fixed on each article of trade'. The leader was also 'to recommend to every person among the crews, to live in a good understanding with the natives, to endeavour to conciliate their friendship by a proper way of acting and respect; and must forbid them … ever to employ force for taking from the inhabitants what they may not be willing to part with … On every occasion [he] will act with great mildness and humanity towards the different people he may have any intercourse with during his voyage'. 'His Majesty', it concluded, 'will look upon it as one of the most successful parts of the expedition that it may be terminated without costing the life of a single man.'

In similar vein, Part V required that the safety of the crews be assured. 'Knowing the intentions of his Majesty', we read, 'with regard to the conduct he should observe towards the savage nations … [the leader] will certainly foresee what particular care he ought to pay to the preservation of the crews employed in the expedition.'[7]

The resemblance between these instructions and those given to Abel Tasman (by the United Netherlands Chartered East Indian Company) a century and a half before could appear almost too striking to be coincidental. Tasman was told to 'find out … the form and appearance of the inhabitants, their clothing, weapons, customs, manners … [and] war'. He was also instructed to show them 'various samples of goods in order to find out what wares and materials they have, and what they want … in return' and to 'make contact properly and amicably with them'. 'All insolence and hostility towards the discovered peoples,' he was told, '[you] will carefully prevent.'[8]

Lapérouse himself had had serious reservations about many of his instructions even before setting out, and his subsequent Australian and other experiences would confirm his beliefs. He conveyed these to his 'good friend' the Comte de Fleurieu in a letter from Botany Bay on 7 February 1788, but Fleurieu appears to have taken little or no notice of them when drawing up instructions for D'Entrecasteaux. 'My opinion,' Lapérouse had said, 'concerning barbarous nations was long since fixed, and my voyage has only served to confirm it.' '*J'ai trop, à mes périls, appris à les connaître.*' ['I have learned too well at my peril, to know them.'] 'I am however,' he continued, 'more angry with the philosophers who extol the savages than with the savages themselves.'

In this, his last letter, he says that he planned to 'sail from Botany Bay on the 15th of March' but expected to have 'very mischievous people to visit' in 'the island situated to the south east of New Guinea' (where he will disappear). However, he wrote, 'I do not answer for not firing a few cannon-shot at them; for I am convinced that fear alone can prevent the effect of their bad intentions.' He hoped to arrive at *isle de France* (renamed Mauritius by the British in 1810) in December of that year, and then back in France in June 1789.[9]

Although D'Entrecasteaux failed to find any trace of Lapérouse, and both he and his second-in-command Huon de Kermadec died before being able to return to France, his expedition is nevertheless of great interest, for he and his colleagues kept detailed accounts of their encounters with the indigenous inhabitants — and perhaps of especial interest with those in Tasmania where, after some forty years of European settlement, these people will become virtually extinct. On one occasion in Tasmania this expedition met with some fifty inhabitants: '4 old men [over 50], 6 men [from 15 to 45], 14 women ... and 24 children,' noted D'Auribeau in 1793.[10] The total complement of D'Entrecasteaux's ships was over four times this number: 113 men on *La Recherche* and 106 on *L'Espérance*.[11]

The next French expedition to arrive in Australia was led by Nicolas Baudin who, like so many of his unhappy predecessors, will die before returning home. Sponsored by Napoleon, Baudin set out from Le Havre on 19 October 1800 with two ships, *Le Géographe* and *Le Naturaliste* (the latter commanded by Captain Hamelin). The expedition carried a team of scientists interested — as the ships' names suggest — essentially in the fields of geography and natural history. As sources here we have the journal of Baudin himself, and those of the zoologist François Péron (also on *Le Géographe*), of Lieutenant Pierre Bernard Milius and of a junior officer, Louis de Freycinet (both on *Le Naturaliste*).

The aim of Baudin's voyage, as set out in his instructions (drawn up again by Fleurieu), was to examine 'in detail the south-west, west, north-west and north coasts of New Holland' as well as the east coast and Van Diemen's Land, in order 'to know the entire coast line of this great south land'. Regarding his conduct 'towards the natives of the countries he may visit' and 'the manifold precautions to take for preserving the health of the crews', Baudin — like D'Entrecasteaux — was simply referred to 'the instructions which were given to General La Pérouse [sic]'.[12] There was thus no evolution at all in the nature of these instructions. In his journal, however, François Péron would note the importance of the advice of a young member of the newly-formed (and to be short-lived) *Societé des Observateurs de l'Homme*,[13] Joseph-Marie Degérando, who, he said, 'prepared for us an interesting work on the rules to be followed in the observation of barbarous nations'.[14]

Degérando clearly appears to have learnt from the experiences of earlier expeditions, for the first six pages of his work examine the 'faults in the observations made up to the present'. He then suggests to future explorers what they might do, and how they might set about it. 'The first means to the proper knowledge of the Savages,' he wrote, 'is to become after a fashion like one of them, and it is by learning their language that we shall become their fellow citizens.' Few French explorers had lingered long enough to learn a language (although some had made lists of vocabulary), but some of Degérando's other advice would have had more practical application, especially perhaps on first encounter. 'Explorers have failed to consider sufficiently,' he said, 'that their presence was bound to be a natural source of fear, defiance and reserve … [and] that a community might be gentle and sociable, and yet believe itself in a state of natural war with strangers whose intentions are unknown.' 'One should first leave time,' he suggested, 'for the reactions of astonishment, terror and anxiety … to be dispelled.' Among the many subjects he examined, Degérando looked into the question of property, which had caused the French (and other explorers) much confusion. 'Has a savage people the idea of property?' he asked. 'If it is a grazing or hunting tribe, it lacks no doubt the idea of territorial property; but has it not at least the idea of property in its instruments, and in the objects won by its efforts?' Degérando proposed that, because 'often explorers make the savage reason as we do, so they often pronounce excessively severe judgements on a society accused of cruelty, theft, licentiousness and atheism'. In a word, one needed to put oneself in the place of the others in order to understand them better. 'Explorers,' he continued, 'historically judge the customs of Savages by analogies drawn from our own customs, when in fact they are so little related to each other.'[15]

The final recommendation in Degérando's memoir could appear to be strangely out of step with the rest of his advice. 'We shall not finish,' he wrote, 'without recommending to the travellers to bring back for us if they can Savages of both sexes … [and] it would be desirable if a whole family could be persuaded to come back … [as this] would better preserve their natural characteristics … and make the spectacle of their life more interesting and instructive for us.' Bringing back such live anthropological specimens (for this is clearly how they were seen) was important because, thought Degérando, 'we should [thus] have in miniature the model of that society in which they were reared'. 'So the naturalist,' he continued, 'is not content to bring back a branch, a flower that is soon withered; he tries to bring back the whole plant, to give it a second life in our soil.' Although today such advice seems not enlightened at all, the Dutch, British and French explorers had all taken indigenous people (voluntarily or otherwise) away from their homelands in the seventeenth and eighteenth centuries, usually with the most unhappy results. In November 1789, to give but one example, Governor Phillip had ordered that some 'natives' be captured and brought to Sydney. 'The noise of the men crying and screaming,' reported Lieutenant Bradley (responsible for their capture), 'was really of a most distressing scene.'[16]

Consciously or not we do not know, but Baudin did not follow this recommendation. In the very last words of his *Observations*, however (just three pages later), Degérando would appear to be more fraternal when he declares that, in their aims, the travellers should 'aspire only to the good of all' and would thus, upon their return, be 'the bearers of happy tidings of our brothers scattered in the uttermost confines of the Universe'.[17]

In late May 1801 Baudin arrived off the shores of west Australia, and then sailed to Timor. From here he travelled back down the west coast of Australia and to Tasmania where he arrived in the D'Entrecasteaux Channel in January 1802. After a few days here, *Le Géographe* set off north, and in April crossed the Bass Strait and met Matthew Flinders at what is now called Encounter Bay. Although the pitiful health of his crew, racked by scurvy, required him to make speed for Port Jackson and immediate assistance, Baudin instead turned south again for Tasmania, and would not arrive off Port Jackson until mid-June, when his crew would be too weak to sail into the harbour without help from the British! Baudin, indeed, 'had only four men in a fit condition to be on duty'. François Péron described the appalling condition of his colleagues.

> On their bodies rose up in different places, tumours covered with black scabs; all over their skin, at the base of the hair, were small round wine-coloured spots. Their joints stiffened, their flexor muscles seemed to shorten and so held their limbs half-flexed. But nothing could be more repulsive than the appearance of their faces: to the leaden colour common to scurvy patients were added swollen gums sticking out of their mouth showing dead patches and other ulcers … The completely weak state of these unfortunate people did not prevent them having full possession of their intellectual faculties, which only allowed them to feel more acutely their hopeless situation.[18]

This situation, among a civilised people on an expedition for which the food and hygiene had been meticulously planned, was much worse than anything Péron would ever see among the indigenous peoples.

The French stayed at Port Jackson for five months, during which they were offered every assistance by their hosts. 'The Governor [King] having give us open credit on the Public Treasury,' wrote Péron, 'our Captain [Baudin] was issued with vouchers bearing the Royal stamp, that he could make out for whatever sum he thought convenient.' 'The behaviour of the English authorities to us was so splendid and generous,' he acknowledged, 'that it would be unworthy of all the principles of honour and justice not to record the expression of our gratitude.'[19]

Baudin left Port Jackson in November, and set forth to the south. Governor King feared Baudin was about to claim Van Diemen's Land for France so hastily set the schooner *Cumberland* and Acting-Lieutenant Robbins (with seventeen crew, in face of Baudin's 170) to pre-empt the French. Robbins found Baudin on King Island — quietly catching insects and collecting plants with no tricolour in sight — and fastened a British flag to a tree. While this could have caused offence, it fortunately did not. 'This childish ceremony was ridiculous,' wrote Baudin to King on 23 December 1802, 'and the flag ... was upside down and in a not very dignified position ... I thought at first it might have been a flag which had served to strain water and then hung out to dry.' The *Cumberland* having lost an anchor, Baudin's 'forge worked two days' to help Robbins replace it, and also provided him with 'gunpowder, sails, thread, needles, lead and sounding line, old ropes, etc'.[20]

From King Island Baudin sailed west and stopped in King George Sound in February 1803 before continuing north to Shark Bay on the west coast. From here he set out for France, but died of tuberculosis at Isle-de-France on 16 September.

The greatest number of inhabitants Baudin had encountered at one time would appear to have been at Shark Bay (Western Australia) in March 1903 when a landing-party had been unable to go ashore 'because a band of natives, which the men numbered at more than a hundred' had opposed them. However, Baudin himself admitted that estimates varied from 'as high as two hundred' to just 'thirty or forty' according to how frightened the crewmen in question had been.[21] The French themselves were not numerous. While in Australian waters Baudin's ships *Le Géographe* and *Le Naturaliste* had been manned by only some twenty people on each vessel, several having left ship 'for health or other reasons' before arriving in Australia.[22]

The next explorer, Louis de Freycinet (who had travelled with Baudin), would, unlike his predecessors, arrive back in France safe and sound, despite being shipwrecked in the Falkland Islands on the way. Unlike his predecessors too, he was accompanied by his wife Rose, whose diary will be of interest to us here.

Freycinet set out in the corvette *Uranie* from Toulon on 17 September 1817 and arrived at Shark Bay exactly a year later, before setting off for Timor and Hawaii and thence to Sydney in November and December 1819, where he was generously welcomed by Governor Macquarie. Some have tried to ascribe a political motive for Freycinet's expedition (as had been ascribed to Baudin's) but his aim would appear to be purely scientific. 'The principal object of the expedition,' we read in the official 'Report made to the Academy of Sciences', dated 23 April 1821, 'was the investigation of the figure of the earth, and of the elements of territorial magnetism; [and] several questions of meteorology … Though no professed naturalist was attached to the expedition, our navigators undertook the task of collecting for the Museums … [and] finally it was to be expected that Captain Freycinet and his companions would add new particulars to the history of the savage nations.'[23] Jacques Arago, who kept detailed records of the voyage, is our major source here. In Shark Bay the expedition had encountered 'about fifteen' inhabitants,[24] and in and around Sydney they had of course made the acquaintance of many more.

The next expedition that set out for the South Pacific was in 1822 and commanded by Louis-Isidore Duperrey, with Dumont d'Urville as executive officer and René-Primavère Lesson as physician. In the corvette *La Coquille*, Duperrey circumnavigated the globe from east to west, past Cape Horn and across the Pacific to New Guinea, before going down the west coast of Australia and around to Sydney, where he stayed in February and March 1824. A major aim of this expedition was to explore the possibilities for commercial exploitation and colonisation as well as matters of scientific interest concerning terrestrial magnetism. Duperrey also had specific instructions which would cause the British authorities some concern. In the *Itinerary of the Voyage of Discovery ordered by his Excellency m. le marquis de Clermont-Tonnerre, Minister for the navy and colonies* we read that Duperrey was to 'put in to … the south-west coast of New Holland, principally to examine the nature of the soil at Swan River and King George Sound and to see whether this part of New Holland is suitable for a colony'. The Minister recalled too that this part of Australia (i.e. Western Australia) 'was discovered and possession taken of … in the name of the King of France by Saint-Allouarn' back in 1772. Fortunately perhaps for Franco-British relations, Duperrey failed to do this. 'Contrary winds,' he wrote to the Minister on 15 February 1824, 'carried me a long way from the coasts of New Holland and did not allow me to put in at Swan River … Had I persevered with this plan I would have wasted an enormous amount of time.'[25] While a guest of the British in Sydney, however, this French expedition had several encounters with the Aboriginal people, and both Lesson and D'Urville wrote in detail of their experiences.

Shortly after Duperry's visit the British took steps to pre-empt any attempts by the French at colonisation. Late in 1826 the Governor of New South Wales, Sir Ralph Darling, received instructions from London to send a contingent of soldiers and convicts to King George Sound, and on Christmas Day of that year this part of Australia was formally annexed. Then, in May 1829, Captain Fremantle, near the mouth of the Swan River, would confirm British claims to the entire western coast.

The visit to Port Jackson in 1825 by Baron Hyacinthe de Bougainville (son of the earlier explorer Louis-Antoine de Bougainville) was to be in the best traditions of true adventure and romance. Hyacinthe had received nothing less than the *Most Secret*

Instructions from his Minister for the Navy and Colonies (the Marquis de Clermont-Tonnerre) regarding his visit, and would fall passionately in love with a beautiful woman from Sydney's high society, whom he would have to leave and never see again.

An experienced sailor and officer (he had been with Baudin's expedition already in 1802), Hyacinthe sailed from Brest on 2 March 1824 with two ships, *Le Thétis* and *L'Espérance*, and set out for the China Sea and the South Pacific. His official instructions were not unusual: to continue research in hydrography, and to observe the commercial activity and resources of the countries he visited. Just before departure, however, he received a personal letter (dated 17 February) containing the *Most Secret Instructions*. 'Europe is at present enjoying a period of peace …' noted the Minister. 'However, in the event of war breaking out … [and if] England were to become our enemy, the French navy may as a result of our forward planning enjoy considerable success … But for this to happen, we must have at our disposal precise information concerning the fortifications of the targeted positions [i.e. Sydney]. You must therefore attempt to gather such information, while at the same time taking every precaution to avoid acting in any way which may arouse the suspicion of others as to our secret plans.' Bougainville would appear to have been successful in this undercover work during the months of July, August and September 1825, for he was cordially wined and dined by his British hosts, and invited to explore Sydney and its environs at his leisure. On his return to France in June 1826, he submitted a full report to the Minister on the defences of Port Jackson, and detailed information on the garrisons of Sydney and Parramatta, Newcastle, Port Macquarie, Moreton Bay and even Melville Island.

Bougainville also made an interesting observation on the problems the Sydney authorities might have should an enemy appear upon the horizon. 'As well as the enemy,' he wrote, 'they would probably have to fight approximately 19 000 convicts who would be motivated by the desire to regain their freedom and thus are likely to form an alliance with anyone who would provide them with an opportunity to do so.' Having said this, however, Bougainville paid his hosts a handsome compliment. 'Australia,' he wrote, 'is a model of what can be achieved by the spirit of colonisation and perseverance, and any civilized nation ought to strive to imitate rather than destroy such a magnificent organisation.' On leaving Port Jackson, he said, 'we regretfully bade farewell to a country where we had been the object of such deep regard and kindness ... We left behind some good friends'.[26]

Although among these friends he named Captain John Piper, Sir John Jamison, Police Superintendent Nicholas de Rossy, harbour-master John Nicholson, surveyor-general John Oxley and others, Bougainville does not mention at all in his official publications a person to whom he had become passionately attached, and for whom indeed he may have delayed his departure for several days. Her name was Harriott (née Blaxland) and she was married to a merchant from Calcutta, Alexander Ritchie.

The story of this romantic encounter is to be found only in Bougainville's personal diary. It would have little interest in an official report. It does, however, show that, while life at sea could pose the ever-present dangers of shipwreck, of sickness and disease, of hostile encounters with inhabitants and privation from the joys of everyday life at home, there could be moments of relief in pleasant company and society.

The first time Hyacinthe and Harriott appear to have met was at the home of Harriott's father, on Sunday 21 August where, wrote Hyacinthe, 'we had a pleasant dinner and spent an enjoyable evening'. 'Three pretty young ladies were present', he noticed, among whom 'Mrs Ritchie is jolly and lively'. Two weeks later he met 'the attractive Blaxland family' again and invited them to come aboard his ship for lunch, and that evening attended a ball in his honour at which Harriott was present and where Hyacinthe himself danced, he thought, 'not too badly for a 40-year-old adolescent' (he was 43). On Saturday 10 September he was at Captain Piper's house where 'there was a charming small ball where I danced like a young beau'. Again Harriott was present. 'Mrs Ritchie,' declared Hyacinthe, 'is a beautiful woman with a jealous husband.' The next day saw them together at the Blaxland residence where, in the company of others, a 'very merry' and 'most pleasant' evening was spent. The next morning Hyacinthe breakfasted with the Blaxlands, and bade what he thought would be 'our last farewell'. 'I found,' he wrote, 'that I was more and more attracted to Mrs Ritchie, perhaps a little too much.' Harriott's husband, Alexander, we shall see, certainly thought it was too much. On Friday 16 September Hyacinthe was preparing to sail. By now his emotions were explicit. 'At 11.30', he wrote, 'I went and fetched my beloved (Mrs R.) and Mrs de Rossy and accompanied both ladies back to the ship' where they took lunch. In the evening they went to Captain Piper's home, where, wrote the Frenchman, 'I wooed the lady in question most assiduously despite the jealous husband, made rapid progress and fixed a *rendez-vous* for the next day'. That day saw him at the home of William Balcombe (colonial treasurer) with Harriott where he says 'we enjoyed a romantic *tête-à-tête* and promised to meet the next day at midnight on board'. The situation was becoming quite serious. That next day, however, was not to be the joyous one Hyacinthe had hoped. 'Received a letter form Mrs R.,' he wrote, 'who has … a prior engagement. I suffered from deep melancholy, struck off a reply and felt indisposed. Our preparations for casting off have been interrupted … Mrs R. haunts my thoughts … Beloved Harriott!' The following day he dined on shore at 'a very merry session' where 'Mr and Mrs R. were seated next to each other to my deep chagrin'. Alexander Ritchie must have expressed his feelings to his wife, for he certainly did to her suitor. 'Letter from Mr R.', noted Hyacinthe, who feared greatly 'the prospect of being confronted with an angry husband', and probably 'the angriest in the world'.

He never saw Harriott again. On Wednesday 21 September he set sail from Sydney harbour and 'at 4.30 pm', he wrote, 'we lost sight of the lighthouse from the topmast … I shall perhaps never again set eyes on those shores where … I have experienced the joy of loving and being loved … And how painful are the days that follow a parting that is bound to last for ever!'[27]

We have, alas, no record of the thoughts and feelings of the lady in question. After the death of her husband, Harriott became (in September 1835) the second wife of Sir James Dowling, who became Chief Justice in August 1837. Harriott died Lady Dowling in England in 1881. Her unhappy French suitor, who never married, died in Paris on 10 October 1846.

While he was in Sydney, however, Bougainville did successfully achieve negotiations for the erection of a monument to his compatriot Lapérouse. With the assistance of Governor Brisbane, plans were drawn up and costs arrived at and, on 6 September, a ceremony was held where Lapérouse had landed and where now the first stone of the monument was laid. Bougainville arrived back in France in June 1826 with many geological and botanical specimens, as well as nine live animals (3 kangaroos, 3 black swans, 2 emus and a goose). That his expedition was generally considered a success is confirmed by a letter to him from the Ministry for the Navy dated 15 August 1826. 'I have the agreeable duty to write to you once again, dear Baron,' wrote the Minister, 'to confirm that you have completed in a most satisfactory manner the mission entrusted to you.'[28]

Just two months before Bougainville arrived back in France, Dumont d'Urville had set out with his own expedition from Toulon on 22 April, and would arrive in King George Sound in October that year. From here, he sailed east towards Sydney where he arrived in December, and where he stayed for ten days. Governor Darling did not fail to mention to Dumont that he must have narrowly missed seeing the ships sent to annex King George Sound for the British Crown! D'Urville may indeed have been disappointed to learn of this annexation, for Dr Quoy, *Astrolabe*'s naturalist, remarked how King George Sound would have 'suited us very well and perhaps through too much slowness … we have lost it'.[29]

From Sydney D'Urville moved on to New Zealand where he looked carefully at Hauraki Gulf (the site of the future Auckland) with a view to settlement. From here he sailed north, circling Australia, and in December 1827 arrived in Hobart Town where he stayed for just over two weeks. Hence he would sail north to Vanikoro in an endeavour to discover the fate of Lapérouse (D'Urville's own ship, like that of Lapérouse, was named *L'Astrolabe*) before setting off for home, where he would arrive in February 1829.

D'Urville's instructions, like those of Bougainville, did not mention specifically relations that were to be established with the indigenous peoples. In his *Official Instructions*, however, the Minister for the Navy and Colonies (then the Comte de Chabrol) did advise that, 'among people of less advanced civilization', D'Urville was 'to compensate for the lack of official recommendations with articles of trade'. The voyage would officially be a scientific one: 'to augment the mass of scientific documentation which resulted from the voyage [of *La Coquille*] in 1822, 1823 and 1824'. D'Urville was also told to seek traces of Lapérouse, as 'an American captain' had said 'that on an island situated ... between New Caledonia and Louisiade he saw in the hands of natives a Cross of Saint Louis and some medals which appeared to come from the shipwreck of that famous navigator'. D'Urville made every effort to discover the facts of Lapérouse's disappearance. 'Everything leads us to believe,' he concluded, 'that Lapérouse ... ran unexpectedly on to the terrible reefs of Vanikoro, the existence of which was completely unknown.'[30] One ship had gone down first, he thought, and the other had sunk when coming to its assistance.

Before D'Urville's second visit another French explorer of interest will arrive in Australia. Cyrille Laplace set out from Toulon on 30 December 1829 with 160 men on the frigate *La Favorite*, and would circumnavigate the globe, calling at Hobart Town, and then staying in Sydney for two months (in August–September 1831) before moving on to New Zealand where, like D'Urville, he looked about him with an eye to settlement. If the British had worries about Laplace annexing New Zealand, these could have been eased somewhat by a reading of his journal, in which he echoes experiences and sentiments already known by his compatriots Marion Dufresne and Lapérouse. Laplace witnessed some Maoris in North Island who had just waged battle with a neighbouring tribe. 'Some,' he wrote, 'standing in the bows of their canoes, held out before us on bloodstained poles the heads of the enemy chiefs killed in the battle ... I should like to know what one of these philosophers, who consider man in his wild state to be a model of innocence and goodness, would have said if they had been present at this spectacle ... we found that such a scene helped considerably to sicken us of their savage country.'[31] The British government, however, would effectively put an end to any French speculation here when, in 1840, Captain William Hobson signed with the Maoris the Treaty of Waitangi — shortly before a group of French colonists arrived to establish a settlement at Akaroa (in South Island).

Laplace's instructions in fact do not mention colonisation or annexation at all. His aim was to be essentially hydrographic, and many details were given as to what he was to achieve. This, however, was not to be his sole aim. 'Busy yourself too,' instructed the Minister for the Navy and Colonies (Baron d'Haussez), 'in gathering information which would appear to be useful to commerce.' Any natural history research was to take a 'completely secondary' place, and be done solely by the 'officers of health [*officiers de santé*]'.[32] Laplace arrived safely in Toulon in April 1832.

Dumont d'Urville's second expedition set out westward around the world from Toulon on 7 September 1837 with two corvettes, *L'Astrolabe* and *La Zélée*. One of the expedition's aims was to visit the Antarctic, which Dumont did on two occasions: in 1838 (in the Weddell Sea) and in 1840 (in what he would call Terre Adélie, in honour of his wife). In March and April 1839 he stayed in Raffles Bay and Port Essington (not far from present-day Darwin) where the British had hoped — but failed (in 1829) — to establish a colony. Dumont did not like at all what he saw. 'Nothing could be more depressing than our stay in Raffles Bay,' he declared, 'the heat there was intolerable ... The flies harassed us during the day, at night they were replaced by the mosquitoes ... Our beds, even though they were suspended, and our food supplies were invaded by ants.' After extensive travel among the islands of south-east Asia and a two-month journey from Sumatra, the two ships arrived in Hobart Town in mid-December 1939 where, wrote D'Urville, 'everywhere we went we encountered great kindness and received a most flattering welcome'.[33] He had already been here during his first expedition, but now he noticed how the population 'had almost tre-bled' (to 'twelve or fourteen thousand') and how all the streets were 'almost all lined on both sides with charming houses, small, certainly, but remarkably clean'. On 1 January 1840 he set sail for the Antarctic, and arrived back in Hobart for a second stay on 17 February. Although he would stay here only a week, these few days, he wrote, 'were agreeably employed in an endless round of pleasure'.[34] On 25 February the two ships set sail for New Zealand, where they arrived at Akaroa on 8 April.

The group of French settlers who would arrive at Akaroa some four months later may have been lucky that the English had declared possession of this land just before their arrival. 'The port of Akaroa', wrote D'Urville, had 'no advantages for the foundation of a settle-ment'. 'It would be a crazy undertaking,' he thought, 'to go and start, at the other end of the globe, French agricultural settlements in New Zealand opposite England's Australian possessions ... In time of war with England, she [i.e. France] could not think of defending such iso-lated possessions against British forces.' From Akaroa D'Urville sailed west, around the Cape of Good Hope, and arrived back in Toulon in November 1840.

It is perhaps indeed fortunate that the French precipitated the British acquisition of (at least) parts of Australia and New Zealand. Divided sovereignty here could have engendered serious conflicts of interests — resembling perhaps the future 'pandemonium' in the condominium of the New Hebrides. Even a century and a half later such conflicts will still be latent. In the 1980s the French in New Cal-edonia will be suspicious of the 'colonial' intentions of Australia when the Australian government openly supported Melanesian independence, and in the 1990s Australians will protest loudly against French nuclear experiments at Mururoa, still considered to be in Aus-tralia's 'backyard', although over 6000 kilometres away and indeed nearer to Chile than Australia.

D'Urville's official instructions had again made no mention of establishing relations with the indigenous people he may have encountered. Like Laplace, his main interest was to be the advancement of hydrography, although he was again to visit Vanikoro and attempt to collect 'fresh information from the natives'[35] there regarding Lapérouse. He was also instructed to protect the interests of French trade along his route, and to seek future markets for French manufactured goods. Like all the other French explorers since Nicolas Baudin, D'Urville thus received no specific instructions as to the anthropological aspect of his voyage.

Just eighteen months after his return to France, and having now survived three long and rigorous expeditions to the South Seas, Dumont d'Urville was returning to Paris from a day-trip (on 8 May 1842) to Versailles when the train on which he was travelling left the rails and burst into flames, killing him, his wife and their only remaining child in the ensuing inferno.[36]

Other expeditions had landed in Australia and communicated with the Indigenous inhabitants before the French arrived. They were either Dutch or English, and on occasion in this book their experiences will be compared with those of the French.

The first expedition was that of the Dutch ship *Duyfken*, skippered by Willem Jansz, who sailed along the west coast of Cape York Peninsula, without knowing that Australia was separate from New Guinea, early in 1606. This was indeed the first authenticated sighting of this continent. While searching for water near today's Duifken Point, a crewman was speared by Aborigines and died of his wounds.[37]

In April 1623 another Dutch expedition, led by Jan Carstensz, arrived in the vicinity of the Mitchell River, again on the west coast of Cape York, and, wrote Carstensz, 'when the men were engaged in cutting wood, a large number of blacks upwards of 200 came upon them and tried … to overcome them'. Carstensz also described how his men captured two 'blacks' to take to Batavia. He himself 'seized [one of them] round the waist, while at the same time the quarter-master put a noose round his neck, by which he was dragged to the pinnace'. There followed a scuffle with 'the other blacks', whereupon, wrote Carstensz, 'in defending ourselves we shot one of them'. As previously discussed, the taking of indigenous people away from their homes was not then necessarily considered reprehensible, and indeed Carstensz was instructed 'by adroit management or by other means' to 'endeavour to get hold of a number of full-grown persons, or better still, of boys and girls, to that end that the latter may be brought up here [i.e. in Holland] and be turned to useful purpose'— possibly, one supposes, as interpreters for trade.[38]

Three other Dutch expeditions in the seventeenth century — those of Pelsaert in 1629, Peereboom in 1658 and De Vlamingh in 1696-97 — all went ashore on the west coast of Australia, and either saw 'natives' who fled on being approached or came across signs of their presence in the form of fires, weapons, tools or 'huts'. Tasman in 1642, as already noted, did not see any inhabitants or any real sign of them.

During this same century the west coast also received two visits from an Englishman, William Dampier, who on both occasions made contact with the 'Natives', or 'New-Hollanders' as he called them. On his first visit (to King Sound, near Derby) in 1688, he met some forty natives and presented detailed descriptions of their appearance, way of life, and the relations established with them. 'The Inhabitants of this Country,' he declared, 'are the miserablest People in the World.' On his second expedition (this time to Lagrange Bay, just south of Broome) in 1699, he met '10 or 12 Natives' but this time hostilities developed, resulting in one man being wounded on each side. 'They all of them,' concluded Dampier, perhaps rather bitterly, 'have the most unpleasant Looks and the worst Features of any People that I ever saw.'[39] Here alas, as always, we can only try to guess what the 'New-Hollanders' may have thought.

In 1705 an expedition of three Dutch ships (the *Vissenbosch*, the *Waijer* and the *Pattsjallang*), under the command of Martin van Delft, landed on Coburg Peninsula and Melville and Bathurst Islands where, on occasion, according to the notes of the captain of the *Waijer*, 'about five hundred people with women and children were met'.[40] The expedition's report gave detailed descriptions of these people, and of the unhappy nature of the relations established with them.

The last Dutch expedition to Australia, led by Lieutenant Jean Etienne Gonzal in the *Rijder* in 1756, explored once again the western side of Cape York. Here Gonzal encountered 'upwards of fifty natives' and, in his report, described them, their 'primitive dwellings', their 'prows' (boats) and their weapons. 'The natives', he said, 'enjoyed the liquor with which our men plied them' and, with the help of this, the Dutch succeeded in taking two prisoners.[41]

When Captain James Cook arrived in April 1770 on the south-east coast of Australia (at what he will call Botany Bay) he had, as far as we know, been preceded by no one on this side of the continent. His reception was hostile. 'They calld [sic] to us very loud in a harsh sounding Language ... shaking their lances and menacing, in all appearance resolved to dispute our landing,' wrote Cook's colleague, Joseph Banks. 'We parleyd with them for about a quarter of an hour [but], they waving us to be gone ... a musquet was fired over them.'[42] A second load of 'small shot' was fired, whereupon the inhabitants withdrew and Cook was able to go ashore. Here he stayed for about a week,[43] and in his journal he gives long and detailed descriptions of the inhabitants (or 'our neighbours', as Banks later called them) and their way of life, although, he admitted, 'we were never able to form any connections with them'.

Cook then travelled north in his ship the *Endeavour*, and six weeks later he became stranded at today's Endeavour River, where Cooktown is situated. Here he had several meetings with the 'Indians', some of whom paddled in a 'canoe' to come alongside his ship. Banks and Cook again describe their encounters at great length and in great detail. Although they stayed for six weeks, very little contact was established, the inhabitants 'shunning us', wrote Banks, leading him to conclude that 'they are a very pusillanimous people'.[44]

It is difficult to ascertain, but one may calculate that Cook met at least fifty inhabitants along this eastern coast. 'This immense land,' concluded Joseph Banks, 'is thinly inhabited even to admiration ... we never but once saw so many as thirty Indians together, and that was a family, Men, women and children assembled on a rock to see the ship pass by.'[45]

CHAPTER 1

Descriptions of the Aboriginal Australians

T HIS chapter examines first the Aboriginal Australians' lack of clothing, and the French attitudes and reactions to this. The second section presents details of the French explorers' physical descriptions of the Aboriginal people, and the measurements of their physical strength as made essentially by Baudin's expedition. Subsequent sections examine the inhabitants' nutrition, their dwellings and the 'home' fires they often kept burning, their canoes (in which on occasion small hearths were also kept alight) and, finally, some of the implements and utensils they made and used.

Where there are important differences, the Tasmanian people and their way of life are discussed before those of the mainland.

Clothing

One of the first observations the European explorers made about the Aboriginal people was that they were generally 'naked'. This was the case around the coast of the entire continent (except perhaps for one small corner in the south-west), and the word 'naked' is found recurrently, preceded by a diversity of emphatic adverbs.

'These natives,' wrote the Dutchman Cartensz on the west coast of Cape York in 1623, 'are coal-black, with lean bodies and stark-naked.' Six years later, on the north-west coast of Australia, his compatriot Pelsaert saw four 'black men, quite naked, having no covering', and in this same area in 1696 De Vlamingh's expedition would encounter twelve 'natives, all as black as pitch, and stark naked'.[1]

In 1770, in his general account of the Aboriginal people on the east coast, Joseph Banks would write more loquaciously about this aspect of the inhabitants' appearance. 'Of Cloths [sic],' he wrote, 'they had not the least part but naked as ever our general father was before his fall' and, he continued, 'they seemd [sic] no more conscious of their nakedness than if they had not been the children of Parents who eat the fruit of the tree of knowledge.'[2] Cook would add later: 'They have very little need of clothing and … many to whome [sic] we gave Cloth etc., left it carlessly [sic] upon the Sea beach and in the woods as a thing they had no manner of use for.'[3] On Bruny Island in 1777 Cook would again note that the 'natives' (both men and women) were 'quite naked'. However, he remarked, 'the women wore a Kanguroo [sic] skin … tied over the shoulder and round the waist, but it was evidently intended for no other purpose than for the conveniency of carrying the child, for in all other respects they are as naked as the men'.[4]

When Dufresne's expedition had arrived in Tasmania five years earlier, one of the first things to strike his people was the nakedness of the inhabitants.

The men indeed appeared to be almost always completely naked. On first setting foot on shore, Duclesmeur had noted: 'the men, naked … come towards us'. His colleague, Le Dez, who landed at this same time, wrote that there were about forty 'Diémenois' and they were all 'exactement nuds'.[5] Twenty years later, in this same part of Tasmania, one of D'Entrecasteaux's companions, St Aignan, encountered six 'savages … all men' who were 'quite naked', and in February 1793, on their second visit to these shores, Jean-Louis Féron described how they had met a 'large number of natives' among whom, 'like the men, the women are entirely naked', a fact confirmed by his colleague Joseph Raoul who said quite simply 'the men and women are completely naked without any exception'.[6]

In January 1802 Nicolas Baudin arrived in D'Entrecasteaux Channel and his colleague Jean-Baptiste Leschenault went ashore and met 'a number of natives', all men, 'completely naked'.[7] On 4 February another colleague, Citizen Bernier, met 'about twenty natives, as many men as women and children', and 'the men', he reported to Baudin, 'were completely naked'.

Although in 1772 Jean Roux had declared seeing 'the oldest of the natives having ... on their belts straps of long-haired skin',[8] only on very rare occasions did the French see any Tasmanian men wearing any form of clothing. Indeed, only Baudin's expedition reported this. On 14 February on Bruny Island Baudin himself encountered some native people among whom the men were 'naked from head to foot'. There was, however, 'one, alone [who] wore a skin that partly covered his back and shoulders'. A few moments later, he wrote, 'a second group of six or seven natives passed us', and 'amongst this last group, two were remarkable for the elegance of their dress. One wore the skin of a kangaroo, or some other animal, which covered his chest right down to his navel'.[9] Pierre Bernard Milius, who was also present, confirmed Baudin's observation: 'one alone had a kangaroo skin,' he wrote, 'which he wore carelessly on his shoulders'.[10] Two weeks later (on 26 February), in his *Particular Remarks concerning our sojourn in D'Entrecasteaux Channel*, Baudin will recall how on Bruny Island he had seen 'the largest number [of natives] together' and 'once counted fifty-five of them, men, women and children all included'. 'Although,' he continued, 'we saw some with their shoulders and chest covered by a kangaroo skin, the men are more generally naked.'[11]

Two of D'Entrecasteaux's people feared that going naked could cause injury. 'These savages', wrote Labillardière in Recherche Bay (at the mouth of the D'Entrecasteaux Channel) in February 1793, 'going completely naked, are liable to wound themselves, particularly in the lower extremities, when they pass through the woods. We observed one who walked with difficulty, and one of whose feet was wrapped up in a piece of skin.'[12] His colleague D'Hesmivy d'Auribeau also noticed this young man of whom 'one of his toes was wrapped in kangaroo skin tied around the back of his heel'. 'The ship's surgeon, who examined it very carefully,' added D'Auribeau, 'thinks that it was a simple excoriation bandaged with the hairy side of the kangaroo skin. The boy did not limp at all.'[13] In 1777 Captain Cook's surgeon William Anderson had also noticed in Adventure Bay on Bruny Island some 'natives' with 'bits of Kangooras [sic] skin fix'd on their feet ... though it could not be learned whether these were in use as shoes or only to defend some sore on their feet'.[14] In 1802, again on Bruny Island, Nicolas Baudin himself will meet two 'natives [with] fairly large, fresh wounds on their legs',[15] and his colleague Jacques-Félix-Emmanuel Hamelin, captain of *Le Naturaliste*, who accompanied him, wrote that one of them had 'under his foot ... a sole made of kangaroo skin fastened with strips of the same skin'.[16]

On the Australian mainland the men appeared to be just as bereft of clothing as in Tasmania. In June 1801 Baudin and a few of his colleagues had ventured ashore at Géographe Bay on the west coast and, wrote Baudin, 'we saw one [native] up to his waist in the water, busy spearing fish'. As the French came towards him, however, he left the water and 'fled precipitately', whereupon Baudin remarked he was 'naked from head to foot, except for a piece of bark covering his back'.[17]

On this same occasion François Péron reported that some of his colleagues had been assailed by several 'savages' who were all 'absolutely naked [*absolument nus*], with the exception of a cloak [*manteau*] made of the skin of a dog or kangaroo which covered the shoulders of a few of them'.[18] Here again in Western Australia, in September 1818, Rose de Freycinet will meet 'a band of savages, all naked ... armed with assegais and spears'. 'I must confess,' she confided, 'I was afraid and would willingly have hidden myself.'[19]

While lost in the bush near Esperance (at Cape Riche) on the south coast of West Australia in December 1802, naturalist Riche reported seeing men who 'always fled when he was advancing towards them' and who 'were all absolutely naked'.[20] Further east, in March that year at western South Australia (which would be known for some time as 'Terre Napoléon'[21]), François Péron had noted: 'of thirteen individuals we saw, one alone was covered with a black skin; all the others were absolutely naked [*absolument nus*]'.[22] In today's Northern Territory, at Raffles Bay in March 1839, Dumont d'Urville's ship was visited by 'several natives', all of whom were 'stark naked'.[23]

In Sydney and the surrounding countryside the situation was similar. On a visit to the country in the company of John Oxley in November 1819, Jacques Arago had met '*un sauvage absolument nu*' who begged him for food. 'These unfortunate people,' he wrote, 'sometimes escape from the profound solitudes to which they are relegated, and come as far as Port Jackson, audacious and naked, thus seeming to mock the civilisation which surrounds them without seducing them.'

Shortly afterwards in Sydney itself, Arago would declare: 'These savages [*sauvages*] are permitted to come to Sydney; they are allowed, I don't know why, to walk about in the town naked, absolutely naked, as also their wives'.[24]

Our last visitor, Cyrille Laplace, in 1831 encountered on the banks of the Nepean ('twelve miles from Regentville'), a 'savage [*sauvage*], accompanied by his wife and his two children'. 'The husband,' noted Laplace, 'had for sole vestment [*vêtement*] a narrow belt from which hung behind a wooden hatchet.'[25]

One feature often commented upon by the European visitors was the way the Aboriginal men habitually stood on one leg holding their foreskin. Joseph Banks had noticed this as far north as Endeavour River in July 1770, and expressed himself as became an English gentleman. Speaking of the 'Indians', as he called them, he wrote (his spelling), 'Cloaths they had none, not the least rag, those parts which natives willingly conceal being exposed to view compleately uncovered; yet when they stood still they would often or almost always with their hand or something they held in it hide them in some measure at least, seemingly doing that as if by instinct'.[26]

Far to the south and across the sea in Tasmania this would also be observed, although in a somewhat less circumlocutory way. 'The men have small natural parts [*les parties naturelles petites*] and are not circumcised,' wrote Julien Crozet[27] in 1772, but the foreskin would appear to have been elongated by this 'bad habit', as Labillardière considered it. 'We were rather surprised,' he wrote in Adventure Bay in February 1793, 'to see most of them holding the extremity of the prepuce with the left hand; no doubt from a bad habit, for we did not observe any thing of the kind among some others, who soon after joined them.'[28]

'The action which is the most striking and the most constant,' would confirm his colleague, chaplain Louis Ventenat, 'is to touch unceasingly their penis and to swing it from side to side'. 'Their prepuce is extremely long,' he concluded.[29]

Again in Tasmania, Baudin would write in his *Particular Remarks* how 'the men have a rather curious habit that greatly amused our sailors; it is to hold the end of their prepuce between their fingers nearly all the time. Consequently it is very long'.[30] In Sydney too Pierre Milius will remark that 'when they [*les naturels*] chat together they are in the habit of holding the foreskin [*prépuce*] with the left hand and their weapons always in the right'.[31]

This characteristic stance of the Aboriginal men is seen in the illustration by the artist Nicolas–Martin Petit (who accompanied Baudin) in the photographic section.

The Aboriginal women, as we have seen, were generally observed to be 'naked', whether in Tasmania or on the mainland. 'The women were all naked [*toutes nues*],' noted Milius in Tasmania in January 1802, and four months later in Sydney he would see 'the women go about absolutely naked [*absolument nueds*]'.[32] On the Péron Peninsular in September 1818 Arago would see a 'woman [who] ... carried an infant seated on her hips [who was] ... perfectly naked'.[33]

It is clear, however, from the observations of other explorers (including Captain Cook) that not all the women were 'naked', and especially so if they had children. The women Duclesmeur had seen in Tasmania in 1772 had 'appeared to be covered as far as the waist with a skin or a kind of fabric'. His colleague, Crozet, described them more simply: 'Some of the women,' he wrote, 'carried their children on their backs, attached with rush cords.'

Le Dez's evidence may give an explanation for the varying descriptions. 'The women we saw only from a distance,' he said. 'They … seemed to have as their only clothing a piece of skin which covered their breasts and reached to their thighs.' Jean Roux also suspected minimal clothing. 'The women never came close to us,' he wrote. 'All those I could distinguish were completely naked.'[34]

Several members of D'Entrecasteaux's expedition actually made close acquaintance with some of the women, and their first-hand testimony is thus more accurate and detailed.

In February 1793 Labillardière met a group of forty-two natives. 'Even the women,' he wrote, 'were for the most part entirely naked … some of them only had the shoulders and part of their back covered with a kangarou's skin, worn with the hair next to the body. Among them we observed two, each of whom had an infant at the breast. The sole garment of one was a strip of kangarou's skin, about two inches broad, which was wrapped six or seven times round the waist. Another had a collar of skin round the neck, and some had a slender cord bound several times round the head.'[35] La Motte du Portail was also present. 'The skin of the kangaroo,' he thought, 'is used rather for the children to lie on and to sit on themselves rather than serve as clothing, using it in the latter way when on the march, when they spread it over their shoulders, doubtless more for convenience than necessity.' Joseph Raoul, who was also present, discovered a name for these pieces of the skin of the kangaroo which, he wrote, 'they call "cagura"!'[36]

In January 1802, again in Tasmania, François Péron also gained the impression that the kangaroo skins were more for convenience than clothing when he met a woman 'who appeared to be about forty [and …] had been the mother of many children' and who was now 'entirely naked'. Accompanying her was a 'young woman [who] was about twenty-six to twenty-eight years of age' who was 'also entirely naked with the exception of the skin of a kanguroo [sic] wherein she carried a little female infant, to whom she gave suck'. Two weeks later, on Bruny Island, Péron and a few colleagues met 'about twenty savages' among whom 'there was not a single male'. 'All these women,' he wrote, 'with the exception of some few who had the skin of a Kangarou over their shoulders were all naked but without seeming to think at all of their nudity; they so varied their attitudes and postures it would be difficult to give any just idea of meeting all that this presented us of the bizarre and picturesque.'[37]

On this same occasion, Nicolas Baudin met 'two girls who had not yet reached the marriageable age' who were 'absolutely naked'. 'The adult women, however,' he noted, 'wore kangaroo skins which seemed to cover their shoulders and a little of their bosom.' Baudin thought these skins were 'intended principally to form a sort of bag, in which they place what they are given or what they gather when out walking'.[38] Jacques de St Cricq had the same opinion. 'The women,' he noted, 'carry their infants behind their back, and then they arrange the skin in such a way that it makes a sack in front [and] they put in it the provisions they have been making for themselves and their families.' Their colleague Leschenault de la Tour found these skins olfactorally and visually distasteful. 'They were all covered with stinking and torn kangaroo skins,' he declared, 'but the skins did not cover at all the parts of the body that European modesty takes great care to cover.'[39]

On the mainland there are only a few testimonies as to women's clothing. Among them is that of François Péron, on the west coast of the continent, at Géographe Bay in June 1801. Some of his colleagues had chased and managed to catch up with a woman who 'was far advanced in her pregnancy'. Despairing of being able to escape, she had stopped and 'remained as one stupefied and overcome with fear and astonishment'. 'This miserable woman,' wrote Péron, 'was entirely naked in all parts of her body. A small bag, made of kangaroo skin and attached around her forehead with a kind of string made of rushes, hung behind her back. Our friends found nothing in this bag but a few bulbs of the Orchidia [*Orchidées*]'.[40] As the word 'miserable' in French has several implications, including 'worthy of pity', 'deplorable', and even 'contemptible', it is difficult to ascertain Péron's attitude here. Two centuries later, however, historian Inga Clendinnen will suggest that 'these heirs to the French Revolution certainly recognised her as a fellow human, black and near naked though she was ... and they molested her only in so far as their scientific purposes required'.[41]

The attitudes of the Frenchmen to this nakedness are quite explicit when they report the manner in which the women sat. No fewer than five members of D'Entrecasteaux's expedition, including D'Entrecasteaux himself, observed this when in Tasmania in February 1793. 'We all noticed,' wrote D'Auribeau, 'that when the women sat down, one of their feet was always placed in front of their private parts, covering them completely. Two or three men were seen to take up this position for a moment, but at their meal they sat with their legs drawn up beneath them ... The women, however, all sat as I have just described.' His colleague, La Motte du Portail, seems to suggest that the women may have felt some embarrassment before the men's 'gaze'. 'They seemed,' he wrote, 'to feel a sort of shame in displaying themselves to our gaze, one of their feet serving always to hide their most secret charms', and, 'the young girls [were] even seeking to hide their breasts from view with their arms'.

D'Entrecasteaux himself did not think 'prudery' was the cause for this manner of sitting which, he thought, was 'remarkable enough'. 'One heel is placed in such a way as to cover the natural parts, but their complete nudity in every other situation does not permit us to suppose that it is prudery that causes them to hide what they are not afraid to let us see when they are not seated.'[42]

The Aboriginal women may indeed have been puzzled and embarrassed if they had realised the interest these men took in their quite 'natural' parts. They did not know that from Adam's rib 'the Lord God' had made 'a woman, and brought her unto the man ... and [that] they were both naked ... and were not ashamed' until they both ate of the fruit of the 'tree of knowledge' (of which, we have seen, Joseph Banks spoke in a similar context), whereupon 'the eyes of them both were opened, and they knew that they were naked, and they sewed fig leaves together and made themselves aprons'. Perhaps indeed the French felt — however unconsciously — that the Aboriginal women (and men?) should have, like Adam and Eve, hidden themselves 'from the presence of the Lord God amongst the trees'[43] and not revealed their reproductive parts (for it is these that Adam and his 'wife' were no longer 'not ashamed' of) for all to see.

The ship's chaplain, Louis Ventenat, would have been cognisant of this extract from the Old Testament, and his position here is quite clear, although (one hopes) expressed with tongue firmly in cheek and a large pinch of salt. 'What has struck everyone,' he wrote, 'is the manner in which the women sit; as soon as they do so they cover with their toes what prudery forbids us to name and in such a way that it is extremely hidden. We have all been witnesses of this invariable custom. I have made several of them stand up and change their position, and always on going back to their place they adopt the same attitude. You ask me why? I will say firstly that it is not in any way a matter of prudery, for these fine honest people have not yet made sufficient progress in depravity to know how to blush.'

Probably without knowing it, the chaplain was echoing here a remark by Jean-Jacques Rousseau in 1758: 'Savage women [*les femmes sauvages*]', he had written, 'have no "pudeur" for they go naked ... Our women have even less, for they go about dressed'.[44] Ventenat went on to conjecture as to why the women sat in this way. 'Do they fear,' he wondered, 'that when they are seated, and all are eating, that some shellfish may chance to fall on this sensitive place and it will wound them? Is it to warm their toes (for they often change their feet)?' 'The extremities of the body are always cold,' he concluded, and especially so in this 'cold country' which he considered Tasmania to be (even though D'Entrecasteaux's visit was at the height of summer). His botanist colleague Labillardière was more straightforward, although his turn of phrase is again carefully circumlocutory. 'We remarked with surprise,' he wrote, 'the singular appearance of the women when they are seated on the ground. It appears that it is the fashion among these ladies, when they have their knees very widely spaced, to conceal, with one of their feet, that which is contrary to decorum to suffer to be seen in this posture.'[45]

Ten years later, in a letter to the Minister of Marine and Colonies from Port Jackson and dated 11 November 1802, Nicolas Baudin spoke of his stay on Bruny Island. 'When they were with us,' he declared, 'the [Aboriginal] women did not employ the same means of hiding their nudity that Citizen Labillardière mentions.'[46] It is thus perhaps possible that the 'gaze' of D'Entrecasteaux's men may have been a little too persistent and unusual for the comfort of their female hosts.

The Frenchmen were certainly concerned about the physical comfort of their 'naked' hosts.

Even in that one small corner of Australia where the inhabitants did appear to wear some form of clothing, they still appeared to suffer from the cold — and this during the spring. In King George Sound (in Western Australia) in October 1826, Monsieur de Sainson, D'Urville's artist, and two colleagues went ashore at dusk in the rain, with a native who 'appeared to suffer from the cold, although he was protected by the clothing the sailors had given him, and when he saw that Monsieur Gaimard was putting up his umbrella, immediately went and huddled close to him'. Keeping close and huddling together was indeed one of the Aboriginal ways of keeping warm, and especially so at night. 'By 2 am,' Sainson would note later that night, 'everything was asleep.' He glanced out of his tent and saw 'the savages crouching down with their chins on their knees ... huddled one against the other to keep out the cold'. The fire by then, he noted, 'gave out no more than a dull glow' and at daybreak the natives 'appeared numbed with the cold'.[47]

Another way of keeping warm seemed to be by setting fire to the immediate environment. 'To warm themselves,' wrote François Péron at Western Port in mid-winter (June) 1802, 'or perhaps only as an effect of their indifference, they light in the woods the most disastrous fires.'[48]

In Tasmania too the French thought that fire was the answer to the cold, either at night or in winter. In late summer (March) 1772 Lieutenant Le Dez thought the 'Diémenois' [Diemenlanders], as he called them, 'must suffer very much during the winter, which must be long and hard, because they do not have other ways of fending off the cold than by lighting fires'. 'We noticed,' he continued, 'that … [they] carry a firebrand … and at each time they stop, and often it is only for a moment, they make a fire and gather round it. It is astonishing how many places we have found where they have lit a fire and how much the woods are devastated by it. We have seen few trees which were not injured at the foot and it was the same throughout the whole Bay.' 'The climate of these southern parts of New Holland seemed very cold to us, although we were there at the end of summer,' confirmed Le Dez's colleague Julien Crozet; 'we could not understand how the savages could exist in their naked state.'[49]

Despite being well-dressed, and from a similar climate in the northern hemisphere, the French themselves felt the Tasmanian cold. In February 1793 they again found the ways of the Aboriginal people 'astonishing'. 'We wore,' wrote Labillardière, 'a great many clothes on account of the coldness of the nights … It appeared to us very astonishing, that in so high a latitude, where, at this early season of the year, we already found the cold pretty severe during the night, these people found not the necessity for clothing themselves.'[50] Thirty-four years later Dumont d'Urville and some of his colleagues were entertained in Hobart in mid-summer (December 1827) by the Governor on the banks of the Derwent, 'where a long table was set up where thirty or forty people took their seats'. Soon, wrote D'Urville, 'a few drops of rain fell; the thermometer which only in the morning registered 18° and 20° dropped to 10° … I caught a severe chill, although I had been careful to remain in my heavy uniform … We gathered again in the evening at the Governor's residence, where', he wrote more happily, 'coffee and tea were served in a well heated apartment, which seemed to everyone much more "comfortable"'.[51]

The French did not lack compassion, and on many an occasion offered clothes — even those they were wearing — to their Aboriginal companions. Generally, however, these were declined, or returned or discarded after a brief trial. Neither women nor men seemed to have much use for them. In Tasmania Labillardière gave four young Aboriginal girls some clothes which were 'received with indifference' and, 'not to load themselves with a very useless burden, they immediately deposited them in the coppices bordering on the path that we followed, intending, no doubt, to pick them up again on their return'. Labillardière's supposition floundered, for he himself noted that none of the girls wore any of the clothes that had been given to them the previous day.[52]

Labillardière had indeed, a few days earlier when in the company of no less than forty-two inhabitants, tried 'to obtain the skin of a kangaroo, at a time when among the savages who surrounded us there was only one young girl that had one'. He had offered the girl a pair of pantaloons in exchange — whereupon 'she ran away and hid herself in the woods' (rather as Adam and Eve had, when they discovered they felt 'ashamed'). 'The other natives,' wrote Labillardière, 'appeared really hurt at this refusal. These good people,' he continued (meaning, one assumes, that they were 'good' for him, although rather less for their compatriot), 'interceded for me with this young girl, and called her several times. At length she yielded to their solicitation, and approached to deliver me the skin.' Here the Frenchman made a brief attempt to imagine why the girl had fled.

'Perhaps it was only through timidity,' he suggested, 'that she had made any difficulty in parting with this sort of clothing.' In return she was given 'a pair of pantaloons, which,' observed the botanist, with a well-meaning attempt at cross-cultural humour, 'according to the fashion of these ladies, was far less useful to her than this skin, which served to cover her shoulders'. The girl thus had little idea as to the use of the pantaloons, which had to be shown to her by the French men, entirely clad, who came from she knew not where.

'We showed her the manner of using them,' continued Labillardière, 'but notwithstanding, it was necessary for us to put them on for her ourselves. To this she yielded with the best grace in the world, resting both her hands on our shoulders to support herself while she lifted first one leg then the other to put them into this new garment. Wishing to avoid every cause of offence, we behaved with all the gravity we could on the occasion.'[53] As the Frenchmen felt the need to preserve their gravity, one may suppose they could have found this experience rather comic, but (perhaps to their credit) did not wish to show this to their hosts, who were clearly not manifesting any sign of amusement.

Baudin too tried to clothe these 'naturels'. 'During our stay among the inhabitants of this country [Tasmania] all our efforts to make them understand the purpose and usefulness of most of our presents met with no success,' he wrote. Perhaps, of course, he himself failed to understand just how 'useful' these 'presents' could not be to another people. 'We dressed several of them,' he continued, 'in cassocks and long breeches, but these clothes were too constricting for them to keep on for long. As soon as they could they withdrew to one side and, after taking off the clothes, removed from them the buttons and left them at the foot of a tree. The next day they appeared in their normal attire.'[54]

Clothing was indeed by no means natural for these 'naturels'. Aboriginal people usually seemed scarcely able to wait before disembarrassing themselves of this strange and unnecessary apparel. Only on rare occasions was clothing accepted and worn, and some of these were in that corner of the country where the population generally seems to have already worn some simple form of 'dress' (in and around King George Sound). Already, near here at Cape Leeuwin in 1658, Jacob Peereboom, skipper of the *Elburg*, had reported seeing 'three black men, hung with skins like those at the Cape of Good Hope'.[55] Nearly two centuries later (in October 1826) at King George Sound, Dumont d'Urville met and invited on board for the night 'a man of about forty' who was 'covered by a single animal skin', and the next morning on shore met 'one of his comrades, similar in physique and dress'. The following day D'Urville and two colleagues were again on shore, 'gathering the beautiful plants which are so common in this region', when they heard shouts and saw eight 'natives' coming to meet them, 'all clad in kangaroo skins'.

Monsieur Quoy, D'Urville's naturalist and zoologist, referred more generally to these people when he wrote: 'The tribes of King George Sound … have for clothing only a thin kangaroo skin covering their shoulders' and, he thought, 'because of the thinness of all their limbs … from the distance, covered in their piece of kangaroo skin and climbing over the rocks, they look something like those water birds … called stilt birds.' Quoy recalled too how one of the natives, 'fairly old', had come on board and, 'from being virtually naked … was soon clothed from head to foot, the whole topped with a big black sheep-skin hat'.[56]

Physical descriptions

After spending some two weeks in and about Hobart in 1827, Dumont d'Urville said he thought the native people in Tasmania had 'frizzier hair than their neighbours in Australia'. He also thought they practised 'neither the custom of knocking out the two front teeth of the males, nor of cutting off the first joint of the little fingers of the woman as is widely done by the natives of New South Wales'.[57] To what extent these beliefs were justified may be judged by the observations of his earlier compatriots.

In Tasmania in 1772 Duclesmeur had observed that the men had 'frizzy hair',[58] and twenty years later St Aignan described their heads as 'woolly'.[59] Baudin himself presented a long description of one of the men he met who, he wrote, 'appeared to be wearing a sort of wig-shaped cap which … we thought was made of seaweed. Upon examining it more closely, however, we realised it was his own hair'. Baudin went on to give more detail. 'Divided into small strips about ½ inch wide and 1" long, and smoothed down with grease and red-dish-brown dirt, it formed a skull-cap over his head, and every movement he made caused it to shake in a different way.' Another of the men 'simply had his head shaved, and wore a long strip of hair wound round it'.[60]

The hair of the Tasmanian women is mentioned less often, although Labillardière found it could serve an unusual purpose. Occasionally, he noted, the women 'took the trouble to break branches of trees into short pieces to feed the fire' and, in order to do this, took hold of them 'at each end with the hand [and] bent them over their heads till they broke'. Fortunately, he thought, 'their hair forms a cushion, which diminishes the pressure'. 'Few of the women, however,' he continued, 'could have done as much; for some had their hair cut pretty short, and wore a string several times round the head; others had only a simple crown of hair.'[61]

In Tasmania it is certain that the men rubbed 'reddish dirt' into their hair. In 1772 Julien Crozet noted that the men's hair, 'like the wool of Kafirs [*Cafres*], was tied in rolled knots and powdered with red ochre', and in February 1793 La Motte du Portail would make a remarkably similar statement when describing the forty or so people about him. 'The head,' he wrote, 'is covered with a wool which is longer than that of the Kafirs, and with which some of them make curls, held together with red and greasy clay.'[62] In 1802 Milius, while noting that 'several [of the men] shave their heads', observed that 'others rub their hair with a kind of grease or fish oil [and] put into it lime or rouge according to taste'.

On the mainland the French were less loquacious about Aboriginal coiffure. In Sydney, Milius remarked how the men's hair was 'frizzy [*crépus*] and non-woolly' and that the women 'daub their hair with grease and charcoal'.[63] In New South Wales generally, René Lesson would say that the 'naturels' had 'hair more or less curled into locks [*frisés en mèches*]'[64] and Bougainville that 'some had their hair plastered with grease and red dust, and it was so curly that it appeared half woolly at first sight'.[65]

The question of the native people's teeth, however, may be more clearly resolved. First, their teeth — whether all present or not — appear to have been excellent. In Tasmania the people Le Dez saw had 'very white teeth',[66] and chaplain Ventenat noted how 'their teeth are large, regular and white'.[67] Baudin's second-in-command, Hamelin, was even more emphatic about the natives he met on Bruny

Island. 'Among these thirty-six people,' he said, 'there was only one man who had a tooth missing, but it was evident … that this had been broken. It would be difficult in Paris,' he mused, 'to find thirty-six mouths as well furnished with very white teeth among the same number of people taken indiscriminately from an ordinary gathering.'[68]

In Sydney René Lesson had a very unusual experience. 'Some skulls,' he wrote, 'extracted from the tombs of these "naturels", presented to me the singular anomaly of having thirty-four teeth, beautifully and well spaced.' Of the (living) people about him he noticed too the 'very beautiful and very white teeth'.[69] In Raffles Bay D'Urville's colleague Lieutenant Demas encountered some twenty natives (of whom two were women) and, although he considered them generally 'wretched people', he could not help remarking how they 'displayed two rows of pearly white teeth'.[70]

As concerns tooth avulsion in Tasmania, Labillardière at first was quite unequivocal. 'The custom of extracting two of the front teeth of the upper jaw … certainly has not been introduced into this tribe,' he wrote at Recherche Bay in February 1793, 'for we did not see one among them in whom a single tooth of the upper jaw was wanting; and indeed they all [forty-two] had very good teeth.' At Adventure Bay on Bruny Island he would appear less certain. 'We observed some,' he wrote, 'in whom one of the middle teeth of the upper jaw was wanting, and others in whom both were gone. We could not learn the object of this custom; but it is not general, for the greater part of the [ten] people had all their teeth.'[71] As these missing teeth were seen only once by one observer in a minority in one small group of people, it may be assumed that they had been lost by accident, or perhaps because of advancing years.

On the mainland, however, tooth avulsion had certainly been practised widely for many years (if not centuries) and, if not witnessed at all by Cook, had been clearly seen by Dampier on the west coast (near today's Derby) in 1688. Here — despite the flies which 'will creep into one's Nostrils, and Mouth too, if the lips are not shut very close' — he noted that the twenty or thirty men, women and children he met had 'the two Fore-teeth of their Upper-jaw wanting in all of them, Men and Women, old and young'; but, he continued, 'whether they draw them out, I know not'.[72]

The first Frenchman to mention this is Louis Freycinet on board *Le Naturaliste* with Baudin's expedition in Sydney (over 3000 kilometres from Derby) in 1802. 'Custom requires,' he wrote, 'that the men have one of the front teeth of the upper jaw pulled out.'[73] Here Lesson and Bougainville would also count only one tooth missing. 'One of the fundamental customs of these people is to pull out a tooth on the occasion of some extraordinary event,' wrote Lesson, but, he thought, 'these events cannot be very numerous or their denture equipment would soon be quite depleted'.[74] 'All have lost a front tooth from the upper jaw,' wrote Bougainville, 'but not the same one.' Bougainville believed that the boys lost these at '*une grande cérémonie*' upon arriving '*à l'âge de puberté*'.[75] In Raffles Bay (3000 kilometres to the north) Lieutenant de Roquemaurel observed that 'all [the natives] have a tooth missing from the top jaw, which suggests that in the northern part, as at all other parts of Australia that we have visited, the extraction of a tooth is practised on the children'.[76]

Jacques Arago actually witnessed this dental operation — not on a child or a boy, but on a young woman — at a '*cérémonie de mariage*' near Sydney in 1819 (see photographic section). After the man had bedaubed his wife-to-be with spit and powder, the couple withdrew from the crowd. Arago related what he then saw:

> They placed themselves besides the trunk of a casuarina, the woman with her back against the tree and the man facing her. From a sort of bag he pulled a small piece of red wood … took a polished stone … leant the beautiful head of his queen against the tree, applied the little stick on her two upper incisor teeth, held it between the thumb and the index finger on the left hand as if he were knocking in a nail and, with his right, hit it hard with the stone. And thus his lady found herself beautified with two teeth less.
>
> Her mouth was filled with blood, but the courageous virgin didn't utter a single cry, and showed not the slightest sign of suffering.[77]

While the French do not give (or perhaps even know) the reason for this 'wedding ceremony', such an operation would certainly have made it clear for all — even more so than the European wedding ring — that the woman was married.

Before losing their front teeth, however, many girls had already lost most of the little finger of their left hand. Four Frenchman remarked on this in Sydney and New South Wales generally, among whom Louis de Freycinet in 1802 noted simply that 'the women have the two last phalanxes [phalanges] of the little finger cut off'.[78] In 1825 Hyacinthe de Bougainville observed this too and explained its *raison d'être* and what he thought of it. 'It would indeed seem,' he wrote, 'that these people enjoy torturing and disfiguring themselves! No sooner are they born than the girls lose two phalanxes of the little finger on the left hand, and this just to be able to wrap their fishing-line around their hand more easily!'[79] As D'Urville suggested, this phenomenon is not mentioned at all in Tasmania and this may be because, while the people there ate sea-food, they were never seen actually to eat fish itself as elsewhere — and indeed may not have done so for some 4000 years.[80]

At first sight the French thought that the Aboriginal people had black skin, but later often had cause for second thoughts. In Tasmania Duclesmeur said 'their colour is black', and his colleague Roux thought them 'very black'.[81] In Sydney, however, Bougainville would say quite bluntly that 'the surface of their bodies is coated with grease and grime to such an extent that it is impossible to recognize its colour',[82] and Milius had guessed them to be 'very dark copper-coloured' despite the fact that, because they were 'smeared with crushed charcoal all over', they looked 'very black'.[83]

In Tasmania Leschenault had noticed a baby of some eight days whose 'skin was a reddish colour',[84] and this lighter colour had already been observed — in a very unfortunate manner — by Dufresne's people. Although the sequence of events is not clear, it appears that the indigenous inhabitants became very apprehensive as increasing numbers of French disembarked from their strange vessels, and consequently threw spears at them, wounding at least one. The French responded 'with a fusillade which wounded several, and killed one'. They soon discovered the dead man, and examined him. 'He seemed black,' wrote Julien Crozet, 'but on washing him we found that his natural colour was reddish, and that it was only smoke and dirt which made him look so dark.'[85]

The reason for this application of 'smoke and dirt' was not obvious to the French. In King George Sound in 1826 Quoy assumed it was for 'protection from mosquitoes, insects which are very common in the swampy places where they build their huts',[86] but the practice was also prevalent in the less swampy and less mosquito-ridden Tasmania.[87] Here most French explorers interpreted this (with irony or not, one cannot know, for we can only guess at interpreting their interpretations) as the use of an appearance-enhancing cosmetic. La Motte du Portail wondered if one should 'consider as an ornament the crushed charcoal they cover their face with'. He described it as 'a fairly thick layer', which was 'not nice to look at'. Colleague Labillardière also supposed that 'they consider extreme blackness as a beauty, for in order to heighten this colour beyond its natural state, they rub themselves over, particularly on the upper parts of the body, with powdered charcoal'.[88] Baudin too thought it was 'because they do not think themselves black enough that they daub various parts of their faces with charcoal'.[89] Regarding the women, Milius was more blunt: this 'adornment', he said, was 'to seduce the men'.[90]

In Tasmania, in 1802, two women on different occasions showed how this 'adornment' was applied. The first occasion was quite intimate. François Péron and some colleagues had met a family of nine who had returned from fishing, and had shared dinner with them. After dinner the '*bons Diémois*' were treated to some French singing, beginning with a popular song ('the hymn,' thought Péron, 'which was so unhappily prostituted during the Revolution') and concluding with 'some of our more tender airs'. A young girl named Ouré-Ouré was sitting next to Freycinet who, 'showed us for the first time the nature of the paint of these regions and the particular method of using it'. Péron then recounts what he saw. 'Taking some charcoal in her hands, she crushed it … to a fine powder and, keeping this dust in her left hand, with the right she rubbed some of it on her forehead and then on her cheeks, and made herself most frightfully black. And what seemed to us still more surprising was the air of satisfaction with which [she] seemed to regard us after this procedure, and the look of confidence which this new adornment had brought to her countenance.'[91] On another occasion, this time witnessed by midshipman Breton, a woman simply 'rubbed both hands on a burnt tree, puffed up her cheeks, and rubbed them with her hands from her ears to her nose to her eyes'.[92]

A few days later on Bruny Island Péron and his colleagues met a group of about twenty women and, sitting on the ground together, one of the Frenchmen had again sung to entertain them. One of the women had sung and danced in response, and then came towards Péron. 'She came close to me,' he wrote, 'and taking from a bag of rushes … some charcoal, crushed it in her hand and, with an obliging air, began to apply it on my face as is customary in these regions. I willingly submitted to this obliging piece of caprice.' She then approached one of Péron's companions, Heirisson, who soon 'received a similar mask'. Here again Péron guessed as to what the reason for this 'appeared' or 'seemed' to be. 'We now appeared to be very much admired by these women; they seemed to regard us with sweet satisfaction and seemed to congratulate us on the acquisition of these additions to our beauty.' 'Thus,' he concluded, 'the fairness of European skin, of which we are so proud, is really but a defect and a sort of deformity which, in these distant climes, must yield pride of place to the blackness of coal, or to the sombre red of ochre or clay.'[93]

Some years earlier, not far from here, Péron's quasi namesake, the artist Piron, had actually asked the Aboriginal people to cover his skin, like theirs, with charcoal-dust. 'His request,' wrote Labillardière, who was with him, 'was favourably received.' Unlike Péron, however, Piron was blackened by a man. 'Immediately,' continued Labillardière, 'one of the natives selected some of the most friable coals, which he ground to powder by rubbing them between his hands. This powder he applied to all parts of the body that were uncovered ... and presently our friend Piron was as black as a New-Hollander.' Like the girl who had adorned herself in front of Péron, the man here 'appeared highly satisfied with his performance' which he concluded 'by blowing off the dust that adhered ... taking particular care to remove all that might have gotten into the eyes'.[94]

If we really wish to know a person, it is into the eyes that we look, for it is here, we are told, that we find the 'windows of the Soule [sic]'.[95] When St Aignan came across six native Tasmanian men in May 1792 they at first fled but, after the Frenchman waved a red silk kerchief towards them as a present, they came to him. They then 'stared for long time at [him] ... their eyes almost always fixed on his as if wishing to know his thoughts'. 'Their eyes,' reported St Aignan, 'were very fine and expressed sweetness and kindness.' D'Entrecasteaux's men thought the Tasmanian women had a similar look. 'Their gaze is lively, sometimes pleasant,' thought chaplain Ventenat, and he especially recalled one young woman who was 'pretty, and her look soft and attractive'. His colleague D'Auribeau believed that the women's eyes were 'not so deep-set as the men's' and that 'their expression [was] gentle, kind and pleasant'. Ventenat himself felt that the natives' eyes were so 'deepset [that], when raised to look at the sky, they have to bend the head much more than we do'.[96] A decade later Baudin would note how these Tasmanians' 'glance was keen, but anxious' and how 'their eyes were constantly on the look-out' — not surprisingly perhaps, in view of the strange (but perhaps not new) spectacle before them. 'At the slightest move from us,' continued the Commander, 'they were on their feet.'[97] Not all Frenchmen, however, were so impressed with Tasmanian eyes. In 1772 Jean Roux and Le Dez both thought they had a 'wild [*farouche*] look', while Crozet and Duclesmeur said they were 'small', 'sunken' and 'of a bilious colour'.[98] In Sydney a half-century later Arago was not impressed at all. 'A body lean, and far from robust,' he wrote, 'supports a head void of expression, or rather characterised by brutal ferociousness. They have in general very small eyes, a very flat nose [and] a mouth of monstrous width.'[99]

Noses and mouths had indeed not missed the attention of the visitors. Impressions differed with regard to the former, whether it be in Tasmania or elsewhere. They have 'flattened noses', thought Crozet and Lesson.[100] 'Their nose is not flat, it is broad,' said D'Auribeau, and 'the nostrils are large and flared'. Ventenat concurred: 'the nose is large but not at all flat'. St Aignan, however, struck the middle ground: the nose was 'a little flattened', he proposed.[101] As for the native peoples' mouths, these were considered 'large' by Crozet, St Aignan and Ventenat, and by Milius, who also found their lips to be rather 'full [*épaisses*]'.[102]

The various descriptions of the men's chins are restricted to Tasmania in 1793. 'Generally,' noted La Motte du Portail in his journal for 10–11 February, 'they allow the beard to grow', and in a letter home to France that year he wrote: 'They do not seem to have a definite habit about having a beard or not! Some cut it, while others have it long'. The length of the beard was a matter for conjecture. 'They wear a fairly long beard', thought D'Auribeau, while St Aignan reckoned it 'very short'. Ventenat's description perhaps reconciles the two. 'The beard,' he said, '[is] well developed and worn short.'[103] The illustrations we have of the Tasmanian (or, indeed, other) men support this description of a short beard. The beard may be roughly cut as in the portrait by Petit (see photographic section) or more fully developed and carefully contoured as seen in that by Piron (see photographic section). Indeed, the beards may not have been cut at all. In 1770, on the coast of today's New South Wales, Captain Cook's people had met an inhabitant one day who had 'a beard rather larger than his fellows; the next day he came again,' wrote Joseph Banks, and 'his beard was then almost cropped close to his chin and we found the ends of the hairs all burnd so that he had certainly singd [sic] it off'.[104]

Aesthetic appreciations of all these facial features varied. Speaking only of the Tasmanian men (for few women were seen), Roux said that 'they have a very ugly and mean face'. Opinions of the women were more subtle. Still in Tasmania — but twenty years later when many more women were encountered — Ventenat would reveal his opinion of his compatriots. 'The pretty women of New Holland,' declared the chaplain, 'are of the same character and have the same fickleness and the same temper, and are as frivolous as our pretty ones, our winsome little things and our little birds in France, England and so on.' His colleague La Motte du Portail expressed another viewpoint. 'None deserved the title of pretty,' he thought, 'but in this case one knows what must be the testimony of men in the prime of life shut up for a long time in a ship when they see a girl. What reasons for finding them beautiful!'[105] Speaking of the women of 'New Wales' he met when with Baudin's expedition, Louis de Freycinet was more sober in his appreciation: 'it is not rare,' he wrote, 'to finds physiognomies which, far from being disagreeable, are even quite pretty'.[106]

In Tasmania, his companion François Péron had been more analytical — and less generous. In a whole paragraph dedicated to the subject, he declared:

> The physiognomy of these savage men is very expressive. Strong passions are depicted there, which succeed one another rapidly. Mobile like their affections, all the traits of their face change and modify according to these. Fearsome and ferocious in their menaces, they appear at once suspicious, anxious and perfidious. In their laughter their face displays a mad and almost convulsive gaiety. Among the more elderly, it is sad, sullen and severe. But in general, among all these people and no matter when one observes them, their look always keeps something sinister and ferocious … which corresponds only too well with the depths of their character.[107]

In 1623 the Dutchman Carstensz had written the first European description of the Aboriginal people's bodily physique. On Cape York Peninsula he and his men had been confronted by 'upwards of 200 [natives]' who 'tried every means to surprise and overcome them', thus obliging the Dutch 'to fire two shots, upon which the blacks fled'. Carstensz was not impressed with his adversaries. 'The natives,' he said, 'are in general utter barbarians, all resembling each other in shape and features.'[108] Sixty-five years later the Englishman

William Dampier would be the first European known to mingle and fraternise with these people when he landed in the King Sound region (in today's Western Australia) in 1688. Dampier's judgement is perhaps more infamous than famous. 'The Inhabitants of this Country,' he declared, 'are the miserablest People in the World ... And setting aside their Humane Shape, they differ but little from Brutes. They are tall, strait-bodied, and thin, with small long Limbs ... They are long-visaged, and of a very unpleasing Aspect.'[109] Rarely indeed have one set of human values been applied more scathingly to another.

The French also described the native people's bodily physique as it appeared to them.

One of the most striking features was the extensive scarring on their bodies, which they seemed to have inflicted upon themselves. This was observed everywhere, from Tasmania to New South Wales and to the top of the Northern Territory.

In Tasmania Crozet noted in 1772 that several of the men had 'a kind of cut encrusted on the skin of the chest'.[110] In 1793 D'Auribeau saw how these people had 'on various parts of their body ... raised lines of different lengths straight or curved. They showed us with a shell how they go about this mutilation', which, he thought, 'must be infinitely painful'.[111] His colleague Labillardière said, 'almost all of them were tattooed with raised points, sometimes placed in two lines, one over the other, much in the shape of a horse-shoe, though these points were frequently in three straight and parallel lines on each side of the breast'. He also saw some 'towards the bottom of the shoulder blades'.[112] This painful operation was perhaps spared the children. 'The young men and the children,' noted La Motte du Portail, 'are not at all decorated in this way.'[113] In 1802 Baudin also observed this. 'Their arms, shoulders and abdomen are tattooed in a fairly regular fashion,' he wrote, with 'marks ... raised on the surface of the skin, but ... the children, even those between twelve and fifteen, carried no marks at all.'[114]

In August 1770, after sailing northwards along the east coast of New Holland, Joseph Banks wrote generally about the people he had met. He said that 'on the fleshy part of their arms and thighs and some of their sides were large scars in regular lines, which, by their breadth and the convexity with which they had heald [sic], shewd [sic] plainly that they had been made by deep cuts of some blunt instrument, a shell perhaps or the edge of a broken stone'.[115] In the D'Entrecasteaux Channel in 1802 Leschenault de la Tour confirmed Banks' supposition. All the men, he wrote, 'were covered with scars deliberately made. By taking certain precautions (that is, by reopening the lips of the wound when they are about to close) they make these scars stand out sometimes about half an inch. The parts of the body they scar in this way are principally the shoulders, the shoulder blades, the back (region of kidneys), the buttocks, stomach and chest. The scars form straight, circular and semi-circular lines.'[116] Hyacinthe de Bougainville — who did not visit Tasmania — did not notice when in Sydney in August 1826 that the children may have been spared this mutilation. '*Les naturels de la Nouvelle Galles* [New Wales],' he wrote, 'women as well as men, have different parts of the body covered with scarification [which] ... are the result of deep incisions made in childhood with pieces of shell, and which are only left to heal ['cicatriser'] when the edges of the wound have acquired a sufficient elevation: a cruel and lengthy torture for the poor children, accustomed in this way from an early age to tolerate stoically the sufferings which will not be spared them during their miserable life.'[117] In the Northern Territory, at Raffles Bay in 1839, Lieutenant de Roquemaurel will feel no less strongly. 'Tatooing, or raised by incision,' he wrote, 'is practised here in all its glory: the natives have the front of their bodies horribly mutilated. The shoulders, chest, stomach and thighs sport flaps of flesh three or four inches long over as many protruding lines ... All these wounds, on these naked bodies exposed to a burning climate must,' he feared, 'give rise to very serious accidents.'[118] Examples of these scarifications or 'cicatrices' may be seen on the man in *Portrait of an Aborigine Standing* and on the woman in *Woman of Van Diémen's Land* in the photographic section.

The Indigenous people's legs and arms were generally not admired. In Tasmania, Le Dez considered the 'Diémenois' to be 'badly built with thin bodies and slender legs and thighs [and] big knees'. 'It seems,' he said, 'they must often be on their knees, because the skin on them is very hard. Their gait is unsteady and when they run they throw their feet back almost as high as their thighs.'[119] La Motte du Portail thought 'their bust is fine and would be evidence for force and vigour if their limbs corresponded, but generally they are slender'.[120] Nicolas Baudin agreed with one aspect but not the other: 'Although nearly every one of them has spindly legs and weak arms,' he said, 'they nevertheless seem strong and vigorous.'[121]

Péron found there were several differences between the Tasmanians and the mainlanders, but nevertheless maintained that 'the skinniness of the arms and legs'[122] was common to all.

On the mainland this was confirmed by several independent observers. They have 'frail legs', thought Milius in Sydney in 1802,[123] and here too in 1819 Arago would say 'they have excessively slender legs and arms'.[124] Lesson would say that these Sydneysiders' legs were 'thin and spindly'.[125] In Raffles Bay in 1839, D'Urville would consider that 'their skinny legs seem to have trouble supporting their torsos which, proportionately, are long'. 'Their bellies are big,' he thought, 'and only one of those [of the 'several natives'] who visited us today appeared robust and well-built.'[126]

'Bellies' often appeared to be 'big'. In 1793 D'Auribeau thought the Tasmanian women had 'large, wrinkled bellies' as well as 'soft, flaccid buttocks and thighs'.[127] Baudin said that the Tasmanian men had 'a rather protruding abdomen', and Péron went so far as to single out 'a young man of 24 to 25 years called Bara-Ourou' who was 'more handsomely built than all the others' but who nevertheless had 'a belly too large for the rest of his body'.[128] Also in Tasmania (in 1777), Captain Cook's surgeon, William Anderson, had thought that the reason for this physical phenomenon could have been because, unlike so many other peoples, the 'New Hollanders' did not wear corsets! Their 'belly seems rather projecting,' he wrote, and 'this may be owing to the want of compression there, which few nations do not use, more or less'.[129]

The shape of the women's breasts often seemed to be wanting when compared with French standards. In Tasmania D'Auribeau thought the women had 'very pendulous breasts'. This observation may be explained to some degree by his colleague La Motte du Portail's observation: 'I was at first surprised at the size of the children I have seen take their breasts,' he wrote (when in the midst of some fifty Aboriginal people), 'but I have been much more so when, instead of one, I have seen three of them … of whom the eldest was not less than five or six years of age, go one after the other to take their share of milk of these poor mothers.' Some observers were more gentle. 'The bosom is well placed in all,' thought chaplain Ventenat, 'not at all bulky and firm even though they are suckling a child.'[130] Here again in 1802, François Péron would give a more precise view. 'Their shape,' he wrote, '[is] generally lean and shrivelled, with their breasts long and hanging down.' From 'this general tableau, however,' he continued, 'we must except two or three young girls of 15 or 16 years in whom we discerned rather pleasant shapes, and whose breasts were firm and well-placed, although the nipples were a little too large and too long'.[131] Nearly two decades later (in 1819 in Sydney) Arago was less kind, when writing of the young bride he had seen losing her teeth at her husband's hand. 'Her large breasts floated on her belly,'[132] he declared — an observation clearly in conflict with the Europeanised illustration (adapted from his original) two pages later in his book (reproduced here in the photographic section).

Observations of the inhabitants' height reflect that of the observers themselves. All the French estimations were in Tasmania. Crozet thought 'the men as well as the women were of an ordinary height' and his colleague Jean Roux thought the men 'of an average height'. Another colleague, Le Dez, estimated the height of the young man they had killed at 'five feet three or four inches [*cinq piéds 3 a 4 Pouces*]'.[133] La Motte du Portail suggested that 'these savages are of a medium stature: the tallest does not seem to be more than 5 feet 4 inches'.

One must recall here that the old French 'foot' measured 32.48

centimetres, as compared with the English 'foot' of only 30.48 centimetres.[134] These people would thus be some 10 centimetres taller than would at first appear to the English-speaking reader.

At this same port of call (in Blackswan Lagoon) and 'in communication with forty of the natives', D'Hesmivy d'Auribeau confessed, 'I took advantage of their patience and natural gentleness in order to measure the principal dimensions of a man and a woman who were with me at the landing-stage.' He then presented a list of 'the proportions of a man, estimated to be from 40 to 50 years old'. The results of this investigation (from the length of the 'forearm from elbow to waist' to that of the 'male member, natural state') are indeed a testimony to the inhabitants' patience and gentleness, and are as follows (again in old French measurements):

Full height	5 feet 3 inches
Forearm from elbow to wrist	11 inches
From wrist to tip of middle finger	7 inches
From shoulder to elbow	11 inches
Width of shoulders	1 foot 2 inches
Height of head from neck	10 inches
Length of thigh from hip to knee	1 foot 5 inches
Length of leg from knee to heel	1 foot 6 inches
Length of foot	9 inches 6/12"
Breadth of head on opposite side from nose	8 inches 6/12"
Width of mouth	2 inches 8/12"
Length of ears	2 inches
Male member, natural state	5 inches
Small teeth, fairly regular, a little yellow without being dirty	

Details for 'a woman, estimated to be from 50 to 60 years', are:

Full height	5 feet 6/12"
Length of forearm with hand open, to tip of middle finger	1 foot 3 inches
From shoulder to elbow	1 foot

Breadth of head on opposite side from nose	8 inches
Height of head from neck	6 inches
Length of ears	2 inches 6/12"
Length of leg from kneel to heel	1 foot 5 inches
Length of thigh from hip to knee	1 foot 3 inches 6/12"
Length of foot	8 inches 6/12"
Width of shoulders	1 foot
Length of middle finger	3 inches
Width of mouth	2 inches 6/12"

D'Auribeau made no attempt to analyse the significance of these figures, which must have taken him — and the native concerned — considerable time to obtain.[135] In view of the size of his sample, however, their value is clearly minimal.

Still in Tasmania, but in Oyster Bay in 1802, François Péron also indulged in some scientific measurements among fourteen inhabitants, of whom 'most were between about 16 and 25 years, two or three between 30 to 35 [and] one between 50 and 55'. 'Among the grown men,' he said, 'there was one who was not less than one metre 786 millimetres (5 feet 6 inches) but he was much skinnier and lankier than his compatriots. All the others varied in stature between 1 metre 678 and 732 millimetres.'[136]

If the French considered the Tasmanians of 'ordinary' or 'average' height, the opinion of the English at Endeavour River in 1770 had been quite different. Here again the Europeans did not hesitate to measure their antipodean counterparts. 'They are a very small people,' wrote Joseph Banks, 'or at least this tribe consisted of very small people, in general about 5 feet 6 [in English measurement] in higt [sic] and very slender; one we measurd [sic] 5 feet 2 and another 5 feet 9, but he was taller than any of his fellows.'[137]

Like D'Hesmivy d'Auribeau, Matthew Flinders' expedition also took an interest in physical anthropology. Like D'Auribeau too, Flinders measured only one person, and one is thus left to wonder as to the representative value of such details. Again like D'Auribeau, Flinders makes no analysis or comment on these figures, made in

King George Sound (Western Australia) in January 1802. 'The following admeasurement of one of the best proportioned of our visitors,' wrote Flinders, 'was furnished by the surgeon Mr Hugh Bell'[138] (in English feet, inches and 'lines'):

	Ft.	In.	L.
Full height	5	7	6
Circumference of the head	1	11	0
From the transverse nasal suture, to the posterior ridge of the occiput	1	3	0
From the small rim of each ear across the forehead	1	0	0
From the nasal suture, over the nose, to the tip of the chin	0	5	2
From ditto, to the tip of the nose	0	1	0
From the tip of the nose to the edge of the upper lip	0	1	0
Extent of the mouth	0	2	1
Nostrils	0	1	6
Lower jaw from each angle	0	8	6
Length of the arm	1	1	6
Fore arm	1	0	0
Middle metacarpal bone	0	4	0
Middle finger	0	4	3
Femur, from the great trochanter to its lower end	1	5	6
Length of tibia	1	4	6
foot	0	10	0
Length from the protuberance of the inner ankle, to the tip of the heel	0	3	9
Ditto, to the end of the great toe	0	8	6
Circumference of the neck	1	0	6
Chest	2	8	9
Pelvis	2	4	9
Arm	0	10	6
Elbow joint	0	9	6
Fore arm	0	9	9
Wrist	0	6	0
thigh	1	7	6

	Ft.	In.	L.
Circumference			
just above the knee joint	1	1	0
of the knee joint	1	1	0
— leg, immediately below the knee joint	0	11	0
— leg	1	0	0
—the small	0	7	6
— the foot	0	10	6

One of the most intriguing anthropometrical devices must have been the 'dynamomètre', invented by Edmé Régnier in 1796, and used in 1802 by Péron to measure the physical strength of native people. During this Age of Enlightenment (already nearing its end) scientists sought to compare the various faculties of different races around the globe, and such measurements were considered essential. A biologist — and a colleague of Degérando — Georges Cuvier, had submitted a short memorandum to Baudin before his departure, with the rather long title *An Instructive Note on the researches to be carried out relative to the anatomical differences between the diverse races of man*. In this he suggested that one of the best methods to achieve such measurements was to obtain, 'by any manner whatever', an 'entire skeleton', as this would be 'infinitely precious'.[139] Grave-robbing, if needed, was not to be excluded! D'Auribeau, as we have seen, had restricted himself to living people, and here again — this time by necessity (as it is a question more of physiology than anatomy) — this was the course of action taken.

Régnier had in fact devised two machines, one for the hands and one for the back (see photographic section). As may be seen, the strength of the hand was measured by clasping a spring with each hand. The strength of the back was measured by pulling upwards with both hands on a spring while anchoring the machine to the ground with the feet. In both cases, a gauge indicated the degree of strength imposed against the spring's resistance.

In his *Voyage de découvertes* François Péron begins chapter XX with a bitter complaint against Jean-Jacques Rousseau and his followers. 'Their baneful oratory,' he wrote, 'led people astray, and for the first time we saw men of good sense grumble about the progress of civilisation, and sigh for that wretched state, which today we call by the seductive name of "the state of nature" [*l'état de la nature*].' 'Fortunately,' he continued more cheerfully, 'modern travellers, by making us acquainted with so many savage peoples [*peuples sauvages*], have enabled us to appreciate these vain sophisms at their true value; and our expedition in this regard will have been able to serve usefully a true philosophy.' Péron then went on to the precise point of his investigation. 'Of all the advantages which these apologists for savage man [*homme sauvage*] delighted in attributing to him, physical strength is the one on which they insisted most particularly and most constantly.' On Maria Island (on the east coast of Tasmania) and then on the south coast of the mainland, he would put this 'advantage' to the test.

The Tasmanian, he thought, was 'quite different' from the mainlander and was 'par excellence' 'l'enfant de la nature'. 'With men so wild [*farouches*],' he wrote, 'our relations have been, if not rare, at least difficult and perilous … and the dynamometric observations were even more so.' Indeed, Péron could not persuade a single 'naturel' here to undergo the back test, and only a dozen to undertake the hand-pressure test. 'No "Diémenois",' he wrote, 'could make the tension-needle go past the 60 degree mark, and the average figure was … only 50.6 kilograms.' The French and the native people then engaged in hand-to-hand struggles, which ended up in one instance in a free-for-all fight between a French officer, Maurouard, and one of the men. 'The French officer floored him several times with great ease,' noted Péron, and went on to describe his own exploits. 'Myself obliged on Maria Island to undergo a similar trial of wrist strength, I came out of it with equal success.' As always, one must wonder what the inhabitants of this island, undisturbed perhaps for millennia before these recent visits, made of the practices of these peculiar creatures. Péron had his own conclusions. 'One can deduce from this collection of facts and experiments,' he declared, 'that the average strength of the savage people [*peuples sauvages*] of Diemenland and the neighbouring islands is by far inferior to that which, by the same methods and in the same places, we have observed with regard to the Europeans.'

He then went on to describe his experiments with the 'savage peoples of New Holland' (as opposed to Diemenland) who, he thought, were quite different from the 'Diémenois' because of 'the less dark colour of their skin, their long straight hair, and by the remarkable configuration of their head which is not so large and is flattened to some degree towards the top'. These features, however, would not, one assumes, have implied different results for Péron's dynamometer, to which 'seventeen savages of this austral continent submitted themselves'. Fourteen of these (like the Diemenlanders) were between eighteen and forty years of age and so belonging 'to that time of life when man is most vigorous'. 'These savages [*sauvages*],' continued Péron, 'have the same weakness which we observed in Diemenland. Only one could make the tension-needle go as far as 62 degrees, and the average strength of the fourteen individuals scarcely exceeds 51°. Some indeed seemed so weak that they couldn't go beyond 40°.'

These results were for the hands. Those for the back were similar. Except for a young man named Ourou-Mare who got the needle to 19°, none of them could get it to the 18° mark, and the average strength here was 'scarcely 14.8°'. 'We can thus deduce from this second series of observations,' concluded the young zoologist, 'a result analogous to that of the first. That is to say, that the physical strength among the savages of this part of New-Holland is not very great.'

Péron then spoke of the results of the experiments on his French colleagues aboard ship. After examining seventeen of them, he found they had quite superior strength to the 'Diémenois', and also to the mainlanders. Later, in Port Jackson, he measured the strength of fourteen Englishmen. These were the strongest of all — no doubt, suggested Péron, because they were more robust than the French who had just spent several months travelling across the seas.

While in Timor, Péron had also conducted experiments. His general results, for what he called the 'Sauvages de la terre de Diémen [et] de la Nouvelle-Hollande' and then the 'habitans de Timor, des

François et des Anglois' [sic] are given below (a myriagram is equal to 10 kilograms):

	Hands in kilograms	Back in myriagrams
Terre de Diémen	50.6	not available
Nouvelle-Hollande	51.8	14.8
Timor	58.7	16.2
François	69.2	22.1
Anglois	71.4	23.8

Péron drew his conclusions. 'The inhabitants of the "terre de Diémen", the most savage [*sauvage*] of all, "le enfans de la nature par excellence"', he declared, 'are the weakest', and 'those of New-Holland, who are hardly more civilised, are weaker than the inhabitants of Timor', who were 'much weaker' than the English or the French. In one short paragraph he then stated quite clearly (in direct opposition to what he would call elsewhere 'the dreamers') that 'the development of physical strength is not always in direct relation to the lack of civilisation. It is not a fixed quantity, it is not a necessary result of the savage state. Thus, not only did 'the savage' lack powers of reflection (as Rousseau had suggested) but he also lacked physical prowess — and the more he was 'savage' the more he was 'weak'!

Péron goes on to present 'presumed' causes for this 'weakness' [*foiblesse*] among the 'Diémenois' and mainlanders. The first was lack of good nutrition. 'The vegetable kingdom provides them with almost nothing,' he said, and 'the animal kingdom in its term offers few species apart from the emu and the kangaroo … Fishing could provide … more abundant resources,' he thought, 'but the imperfection of their equipment and their fishing methods', along with the harsh winters in Diemensland and storms in New-Holland, all combined to make this resource 'too often insufficient and even at times totally lacking', resulting in 'cruel famines'. In the inland, the inhabitants 'waged active war on frogs, lizards and snakes, various kinds of larvae, and above all fat caterpillars'. 'Even spiders,' he continued, 'form part of their disgusting meals … and even the swarms of ants which devastate the ground have had to be used for food.' Péron then spoke of a 'horrible paste which the *naturels* prepare by kneading these insects and their larvae with fern roots'. This was a 'repulsive custom', he thought, of which he had not found 'the least trace in all the rest of the universe'. Perhaps indeed he had not; but perhaps people he had met elsewhere in 'the universe' did not live in conditions such as those here, and would surely have died if they had tried to. Edward Eyre and other later explorers would not have survived without the assistance of their native guides (Eyre's companion, Wylie, for example), who themselves would have had few problems maintaining their existence in what was of course their homeland.

Péron also considered insufficient continuous physical exercise to be a cause for this 'weakness'. 'The savage,' he declared, 'compelled by the imperious need to procure food to appease his hunger, indulges over several days in long and arduous hunting, only resting when his body collapses from fatigue and exhaustion.' The 'savage' then stayed by his 'prey' for several days, sleeping and eating, before setting off on a new hunt. 'What could be more harmful to real development, and to the harmonious maintenance of strength, than these alternations of excessive fatigues, of forced rest-periods, of overwhelming privations, of excesses and [then] orgies of famine!'

Again here, Péron may be misreading the situation by judging it with his 'civilised' eye. The hunter hunts when he needs to, and rests when there is no need to do otherwise.[140]

Péron goes on, however, to suggest that these 'savages' could improve their strength if they became more 'civilised' by, for example, domesticating the kangaroo and emu for a more regular food supply. They could also 'assemble in villages' and get to know the 'privileges of property' and the 'benefits' of 'social organisation'. But perhaps these indigenous hunting and gathering Australians did not seek such a way of life — and, indeed, according to Rousseau and his acolytes, were better off without it.

To return to Péron's anthropometric experiments, it should be said that their very nature is indicative of their inventor. Perhaps such muscular actions of the hands and loins were much less required by the Aboriginal way of life than by that of the Europeans, and so the Aborigines appeared 'weak' in these actions. Elsewhere they may have been much stronger than the Europeans, who would then appear 'weak' if the Aborigines had chosen and conducted their own experiments. If the French were 'stronger' in the hands and loins (they had been hauling ropes on ship for months), would they have been so strong in running down and spearing a kangaroo? These tests — like the IQ tests and others of later years — are culturally specific, and are limited as such.

In a concluding section before presenting the complete, detailed results of his tests, Péron waxed lyrical against what he again called '*le langage des sophistes*'. 'What can one think from now on,' he exclaimed, 'about those eloquent declamations against the continual *perfectionnement* of the social order deduced from the extraordinary strength of savage man, or rather, to use the language of the *sophistes*, of "*l'homme de la nature*"!' 'I am very pleased,' he concluded, 'to have … opposed actual experiments and numerous facts to that opinion which is all too prevalent … that *the physical degeneration of man follows the perfection of civilisation*.'[141]

A copy of Péron's complete results would be too onerous to present here. However, the following details of his study with the Diémenois and mainlanders may serve to give an idea of the nature of his work. The 'strongest' Diémenois is twenty-two to twenty-four years of age, and the 'weakest' just two years his junior.

Péron's experiments with the dynamometer: Savages of Van Diemen's Land

No.	Name	Age	Strength of hands	Observations
1	—	18 to 20 years	41.0	Of a family strong constitution for this country.
2	—	20 to 22 years	40.0	Arms and legs thin and feeble; large tummy.
3	—	22 to 24 years	60.0	Torso fairly robust; limbs feeble.

No.	Name	Age	Strength of hands	Observations
4	—	24 to 25 years	50.0	Body thin and miserable; tummy rounded.
5	Ouriaga	25 to 27 years	57.0	Fairly good constitution; shoulders broad and strong.
6	Bara-Ourou	28 to 30 years	54.3	One of the best constitutions, and one of the best looking individuals among the nation.
7	—	30 to 32 years	51.7	Constitution listless; legs very feeble.
8	—	32 to 34 years	46.2	Face cruel; beard very strong; much hair on his back.
9	—	34 to 36 years	55.0	Appearance wild; attitude of body tired.
10	—	34 to 36 years	49.0	Back poorly muscled; limbs feeble; tummy swollen.
11	—	35 to 38 years	59.0	Expression fierce; beard thick and black; much hair on the body.
12	—	38 to 40 years	44.0	Legs and arms feeble.

NB,

1. I have not been able to obtain the names of the majority of the individuals listed in this table.
2. None of them would try the strength of their back with the dynamometer.
3. The age indicated in this table is only approximate. The system of numbering found among the peoples of Van Diémen's Land and New- Holland does not extend beyond three, and the individuals tested had no idea of their age.

Average score for this table:

> Hands 50.6 kilograms
> Back —

The mainlanders' results include those for the back test. Here the person with the highest total score (hands and back) among those aged at least eighteen is a man named Pa-ra-ma-ra, some thirty to thirty-three years of age, who is of a 'vigorous constitution' but has a 'cruel look'. His total is 78. The least strong, with a total of 45, is a man of the same age named Mou-guean. Among the Frenchmen the highest score was 109 and the lowest 85, both well above any of the Indigenous totals. Péron's personal total was 'a modest 87'.[142]

Here are details of results for the Indigenous mainlanders.[143] As elsewhere, only men (and some boys here) are measured:

Péron's experiments with the dynamometer: Mainlanders

No.	Name	Age	Strength		Observations
1	Cou-de-Cou-del	10–12	30.0	10.0	Pretty little child, weak constitution.
2	Toul-gra, called Bouldog	14–15	31.0	16.0	Quite well built, very lively, excellent mimic.
3	Mo-ro-e	16–18	43.0	16.0	Small, but quite well built.
4	Ca-pou-er-re	16–18	45.0	14.0	Quite well built for this country.
5	Eutelor	18–20	56.0	15.0	Brave, audacious, one of the most robust for his nation.
6	Ou-rou-Ma-re-Ga-la	18–20	47.0	13.0	Not very strong. Wild-looking.
7	Ou-rou-Mare	19–21	55.0	19.0	As strongly built as his nation can allow.
8	Aca-ra-da Pa-ra	25–28	44.0	13.0	Very weak, hard and wild expression.
9	Oui-roue	27–30	52.0	16.0	Well developed torso, thin legs, wild expression.
10	Ouca-la-ga	27–30	58.0	14.0	Rather well built. Sombre physiognomy. Haggard-looking eyes.
11	Bourra-Bourra	27–30	50.0	13.0	Short, stocky, many hairs on his body. Ferocious man.
12	Pa-ra-ma-ra	30–33	60.0	18.0	Vigorous constitution, very long arms and legs, cruel look.

No.	Name	Age	Strength		Observations
13	Mou–guean	30–33	32.0	13.0	Quite slim, hairy over his whole body.
14	Coure-Oure-Oulou	33–35	55.0	13.0	Thin-looking, weak limbs, prominent tummy.
15	Dal–re	33–35	46.0	14.0	Short, stocky, dark–brown skin.
16	Benil–lon	35–36	57.0	16.0	The Chief. Quite good constitution, but a bit thin.
17	Ma–ra–ora	38–40	62.0	15.0	Very thick beard, very long thin limbs.
Average score for these last 13 people: Hands 51.8 kilograms					
Back 14.8 myriagrams					

In Port Jackson in 1819, Paul Gaimard (with Freycinet's expedition) used this same machine to measure the 'average strength' of sixteen male 'natives of New South Wales' aged '18–53 years'. His results were 48.5 kilograms for the hands and 10.0 myriagrams for the back (and thus slightly weaker than those obtained by Péron). For no fewer than eighty-nine Frenchmen on board the *Uranie* (aged 18–55) he obtained figures of 59.6 and 16.4 respectively. If one should feel, however, that these decreased results for the native men may be due to their oft-cited '*dégénération*' at the hands of the British, one may wonder as to the reason for the similarly decreased results for the French. Freycinet's earlier suggestion that, among the natives, 'the individuals in our experiments were sometimes far from co-operative and would not keep still, which is a possible source of error in making measurements' could scarcely have applied to his compatriots.[144]

In conclusion, one may say that, generally, the French opinion of the physical appearance of the Indigenous people was rarely favourable. Dampier's opinion that those he saw were 'the miserablest People in the World … And setting aside this Humane Shape, they differ but little from Brutes' was in fact reiterated by some of the French; and indeed Duclesmeur will declare that his observations in Van

Diémen's Land so resembled those of Dampier in New Holland that these two parts of the world were indeed one. He quotes Dampier almost word for word. 'These are the miserablest people in the world,' he wrote, 'and the human beings who approach the closest to brutes [*ce sont Les gens du monde Les Plus misérables. Et ceux des humains qui approchent Le Plus des Brutes*].' His colleague Le Dez would express himself similarly. 'We found a few miserable inhabitants,' he said, 'more like animals than men.' And, he continued, 'I compare them with the inhabitants of New Holland of whom Dampier speaks.'[145]

In Tasmania in 1802 Milius and Péron expressed their opinion on the appearance of the women. 'They were all very ugly,' wrote Milius, 'and their excessive dirtiness [*malpropreté*] made them very disgusting.'[146] 'In a word,' Péron concluded, 'all the particulars of their physical constitution were repulsive [*repoussans*].'

In Western Australia Péron would be no less uncomplimentary. Describing the unfortunate pregnant woman they met and who attempted to flee, he spoke of what he called 'this natural ugliness' and how this, added to 'the most extreme dirtiness [*la malpropreté la plus grossière*], ... would have sufficed to repulse the most brutish [*brutal*] of our sailors'.[147]

In Sydney, too, standards of 'cleanliness' were clearly different from those of the British or French, and Milius would describe how the Indigenous women's 'bodies are extremely dirty [*d'une très grande malpropreté*]'.[148] In Sydney Harbour at the end of July 1825 Hyacinthe de Bougainville watched the fishing canoes coming in, laden with their catch, and manned by Indigenous men and women. The picturesque attraction he found in the panorama, however, may have been somewhat diminished by the 'poverty' he perceived in the people. 'Nothing could be more hideous and more disgusting,' he reflected, 'than these poor creatures, whose bodies, wasted away and scar-covered, bore testimony to the abject poverty and primitive state of these savages [*la misère et la barbarie de ces sauvages*]'.[149] Jacques Arago had written, a few years earlier, of the Sydney people: 'I do not believe that any of them has ever been young, for they are ugly, hideous and decrepit at birth.'[150]

Nutrition

When reading the accounts of explorers to Australia of any nationality one could believe that the staple diet of the Aboriginal people generally consisted of seafood, but of course these explorers never ventured far inland. It would appear, however, from archaeological research that for some 4000 years the Tasmanian Aborigines had not eaten fish at all but had limited themselves to shellfish.[151] The French experience confirms this puzzling practice.

In 1772 Dufresne's people never saw the inhabitants actually eating, although Crozet deduced, 'by the considerable pile of shells we encountered … that the usual food of the savages [*sauvages*] was mussels, pinna ['*pinnes marines*'], scallops, cockles and other similar shellfish.'[152] In February 1793 Labillardière did see Tasmanians 'make their meal about the middle of the day.' To his consternation, several women plunged into the sea 'in search of lobster and other shellfish'. Upon emerging from the depths, they were immediately 'employed in broiling [the] shellfish which they put on the coals with the greatest precaution' but they simply threw the lobsters 'carelessly into the flames'.[153]

His colleagues confirmed his observations. Joseph Raoul added to the list 'earshells [*oreilles de mer*], haliotis [and] mussels' and La Motte du Portail included 'crayfish and abalones'. Ventenat would note that after '10 to 12 minutes' of diving the women brought back 'at least twenty-five pounds weight, as many lobsters as earshells, oysters, mussels and other shellfish'.[154] A veritable seafood feast!

When offered vertebrate fish, the Tasmanians would flatly refuse them. One evening in January 1802 some of Baudin's men were dining on shore on some fish they had caught when they were joined by seven natives. 'They invited the natives sitting amongst them to have some of what was left,' wrote Baudin, 'but they would take nothing.' Nor would they even taste the rum that was offered to them, although they accepted with delight the bottles after emptying their contents onto the ground. A few days later Baudin had this same experience when, after hauling in a net of fish, he offered to share his catch with the sixteen natives accompanying him, 'but they would accept nothing', he wrote, 'making signs that they did not eat fish, but only shell-fish or crustaceae'. After Baudin and his men had cooked their catch and were eating it, 'the natives … appeared quite amazed to see people eating fish'. In his *Particular Remarks concerning our sojourn in D'Entrecasteaux Channel … and our stay at Maria Island*, Baudin presents a résumé of the Tasmanians' attitude to any food offered to them. 'These people,' he wrote, 'appear to obtain most of their food from the sea and eat shell-fish more than anything else. They seemed not to set much store by fish, and we did not get them to accept any, whether of those caught alive in the net, or whether of what our men prepared for their dinner … They were also very little interested in our biscuit and fresh bread … [and] threw it away.'

The French explorers' fishing fortunes varied. On Maria Island Baudin's catch was not plentiful. 'We were not lucky with our fishing during this visit,' he declared. 'The fish we did catch were very good, but scarce. This was not the case with oysters and a type of lobster, for every day we caught more than the crew could eat. The oysters were of good quality, but the lobsters were far superior to those eaten in Europe by reason of the delicacy and lightness of their flesh.'[155] In 1792, however, in the D'Entrecasteaux Channel, Huon de Kermadec had declared that 'fish abound to such an extent … that one can be sure … of being able to provide for the crew every day at discretion'. He also discovered 'a considerable quantity of mussels and other very tasty little shells' and 'rock oysters of excellent quality'. His companion La Motte du Portail tasted some of the earshells his companions had cooked and 'was surprised to find it so tender on taking straight from the water, while in our parts we have to keep them for several days, to beat them so as to soften them'.[156] Rhys Jones has suggested that the Tasmanians' ichthyophobia may be due to 'an intellectual decision which had the result of constricting their ecological universe'.[157] If so, then this would appear to be a superb decision, for why would one struggle to catch fish when such excellent shell-fish abounded? Perhaps indeed, in this way, their nutritional universe may have been more expanded than constricted.

The Tasmanians treated with great circumspection any food or drink offered to them, a fact which is not surprising in view of the life or death importance of this subject, and the strange origin of the people offering them. 'I ate and drank before them,' wrote D'Auribeau, 'as also did the sailors with me, but my offer and entreaties failed to encourage them to taste anything at all.' La Motte du Portail offered 'sugar candy' to some children which, he noted, 'they took with much pleasure and their mothers had to take from their mouths, being careful afterwards to put in a finger to make sure that none remained'. 'That could only arise,' he thought, 'from distrust.' Perhaps instinctively the mothers had guessed that this sugar could only harm the children's teeth — and, one recalls, the French had greatly admired these people's teeth! If the native people's obstinacy in refusing the candy (and, more especially, alcohol) had continued, they would indeed have been spared many future miseries. D'Entrecasteaux suggested that this fear of foreign food 'came, perhaps, for some unfortunate experience they might have had with previous [necessarily British] navigators giving them food', although, he reflected, 'I would be inclined to think ... that they only wanted to eat the sort of food with which their upbringing, acting through instinct, had acquainted them'.[158]

There is little evidence as to the Tasmanians' other foods. We have seen that they ate broiled seaweed and fern-root, but they also appear to have enjoyed bird and kangaroo meat. On Maria Island in 1802, Hamelin, commander of *Le Naturaliste* with Baudin's expedition, stated quite categorically that 'the natives here eat birds'. 'Yesterday,' he wrote, 'we killed one for them and they immediately put it on the coals to cook, without drawing it, and ate it.'[159] In the D'Entrecasteaux Channel Labillardière had suspected that birds formed part of the natives' nutrition. 'A parakeet passed quite close to us,' he wrote, 'and settled at a little distance on the turf. Immediately two of the young savages set off, pursued it, and were on the point of putting their hand on it, when the bird flew away.'[160]

The first European acquaintance in Tasmania with the word 'kangaroo' seems to be by Cook's expedition to Adventure Bay in January

1777, when surgeon Anderson wrote: 'we found that the animal called 'kangooroo' at Endeavour River was known under the same name here'.[161] The first French use of this name was in February 1793 by D'Entrecasteaux's people, among whom Joseph Raoul wrote: 'we presumed that they eat the flesh of the kangaroo [and] … they signified that we had thought correctly'.

Perhaps because of its short supply, the Tasmanians did not appear to be concerned about the quality of their drinking water. 'They appeared to us to be infinitely unparticular about water,' said D'Auribeau, 'for what their women brought them in small seaweed buckets … was extremely turbid and muddy. They drank it without difficulty, however, spitting out the foreign bodies they could not swallow.'[162] As in so many other ways, the native peoples have again lived within their means — where the more 'fussy' or 'difficult' Europeans may have soon died of starvation or thirst.

On the mainland the coastal people had no such reservations about fish. We have seen how in 1801 Baudin's first encounter with the inhabitants of Western Australia had been with a man busy spearing fish. In King George Sound in 1803 Péron would see another method of fishing, here involving the construction of stone dams across a river which allowed the fish to enter but not to escape. Péron named this river '*la rivière des François*'.[163] In 1826 D'Urville's people arrived here and saw these same constructions. 'The industry to which they [the natives] apply the most intelligence seems to be the construction of their fisheries,' observed Quoy and Gaimard, 'which are made of stones, like the ones on the French River, or with ordinary small stakes. The fish enter with the tide through a small opening that they straightaway close; and if the fish are plentiful, the fishing is easy.' The fish did not, alas, appear to be plentiful. 'The neglected state the fisheries were in,' continued D'Urville's men, 'would seem to indicate that this is a very precarious resource.'[164] Further north, on the coast of Western Australia in 1819, Arago felt similarly. 'These poor people,' he wrote, 'live wholly on fish, shell fish, and a kind of pulse resembling our French beans.'[165]

In New South Wales too the Indigenous Australians enjoyed fish. This, however, was not always easy to obtain, as the British observed in June 1788, just five months after the establishment of their settlement at Port Jackson. 'The cold weather … at this time of year,' wrote David Collins, 'was observed to affect the fishing; and the natives themselves appeared to be in great want.' In July the natives in fact attacked some fisherman and 'took by force about half of what had been brought on shore.'[166]

This lack of fish was thus already evident when the British arrived. Some thirty years later Louis de Freycinet saw the natives here and thought 'their existence is very miserable: on the sea-shore they live almost exclusively on fish and shell-fish and, inland, on the produce of their hunting, various roots and a few insects'. 'When winter arrives,' he continued, 'and the fish become scarce, they migrate to the North to seek more abundant food but, despite this precaution, these unfortunate people are often exposed to cruel famines. When a whale is washed up on the shore this is a god-send for them: we've seen them draw blood while fighting over such a disgusting quarry.'[167] In Jervis Bay in 1826 D'Urville had an experience similar to that described by Collins. 'At this mooring,' he wrote, 'a single cast of the net brought in a huge catch … the natives, fascinated by such a novel spectacle, indulged in extravagant exhibition of delight. And especially when they saw that the sailors were leaving for them many of the … small sharks and trigger fish, their joyful shouts were so loud and piercing that … I was afraid some unfortunate incident had occurred.'[168]

Shell-fish were also an important part of nourishment, and here again it was the women who collected it. 'While the men rest,' wrote Laplace, 'the women … go along the rivers or the lakes to find shell-fish which they cook on the coals [*charbons*] and bring to their husbands.'[169]

Kangaroos were of course one of the most obvious food sources, and the methods of hunting these were often observed. In King George Sound Péron noted that the   *naturels* had 'several very handsome and very large dogs with them' which, he thought, 'they use especially for hunting kangaroos which they eat'.[170] At this same spot in 1826 D'Urville's people witnessed a kangaroo hunt. 'The catching of a kangaroo is very important for them,' wrote Quoy and Gaimard, 'and for this a whole tribe has to surround the place where it has been isolated and set the area alight, thus forcing the animal out to be despatched.'[171] At Carabeely just west of Sydney in 1802, French-born Francis Barrallier, sent by Governor King to explore the Blue Mountains, actually took part in a kangaroo hunt and described the natives' strategy in detail. It resembles closely that observed on the opposite side of the continent. Barrallier wrote:

> When the natives assemble together to hunt the kangaroo, they form a circle which contains an area of 1 or 2 miles according to the number of natives assembled. They usually stand about 30 paces apart, armed with spears and tomahawks. When the circle is formed, each one of them holding a handful of lighted bark, they at a given signal set fire to the grass and bush in front of them. In proportion as the fire progresses they advance forward with their spears in readiness, narrowing the circle and making as much noise as possible, with deafening shouts, until, through the fire closing in more and more, they are so close as to touch one another. The kangaroos, which are thus shut into that circle, burn their feet in jumping on every side to get away, and are compelled to retire within the circle until the fire attacks them. They then try to escape in various directions, and the natives frightening them with their shouts throw their spears at the one passing nearest to them. By this means not one can escape. They roast the product of their chase, without skinning nor even gutting the animals, and then divide it among themselves, after having cut each animal into pieces.[172]

Lizards, grubs and birds also formed part of the Indigenous people's protein intake, as Barrallier recorded:

> Besides lizards and other animals, grubs are eaten … and it is more particularly those which are found in the trunks of the trees they look for. For this purpose they always carry with them a switch about 12 inches long and of the thickness of a fowl's feather, which they stick into their hair above the ear. When they discover on the trunk of a tree the mark of

the hole made by some of these grubs, they make the hole larger with their axe and … dip their switch into the hole and, by means of the hook [on the end], draw it out and eat it greedily.

While the grubs were eaten raw, the lizard was roasted before being 'devoured'.[173] Laplace remarked that the women of Port Jackson went hunting for 'lizards and possums into the highest tree-tops'. On occasions too he observed how the women would 'stretch out on a mound [*tertre*], holding in their half-opened hands strips of flesh to attract the birds, and stayed still until they could grab one of them when it came for the bait'.[174]

The native people's vegetable intake seems to have been rather restricted. In Esperance Bay (Western Australia) in 1792, D'Entrecasteaux did not meet anyone, but found 'human excrement [which] contained pips and grains'. 'The pips,' he discovered, 'belong to a very small berry that I have since found … to have a very pleasant taste. The grains are those of the "Mesembryanthemum edule".'[175] Although René Lesson declared that 'the food of the maritime tribes consists mainly of fish', he added that 'the basis of their subsistence is the root of a fern called "dingoua", which they crush and knead'.[176]

Water supplies could sometimes be so difficult that the French wondered how the inhabitants managed to survive. At Dampier's Bay (north of today's Perth) in 1818 Arago wrote that this coast 'exhibited nothing but a picture of desolation; no rivulet consoled the eye, no tree attracted it'. 'Do all the beings that dwell on this inhospitable land,' he wondered, 'drink salt water?' Upon meeting some fifteen 'natives', Arago decided to put his theory to the test. 'Desirous of knowing whether they were destitute of fresh water, as we supposed,' he wrote, 'I fixed their attention by some gestures, and pretended to drink some sea-water out of the hollow of my hand. They did not seem to be surprised at it, and showed no signs of aversion, though I am certain they understood me.'[177] Arago may have thus deduced that the natives drank sea-water. Perhaps too the inhabitants supposed that this strange creature from out of the horizon enjoyed drinking sea–water, and, being more tolerant of others than others were at times of them, expressed no surprise at this.

Some of the scenes observed by the French in and around Sydney were almost too horrible to contemplate, for after the arrival of the British, food supplies for the Aboriginal inhabitants began to dwindle dangerously. 'Their frequent hunting parties,' wrote Arago in 1819, 'have destroyed the greater part of the game that served for food to these wandering tribes; the latter, in consequence of the famines to which they are exposed, have been compelled to approach the European settlements.'[178]

In the Northern Territory too the inhabitants had clearly had relations with the English before D'Urville arrived in 1839. In Raffles Bay in March that year he had been approached by several natives 'for the sole purpose of begging'; 'to all our questions and signs,' he wrote, 'their only answers are a few English words "very good bread", at the same time tapping their bellies … to make themselves better understood'.[179]

It has sometimes been suggested that the Indigenous Australians were cannibals. In 1623, at Cape York, Cartensz had reported seeing 'in various places great quantities of human bones, from which it may be safely concluded that the coast of Nova Guinia [as he believed it to be] are man-eaters who do not spare each other when driven by hunger'.[180] D'Entrecasteaux would also believe for a moment that this was so, but quickly came to another conclusion. 'One of the naturalists has found some bones in this harbour [in the D'Entrecasteaux Channel in Tasmania],' he wrote, 'which he believes were those of a very young female; they were among the ashes of a hearth, where it seems the natives cook their meals.' He reflected, however, 'One such isolated incident is not enough to authorize conjectures injurious to human nature.' On his second visit to Tasmania, and after making acquaintances with the *naturels*, he declared: 'Oh! How much we should blush for having suspected them last year of eating human flesh!'[181] No other French explorer even so much as suspected cannibalism.

Dwellings

The Aboriginal Australians did in fact dwell nowhere, and thus had no need for dwellings. They did, however, have ready-made forms of shelter, but it is the very temporary nature of these constructions which makes their reporting by the explorers appear irregular. Wind-breaks and huts could appear to be anywhere, and then nowhere.

On Maria Island in Tasmania in 1772, Duclesmeur reported seeing 'small huts in different places, made of tree bark'. His colleague Le Dez's description shows these were simply 'a few pieces of bark, badly arranged, with one end resting on a piece of wood set crosswise and the other on the ground, that formed … a kind of hut'.[182] In 1792 Labillardière saw 'some rudiments of huts' in the D'Entrecasteaux Channel which consisted of 'a frame-work of the branches of young trees, and designed to be afterwards filled up with pieces of bark which the natives always use to cover the outside of their cabins'.[183] His colleague, the naturalist Riche, however, gave the best description of the best hut discovered:

On the 7th May [1792] I found a hut [at Recherche Bay] which was more clearly constructed than the others. It was hemispherical, with a little door, and a very large heap of shells showed that it was an old habitation … Of the four layers of which I found the cabin to have been constructed, the first and the most interior was an assemblage of hoops which served to bind together and support the totality of the construction. They were tied together where they crossed by strands of rush tied in flat nests and in rosette. The second layer was formed of rushes which served as a bed for the third layer of very short grass, but thick and soft, which served to prevent the wind and cold from penetrating the hut and then for keeping off the rain. The fourth and exterior layer was formed by large pieces of bark from the peppermint eucalypt, placed one on the other to cover the whole convexity of the hut. I had observed before that all the remains of huts I had come across had presented to me about the same order of construction in the way the layers were formed. In all those I have seen, some of which were complete, I have never found more than I have described; sometimes the covering could be no more than a single layer composed of the bark of trees. This one was a palace in comparison with all those others I had seen. It was in the form of a skull–cap, being at least sixteen feet in diameter at the base. Twelve men could quite easily sleep there. The hut was about six feet high in the middle, the entrance was about three and a half feet high and it had been closed up tightly. The cabin had been in existence for more than a year because the branches which formed the framework of its arch must have been bent while they were green, and they were dry and quite easily broken.[184]

Baudin would also see several huts near here and on Maria Island, but these appeared to be of a very different quality. They were, he declared, 'the most miserable things imaginable. A curved piece of wood is all the framework, and this is covered by some slabs of eucalyptus bark that they lift off the trees'.[185] His companion Louis de Freycinet noticed that 'the huts [*les huttes*] constructed by the savages all faced NE or SE' which led him to conclude that the 'winds from the east are never very strong in these parts'.[186]

Huon de Kermadec and his colleagues had believed in 1792 that the Aboriginal Tasmanians had also sought shelter in purposefully hollowed-out trees. 'They construct them,' he wrote, 'very simply … They burn the very large trees at the base so skilfully that all the interior up to a height of five or six feet is consumed by fire so that there remains only the sapwood and the bark connected with the roots to form the walls of the house … I have seen several of these shanties hollowed out in this way which could easily contain eight or ten people.'[187] None of the French ever actually witnessed anyone inside these trees, and the supposition of their 'habitation' is based on finding 'in some of them the remains of shell-fish on which they feed, and frequently the cinders of the fires at which they dressed their victuals'.[188] In 1777, with Cook's expedition, surgeon Anderson had also supposed that the native peoples lived in trees converted into 'comfortable habitation'. These trees, he noted, 'have their trunks hollow'd out by fire, to the height of six or seven feet'. Like the French, however, neither Anderson nor Cook himself (who also saw 'evedent [sic] signs of them some times takeing [sic] up their aboad [sic] in the trunks of large trees') ever actually saw people inside them.[189]

On the mainland 'huts' were also found on the west coast, at King

George Sound, and on the south-east coast. On what is today called the Péron Peninsula, François Péron saw several *cabanes* which, he considered, 'indicated a more advanced civilisation than elsewhere in New Holland', although, he thought, brought about only 'as a result of a deeper misery and a more imperious need'. Péron described these in detail, while his colleague Lesueur drew them (see photographic section). 'They have a semi-spheroid shape,' he wrote, 'slightly compressed at the top. They are spiral ... rather like the shell of a snail. They are about 4 to 5 feet high, with a diameter of 6 to 8 feet. They consist of branches stuck in the sand ... intertwined in all directions to form the roof ... On the outside of this roof are several layers of leaves and dry grass covered with a great amount of sand.'[190] At this same spot sixteen years later, Arago found 'ten or a dozen miserable ruined huts ... formed of a few branches, crossing each other, covered with brushwood and clay, six feet in depth, four or five in breadth, and three and a half above the ground'. 'The entrance,' he noted, 'is always on the side facing the wind.'[191]

At King George Sound D'Urville's naturalist, M. Quoy, found similar constructions. 'Their huts,' he wrote, 'are tree branches bent over into a curve and covered with dried grass-tree leaves. They cannot stand up in them, and can hardly stretch out in them either.'[192] On the south-east coast of Murat Bay (today's Ceduna) Péron discovered 'two wretched huts [*deux misérables cases*] made of branches roughly intertwined and stuck into the ground',[193] and, further north, at Jervis Bay in 1826, D'Urville observed 'two native huts in form ... like an oblong beehive', rather larger than usual for they were 'about six or seven feet high'. They were, he continued, 'built of strips of eucalyptus bark, set upright and brought together at the top, covered with grass and marine plants'. 'Clean and spacious inside,' he noted, 'each of them could easily house a family of eight to ten individuals.' These were clearly more serious constructions than elsewhere and, he concluded, 'evidence a degree of intelligence on the part of these savages superior to any I had so far encountered'.[194]

D'Urville was of course able (implicitly at least) to compare these constructions with the Palace of Versailles (near which town he died in 1842) and to appreciate the technological difference between these two civilisations. Just north of Sydney, however, at Port Stephens in 1826, the Englishman Robert Dawson had been obliged to spend a night in the bush, where his native companions soon made him 'one of their gunyers (bark huts) and,' he declared, 'I slept as well in it as if I had been in a palace; perhaps even better'.[195]

Among the most unusual abodes discovered were the 'sort of underground shelter' examined by Péron at Péron Peninsula in 1803, wherein the inhabitants could find 'a salutory freshness' during the day, escape the cold at night, the 'legions of insects' and 'the fury of the hurricanes [*ouragans*] and rain-storms'.[196] In 1819, however, Arago visited these same 'holes mentioned by Péron ... in which', he wrote, 'he supposes the savages dwell'. 'For my part,' said Arago, 'I do not think so.' Arago could not see how 'the savages protect themselves against the rain', as he could 'not perceive any means they would have for closing it'.[197] As with the hollowed-out trees in Tasmania, no explorer ever actually witnessed anyone in these underground 'shelters'.

Fires

Fires were seen everywhere in Australia by almost everyone. While still some five leagues off-shore, and arriving in Tasmania in 1772, Dufresne's people 'saw numerous fires there and one, by its elevation, we judged was on the summit of a mountain so considerable that it seemed more like a volcano or a conflagration than deliberate. There were three others, much smaller and much lower, which were certainly made by men.' On landing at Frederick Henry Bay they immediately noticed that 'there were traces of fire everywhere' and that 'the ground seemed covered with ashes' and the trees, whether hollow or not, were 'mostly burnt at the foot'.[198] When Milius arrived in Tasmania he saw that 'the great mountain ... to the NW [Mount Wellington?] presented us, during all our stay, with a widespread fire ... During the night we could very easily have read by the light of the flames. It is difficult to explain the cause for this system of destruction adopted by all the natives [*indigènes*] of this country.'[199]

On the west and south coasts of the mainland the situation was similar. As early as 1696 on the west coast, De Vlamingh's crew had seen at night 'fires all over the country',[200] and in December 1792, on the western extremity of the south-west coast of New Holland, Labillardière would see 'fires lighted along the coast [which] sent up large columns of smoke, intended no doubt by the inhabitants to let us know they were there'.[201] On this same coast in 1801 Baudin saw 'many traces of fire everywhere',[202] and in King George Sound in 1803 his colleague Péron would observe 'several columns of smoke' along the shores of 'various lakes' and 'several more towards the mountains'.[203]

Why these fires were lit was a puzzle, and Labillardière's supposition was but one of many. In Tasmania in 1772 Dufresne's people were welcomed with fire. 'The natives showed themselves gracious,' wrote Crozet, 'gathered wood and made a kind of pile.' They then presented the new arrivals 'with some dry lighted branches' and appeared to invite them 'to set fire to the pile'. 'We were ignorant of the meaning of this ceremony,' said Crozet, 'and we lit the pile.' His companion Le Dez thought this was 'a sign of friendship'.[204] Still in Tasmania, in 1802, Captain Hamelin encountered about thirty natives and noted how 'one man was walking in front and carrying a branch with which he set fire to everything'. Hamelin's supposition was quite different from that of Le Dez, for he believed this was 'customary when they want to … begin a war among themselves'.[205]

Some thought, quite simply, that fires were to keep off the cold. 'I think they must suffer very much during the [Tasmanian] winter,' wrote Le Dez, 'because I do not think they have other ways of fending off the cold than by lighting fires.'[206] On the west and east coasts of the mainland, the French and English would draw similar conclusions. In view of the small size of the habitations, Milius thought at Géographe Bay that the fires were 'to keep the feet warm while the rest of the body is under shelter'.[207] On the east coast Joseph Banks also supposed that the people 'trusted their feet to the care of the fire', but he thought too that 'the remains of a fire [were] probably more necessary to defend them from Mosquetos than cold'.[208] Fire was of vital importance to the native people. 'They appreciate fire very much,' wrote Le Dez, 'and … we noticed that most of them … carry a fire-brand [*un tison*] and each time they stop … they make a fire and gather round it. It is astonishing how many places we have found where they have lit a fire, and how much the woods are devastated by it.'[209] When Labillardière met some natives in Tasmania in 1793, he observed that 'one of them carried a piece of decayed wood, lighted at one end', with which he 'amused himself now and then with setting it to a tuft'.[210] La Motte du Portail confessed that his colleagues and he had 'not been able to learn how they obtain fire', and supposed that 'it is the fear of being without it which leads them … to set fire to the places where they are'.[211] Labillardière assumed that Tasmanians 'procure themselves fire by striking two pieces of flint together'— an assumption similar to that of the Englishman John Cox's crew at Oyster Bay in 1789 who concluded that 'they produce fire by collision' of 'a few flints and stones and a little dried grass'.[212]

The mystery of how the Indigenous people made fire on the mainland had, however, already been solved by Joseph Banks some twenty years before. 'They set fire very expeditiously,' he had observed, 'with two peices [sic] of stick very readily and nimbly; the one must be round and 8 or nine inches long and both it and the other should be dry and soft; the round one they sharpen at the end and, pressing it upon the other, turn it round with the palms of the hands … often shifting their hands up and running them down quick to make the pressure as hard as possible; in this manner they will get a fire in less than two minutes.'[213] Baudin's artist, Nicolas Petit, also witnessed this along the same coast (of New South Wales), and his drawing appears here in the photographic section. The same method was employed in King George Sound where D'Urville's naturalist Quoy noted quite simply that 'they make fire by rubbing together two pieces of dry wood, and they always carry some in their hands when travelling in the form of a banksia cone which burns very slowly like a sort of tinder'. 'They all keep this portable heater,' he added, 'under their garment and close to their genital organs, where they seem most susceptible to the cold'.[214]

Canoes

The native people also carried fire in their canoes. Banks had noted that 'in the middle of [the] canoes was generaly [sic] a small fire upon a heap of sea weed', which he guessed was 'to give the fisherman an opportunity of Eating fish in perfection by broiling it the moment it is taken'.[215]

In New South Wales Louis de Freycinet remarked in 1802 how 'they always maintain a fire in the middle of the canoe [*pirogue*]: they place it on a bed of earth or ashes, and use it to cook the fish they catch'. Nicolas Petit made a drawing of one of these small craft, and this is reproduced in the photographic section. In Tasmania Freycinet had seen this same phenomenon where 'they keep constantly a fire in one of the extremities of their canoes' with underneath 'a layer of earth or ashes'.[216] In Sydney Harbour in 1825 Bougainville saw canoes [*canots*] with 'some hots coals' in them 'placed on flat stones, used to grill the fish, which they [the natives] devoured burning hot and half-cooked in their bare hands, casting into the sea the left-overs as bait'.[217] A year later Lesson saw this practice here, and felt perhaps for the poor fish which, he wrote, 'pass fully alive from the water onto the burning coals'.[218]

Some form of water transport seems to have been found on much of the continent, with the notable exception of the south and west coasts. Péron noticed the total lack of inhabitants on all the islands off the shores, from indeed the *détroit de Bass* to the *terre de Nuyts* (west of today's Albany). The 'main cause' for this, he thought, 'was their absolute ignorance of navigation'. Along these coasts, like all previous explorers, Péron 'never saw the slightest traces of any embarkation whatever'.[219] At Esperance Bay, D'Entrecasteaux had in fact concluded that 'the natives ... do not have the skills to build canoes or rafts which could transport them at a short distance across the sea'.[220] Elsewhere, however, canoes or rafts were found in abundance, and especially so in Tasmania where the expeditions of D'Entrecasteaux and Baudin encountered many of these small craft.

Near Adventure Bay in May 1792, St Aignan reported finding 'a kind of canoe, flat both above and below, about seven to nine feet long, in the middle three or four feet wide and finishing in a point at the two ends. It was made of large pieces of bark joined together in bands running lengthwise, and fastened with rushes or strands of grass.' In the D'Entrecasteaux Channel nine months later, another of these canoes was discovered and D'Entrecasteaux's second-in-command, Huon de Kermadec, assumed that 'the savages do not fail to venture on these frail rafts between one island and another'.[221] Baudin's encounters were even more extensive, and he himself saw indigenous people 'crossing from the [Tasmanian] mainland to D'Entrecasteaux [i.e. Bruny] Island in canoes'. His companion, Captain Hamelin, also met two people 'in one of their miserable canoes' making the same crossing and, on one occasion, he actually brought in one of these craft so it could be examined more closely. 'I think the term "raft" or "floating buoy" would be more appropriate than "canoe",' he declared. 'The sticks they propel it with likewise bear no relation to the paddles used in canoes.'[222] On Maria Island his colleague Louis de Freycinet also found some 'canoes [*pirogues*] of the same kind as those already described, and built just as badly'.[223]

As the descriptions of these canoes rather resemble one another, Louis de Freycinet's detailed presentation of those studied in the D'Entrecasteaux Channel may suffice here. 'In a state so cut off from civilisation,' he wrote, 'their arts have not been able to perfect themselves very much' and consequently their 'canoes [*pirogues*] are still of an extremely defective construction [*d'une construction extrêmement défectueuse*]: We have seen and measured many of them which all had the same dimensions and were built in exactly the same way.' He then entered into the detail of their construction and use:

'Three rolls of eucalyptus bark made up the general framework [*charpente*]. The main piece was 4 m 55 long and one metre wide; the two others 3 m 9 long and 0 m 32 thick. These rolls were … joined at the extremities, which made them go up into a point … The whole was quite solidly assembled with a sort of grass or rushes … In this state, the embarkation had the following dimensions:

Length inside	2 m 95 = 9′1″
Width outside	0 m 89 = 2′9″
Total height	0 m 65 = 2′1″
Depth in the middle	0 m 22 = 0′8″
Thickness at the extremities	0 m 27 = 0′10″

The savages [*sauvages*] can number five or six in these pirogues, but more usually they only go three or four at a time. Their paddles [*pagaies*] are simple pieces of wood, from 2 m 50 (7 ft 8″) up to 4 and even 5 metres long (11 ft 6″ and 15 ft 5″), and a thickness going from 2 to 5 cm. Sometimes, when the water is not very deep, they use these sticks [*bâtons*] to push against the bottom …

They usually sit to manoeuvre their pirogues, when they use bales of hay [*bottes de foin*] as seats. At other times they stand. We have only seen them cross the channel in fine weather: such frail and makeshift embarkations could neither advance nor even stay up in a rough sea. Mr Péron has presented, in the collection of plates accompanying the historical part of our voyage, a very exact drawing of the pirogues of the savages of Diemen's Land [*sauvages de la Terre de Diémen*] under no. XIV.'[224] [This drawing, by Lesueur, is presented in the photographic section.]In New South Wales too Freycinet observed similar craft which could also 'not navigate at all off the coasts, but only in the bays, harbours and rivers'. Here, however, the canoes could carry only 'up to three' people.[225] In 1770 Joseph Banks had also counted a maximum of three persons in these canoes at Botany Bay. To the north, however, in the Whitsunday Passage and above, he saw 'far superior' canoes 'regularly hollowd [sic] out of the trunk of a tree and fitted with an outrigger', which could contain '3 people or at most 4'.[226] Further north still, in Raffles Bay some sixty years later (in 1839), Lieutenant Barlatier Demas, in *L'Astrolabe* with Dumont d'Urville, 'saw two canoes coming out to the ship carrying eight or ten savages'. 'These canoes,' he observed, 'were tree trunks crudely hollowed out, without sails, and for paddles they had only bits of poorly trimmed wood.'[227]

Implements and utensils

Other tools of trade among the Aboriginal Australians were relatively rare. In Tasmania, when Dufresne's men had first landed, they had been received quite amicably, but when eventually a third longboat full of Frenchmen attempted to put ashore 'the savages showered us', wrote Duclesmeur, 'with a hail of hatchets and stones'.[228] D'Entre-casteaux's colleague D'Auribeau had a more pleasant encounter with these implements when, after having offered gifts himself, he was 'presented with a stone which [was] used as an axe, and a very hard and rather sharp pebble'. Rather interestingly, when these Frenchmen lent a native man an iron axe, he 'cut down several trees with a dexterity many Europeans would not equal'.[229]

Among the more peaceful utensils encountered were the baskets used by the women. 'The baskets the women use for fishing,' wrote Baudin, 'have some worth from the great amount of work that must go into them, and ... they will only exchange them with reluctance.'[230] The intricate work involved in the fabrication of these baskets may be appreciated in the illustration by Lesueur in the photographic section. These baskets appear to have been used for purposes other than fishing, however. When Labillardière and some colleagues had landed on Partridge Island, they had unintentionally frightened away 'four savages' who left behind them 'about thirty baskets made of rushes, some of which were filled with shell-fish and lobsters, others with pieces of flint and fragments of the bark of a tree as soft as the best tinder'. On another occasion Labillardière saw a man using an oyster shell as a cup,[231] and later Baudin would state that 'their drinking vessels are made from a type of seaweed with very broad, thick leaves'.[232] When the women dived for shell-fish they took with them a small tool which Labillardière observed being made. 'We saw some of the savages,' he wrote in D'Entrecasteaux Channel in February 1793, 'employed in cutting little bits of wood in the form of a spatula, and smoothing them with a shell, for the purpose of sepa-rating from the rocks limpets and sea-ears.'[233]

On the mainland some of these implements were seen by other observers. In King George Sound in 1826, D'Urville's men had seen axes 'like a clumsy rough hammer in shape', which was simply 'a piece of hard stone, shale or basalt, fixed to a thin handle with grass tree resin'. They also saw 'knives [made] the same way, by sticking four or five pieces of quartz together with the same glue on to a sim-ilar shaft'.[234] In 1831 in New South Wales Laplace remarked how, after initiation ceremonies, the new initiate had the right 'to hang a stone axe from his belt'.[235] These tools had been observed as early as 1705 on Melville Island (just north of today's Darwin) by a Dutch expedition which reported that the inhabitants 'possess nothing which is of value … and have neither iron nor anything like mineral ore or metal, but only a stone which is ground and made to serve as a hatchet'.[236] In 1803 Nicolas Baudin would conclude: 'the only mani-festations of industry that we saw were their spears and a not very dangerous club'.[237] The Aboriginal inhabitants of Australia had indeed little with which the Europeans could trade, and this was of course an important factor in the relative lack of interest shown for so long by explorers in this part of the world.

CHAPTER 2

Relations between the Aboriginal Australians and the French

W HEN the French first landed in New Holland the Indigenous inhabitants must have wondered who on Earth these creatures were. They had probably never encountered any people but their own. For the explorers, however, the situation was very different. They were circumnavigating the Earth, and knew to some extent what to expect. Also, the later explorers would have learnt from their predecessors and, in some cases, might have had explicit instructions to follow based on these earlier experiences. The major element of surprise and astonishment was thus reserved for the Indigenous inhabitants. This, as we will see, was to play an important role in the social relations between them and their French visitors.

This chapter examines, in chronological order of the expeditions, first these social relations. It then looks at the French perceptions of the character of their hosts, and the degree to which the French managed to understand their language (both spoken and gestural). Lastly, but no less importantly, the anthropological interest shown by the inhabitants themselves towards these inquisitive and uninvited guests is discussed.

Social relations

When Marion Dufresne and a few of his colleagues set foot in Tasmania on 7 March 1772, this was no doubt the first time the inhabitants had met people from another world. At first (according to the French) they were quite fearless, then happily curious, and finally — as more and more Frenchmen arrived upon the scene — openly hostile.

There are no fewer than five documented eyewitness accounts of this historic encounter and, as may be expected, these vary at times in their detail. Lieutenant Le Dez's account, however, seems to be the most comprehensive, and concurs in general with the others. He wrote:

> This morning we manned three boats to go and reconnoitre the country and M. Marion wanted to go ashore himself in his boat with M. Duclesmeur … The Diemenlanders [*Diémenois*], seeing us coming, came to the water's edge, where they lit a fire and gathered round it to wait for us. When the first boat was within earshot (it was the boat with the two captains in it) they said a lot of things to us as if we could understand them, adding several gestures which did not appear to invite us ashore … There were about forty of them, completely naked, and the only weapons they had were several long spears [*sagayes*] and a few stones they held in their hands. At that moment one of the longboats arrived. They watched it come without showing the least sign of fright.

Marion Dufresne then gave an order which his later fellow-explorers may have done well to imitate. It seemed to meet with immediate approval. 'M. Marion,' continued Le Dez, 'made two sailors undress and go ashore, unarmed, carrying with them some small presents such as mirrors, necklaces etc. The Diemenlanders, seeing them approaching thus, put their spears on the ground and with joy and contentment came leaping to meet them, singing and clapping their hands. Our sailors reached the shore; they [the "Diémenois"] presented them with fire and then … [the sailors] handed out the trinkets [*bagatelles*] they had brought.' The two sailors were 'two big boys, well-built and very white', noted Le Dez and, he declared, 'the Diemenlanders could not leave looking at them and touching them'.

A second boat soon landed. The inhabitants 'were curious of everything they saw' and, thought Le Dez, 'if we had let them have their way we would soon have been dressed Diemensland-style [*à la*

Jean-François de Galaup de Lapérouse

Bruny d'Entrecasteaux

Nicolas Baudin

François Péron
(Source: L.A. Triebel, *The French Exploration of Australia*, Hobart, 1957)

René Primavère Lesson
(original in Mitchell Library)

J.S-C. Dumont d'Urville
(original in Mitchell Library)
(Source: G. Mackaness, *Fourteen
Journeys over the Blue Mountains,
1813–41*, Part 2, 1819–27,
Sydney, 1950, p. 56)

Hyacinthe de Bougainville
(Source: Marc Serge Rivière,
The Governor's Noble Guest, Melbourne
University Press, Melbourne, 1999)

Woman of Van Diémen's Land, in
M. Labillardière, *Voyage in Search of La Pérouse*,
Stockdale, London, 1800.

'The skin of the kangaroo … is used rather for
their children to lie on or to sit on themselves
rather than serve as clothing, using it in the latter
way only when on the march, when they spread
it over their shoulders.' — La Motte du Portail,
February 1793.

Portrait of an Aborigine standing by Nicolas Petit
in Tasmania, 1802, reproduced in *Baudin in
Australian Waters. The Artwork of the French Voyage
of Discovery to the Southern Lands, 1800–1804*,
Oxford University Press, Australia, 1988.

'Ceremony of Marriage' in J. Arago, *Souvenirs d'un aveugle* …, Paris, 1839, tome 4, opp. page 93.

Force des reins   Force des mains

Crémaillère en fer

Mesures dynamométriques

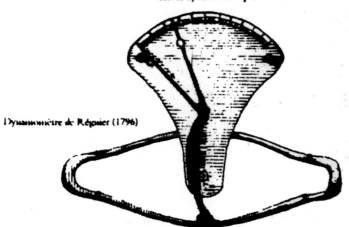

Dynamomètre de Régnier (1796)

Le dynamomètre de Régnier (1751-1825) inventé en 1796 et les manières de s'en servir. (Dessin J. Jasmin d'après Régnier.)

Régnier's 'dynamomètre'. Reproduced from J. Jasmin, 'Faibles sauvages … corps indigènes, corps indigents' in *Mers australes – terres australes, Baudin 1800–4*, Bibliothèque municipale du Havre, 1988, p. 28.

Cabanes des naturels de la Presqu'île
Péron, 1803 (Source: Bonnemains,
Baudin in Australian Waters,
1988, p. 43)

'Homme du Cap de Diémen'.
Drawing by Péron, 1793, in *Atlas du
Voyage à la recherche de La Pérouse*,
reproduced in Hélène Richard, *Le Voyage
de D'Entrecasteaux à la recherche
de Lapérouse*, Paris, 1986, p. 222.

'The beard [is] well developed and worn
short' — Louis Ventenat in Tasmania, 1793,
The General, p. 362.

Aborigines lighting a fire. Nicolas Petit, 1802 (Source: Bonnemains, *Baudin in Australian Waters*, 1988, p. 180)

Aboriginal couple in canoe. Nicolas Petit, 1802. The woman here appears to be holding a net, with which to catch the fish which will be cooked upon the fire. The shadows indicate calm waters. (Source: Bonnemains, *Baudin in Australian Waters*, p. 160)

'Terre de Diémen. Navigation'. Lesueur, 1802.
(Source: Bonnemains, *Baudin in Australian Waters*, p. 50)

'Rush basket' by Lesueur, Tasmania, 1802.
Voyage de découvertes aux terres australes …
Atlas par MM. Lesueur et Petit, Paris, 1807;
plate XIII (detail). (Source: Bonnemains,
Baudin in Australian Waters, p. 121)

Diémenoise], just like them'. Soon 'our third boat arrived', and, 'whether they [the "Diémenois"] had already made the decision to attack us or whether they did not want to let any more people approach them, they made signs for it not to come nearer, threatening with their spears and talking very excitedly among themselves. The people in the boat then took up their muskets ... [and] M. Marion began to withdraw quietly with the people who were with him.' Duclesmeur was one of those people and he too was of the opinion that the inhabitants had 'become alarmed at the arrival of a third longboat'. 'The savages,' he wrote, 'showered us with a hail of hatchets and stones, one of which hit M. Marion on the shoulder, and another bruised my leg. We fired a few shots, and they quickly took flight, uttering horrible screams.' A second landing attempt was made, and again the native people threw spears. This time the French reprisal was serious and, wrote Jean Roux, 'there were several dead and many wounded'. Only one dead man was found, however, pierced by 'three mortal gunshot wounds'.[1]

All accounts indicate that the Europeans fired only in self-defence. 'Our intention,' wrote Chevillard de Montesson, 'was not to do them any harm ... but, seeing that ... they did not cease throwing spears at us (one of which, from sixty paces, hit a black servant in the leg giving him a dangerous wound), we were forced to shoot.' Chevillard goes on to say, however, that 'we immediately sent a detachment of twenty men in their pursuit [a fact confirmed by Duclesmeur], but they did not succeed in catching them'.[2] Apart from the discovery of the dead man, no sign of the 'Diémenois' was seen again and on 10 March, after searching unsuccessfully for much-needed fresh water, the French set sail for New Zealand. The history of the relations between the Europeans and the Indigenous Tasmanians had thus begun quite tragically.

In January 1788 the Englishman Captain Arthur Phillip arrived with the 'first fleet' in Botany Bay and, when preparing to leave for Port Jackson, he was 'surprised by the appearance of two strange sail in the offing'. 'Of what nation this could be,' wrote eyewitness David

Collins, 'engaged the general wonder for some time', until it was de-termined they were 'the Boussole and Astrolabe, French ships … un-der the command of M. de la Perouse [sic] … on a voyage of discovery'. A few days later Collins would have occasion to write that 'the Governor [Phillip] had the mortification to learn that M. De la Perouse had been compelled to fire upon the natives at Botany Bay, where they frequently annoyed his people who were employed on shore'. 'We were, however,' he continued, 'perfectly convinced that nothing short of the greatest necessity could have induced M. de la Perouse to take such a step; as he had been heard to declare, that it was among the particular instructions which he received from his sover-eign, to endeavour by every possible means to acquire and cultivate the friendship of the natives … and to avoid exercising any act of hos-tility upon them.'[3] Lapérouse had thus borne in mind Louis XVI's instructions, and was openly declaring his intention to obey them.

In practical terms, however, such obedience had at times been very difficult. In his letter to the Comte de Fleurieu from Botany Bay on 7 February 1788 he explained in his own words what Collins had ob-served. 'On shore,' he wrote, 'I made a sort of fortified camp to be able to build new longboats [*chaloupes*] … This precaution was necessary against the Indians of New Holland who, although very weak and few in number are, like all savages, very malevolent [*mechans*] and would burn our boats if they could … They have thrown spears [*zagaies*] at us after having accepted our presents and good will.' Lapérouse's mis-trust of native people had been fuelled by events on one of the 'Isles des Navigateurs', 'where M. de l'Angle, the captain of the *Astrolabe*, with eleven officers and men were put to death'.[4] One of the mur-dered officers, M. Lamanon, recalled Lapérouse, 'told me on the eve of his death that these [native] men were better than us'. Lapérouse had thus learnt a hard lesson. He wrote:

> As a firm observer of my instructions, I have always treated [the native people] with the greatest moderation, but I must confess that, if I had to undertake another campaign of this nature, I would ask for other orders. A navigator, when leaving Europe, should consider the savages [*sauvages*]

as enemies, very weak to be sure and whom it would be very … barbaric to destroy, but whom one has the right to warn off [*prévenir*] when one is authorised by justified suspicions.[5]

Lapérouse and his ships disappeared after leaving Botany Bay in March that year.

When D'Entrecasteaux set out to search for Lapérouse in 1792, his instructions, however, contained no such advice, even cast in more gentle terms. Indeed, a reading of D'Entrecasteaux's journal suggests that he would have had little sympathy for such advice, for, as we will see, he appears (during the early months of his voyage at least) to have been a resolute admirer of *le bon sauvage*. Explorers approaching from the sea were usually seen by the Indigenous people long before they could see anyone themselves. And when they landed there was often no one to be found. This was D'Entrecasteaux's experience when he arrived in what is now the D'Entrecasteaux Channel in April 1792. Time and time again he found only traces of the inhabitants. 'No natives have been sighted so far,' he wrote some three days after arrival, 'although traces of their passage, and indeed of their sojourn, have been observed.' A few days later a group of Frenchmen, making their way towards a smoking fire, found four huts hastily abandoned — because, they assumed, 'we had inspired fear'.[6]

Fear seemed indeed to inspire the native people to abandon everything in their flight. On 20 May Labillardière recounts that two officers, 'Cretin and Dauribeau', 'seeing several fires at a small distance from the shore, determined to land'.

As soon as they entered the woods, they found four savages employed in laying fuel upon three small fires about which they were sitting. The savages immediately fled, not withstanding all the signs of amity which they made them, leaving their crabs and shell-fish broiling upon coals … The utensils which they left behind them consisted of about thirty baskets made of rushes, some of which were filled with shell-fish and lobsters, others with pieces of flint and fragments of the bark of a tree as soft as the best tinder … They likewise left behind several kangarou skins and drinking vessels.

The officers brought back to the ship 'two baskets, a kangarou skin and drinking vessel' but, Labillardière assures his reader, 'the savages had no reason to regret the loss of these utensils, as we left, in the place of them, several knives and hankerchiefs, with some biscuit, cheese and an earthen pot'.

On 27 May 'a number of savages' were seen 'landing from a raft', but, when the French arrived at the scene, 'they had made their escape into the woods'. Later that day some form of actual interchange appears at last to have taken place. 'One of the officers of the *Recherche*,' reports botanist Labillardière, following a path beaten by the savages through the woods, met six of them walking slowly towards the south … Their surprise at so unexpected a rencounter [sic] was visible in their countenances, but … they approached at the invitations of the European, and bound round their heads a handkerchief and a neck-cloth which he offered them … He endeavoured in vain to persuade them to come to where our ships lay at anchor [but] the savages walked away.' At the same time, on the other side of the Channel, continued Labillardière, 'some of our men came to a large fire round which eight savages … sat warming themselves under the shelter of four fences against the wind'. Here again, however, 'they immediately ran away as soon as they saw our people'. One 'old woman was so terrified', wrote Labillardière, 'that she leapt down a precipice more than forty feet in height'.[7] In Tasmania, therefore, no meaningful encounters had been established.

On the south coast of mainland Australia, in December 1792, D'Entrecasteaux landed at Esperance Bay and soon noticed 'fires that were lighting up suddenly from place to place'. During the next few days the French visitors saw some 'natives', and assumed that these people 'had probably set fire to the arid bushes to conceal their escape and withdraw from the sight of strangers … who must have frightened them'.[8] Fear, therefore, appeared to be the first and foremost reaction of the native people to their visitors. Unlike twenty years earlier, however, on these occasions spears had not been thrown nor any guns fired.

The first relations actually established by D'Entrecasteaux's expedition with the Indigenous Australians occurred in early February 1793 at Recherche Bay, in the very southernmost part of Tasmania. At about nine o'clock in the morning Labillardière and a gardener (La Haye) 'perceived through the trees a number of natives, most of whom appeared to be fishing on the borders of the lake'. The two Frenchmen returned to camp to avail themselves of muskets 'in case of an assault', and returned with a small party to approach the inhabitants. 'We had gone only a few steps,' wrote Labillardière, 'before we met them. The men and youths were ranged in front … the women, children and girls were a few paces behind. As their manner did not appear to indicate any hostile design, I hesitated not to go up to the oldest, who accepted with good grace a piece of biscuit I offered him of which he had seen me eat. I then held out my hand to him as a sign of friendship and … he gave me his, inclining himself a little, and raising at the same time the left foot … These motions were accompanied by a pleasing smile.' Labillardière's companions approached and 'immediately', he wrote, 'the best understanding prevailed among us'. A few small gifts were offered and happily received.

This encounter was not only with the men. 'The women,' remarked Labillardière, 'were very desirous of coming nearer to us and, though the men made signs to them to keep at a distance, their curiosity was ready at every moment to break through all other considerations', and soon 'the gradual increase of confidence … obtained them permission to approach'. This 'party of savages', he calculated, 'consisted of two and forty, seven of whom were men, eight women [and] the rest appeared to be their children'. The Indigenous people thus greatly outnumbered the visitors.

Labillardière 'showed these savages the effects of our fire-arms', after which he was invited to watch an exhibition of spear-throwing. One man threw a spear 'near a hundred paces' and then 'aimed at an object … and every time was near enough to it', wrote the Frenchman, 'to give us a high idea of his skill'. Some of the native people then insisted on accompanying the French back to their landing-place and 'the attentions lavished on us by these savages astonished us'. 'If our path was interrupted by heaps of dry branches, some of them walked before and removed them to either side', and, to prevent them falling on the slippery and grassy slopes, 'these good savages … took hold of us by the arm and supported us'. Labillardière was most impressed by 'these marks of affectionate kindness'. On arriving at their destination, the French invited some of their hosts to go aboard with them, but the Indigenous people declined and returned the way they had come, walking 'with tranquillity along the sea-side, looking towards us from time to time, and uttering cries of joy'.[9]

Thus ended this historic first encounter. The native hosts had manifested good grace, curiosity, kindness and joy; and there appear to have been no grounds for complaint from either side.

'This first encounter,' wrote D'Entrecasteaux, 'resulted in a great longing by everyone on board the two frigates to visit such kind people.'[10] They did not have to wait long, for 'the next day', wrote Labillardière, 'we returned in a large party' and 'some of the natives soon came to visit us, expressing by their cries the pleasure they felt at seeing us.'[11] On this occasion Labillardière's testimony is supported by other members of this 'large party' — which consisted, according to D'Auribeau, of 'fifty-six people'. On this day, wrote D'Auribeau, they met eighteen 'natives' (eight men, nine boys and one woman) who showed us 'no signs of defiance or fear', despite now being outnumbered themselves. Again gifts were offered, among them the gift of European music, which was quite unanimously shunned. 'The best relations prevailed,' testified D'Auribeau, as he sat with 'some women and children sitting in a circle', and all 'appeared extremely contented and very cheerful'. Then all changed, for 'Mr Saint Aignan played the violin for them several times', which 'did not delight them at all', and 'they gave him to understand that their ears were hurting'. 'They seemed,' wrote D'Auribeau, 'very happy to see him stop.'[12]

We do not know, of course, how well St Aignan played this instrument. La Motte du Portail stipulates that he 'tried' to play it,[13] and Labillardière says he played 'some noisy tunes',[14] so the Indigenous people may perhaps be congratulated on their good taste. When the chaplain, Ventenat, played on his flute, however, 'they lent an attentive ear' and when the French sang some songs (noted La Motte du Portail) 'they seemed to listen to them with pleasure';[15] these two re-actions may lend additional support to the acuity of their critical fac-ulties. The inhabitants also 'attempted more than once to charm us by songs', wrote Labillardière, 'with the modulation of which I was sin-gularly struck ... Several times two of them sang the same tune at once, but always one third above the other, forming a concord with the greatest justness'.

The subject of relations between the Indigenous women and the French men was raised by several people that day. 'None [of the women] deserved the title of pretty,' thought La Motte du Portail, 'but in this case one knows what must be the testimony of men in the prime of life, shut up for a long time in a ship, when they see a girl.'[16] Labillardière reported that all was not always well. 'Two of the young girls,' he said, 'followed the different windings of the shore without mistrust, at a distance from the other natives, with three of our sailors, when these took the opportunity of one of the most retired places, to treat them with a degree of freedom which was received in a very dif-ferent manner from what they had hoped. The young women imme-diately fled to the rocks most advanced into the sea, and appeared ready to leap into it and swim away, if our young men followed them.' Back on board later, wrote Labillardière, 'one of the crew boasted of the favours he had received from one of the beauties of Cape Diémen, but it is difficult to say how far his story is founded on truth'.[17] Ventenat was told by a native on this day that 'one or two sailors' had 'attempted to caress one of the women', whereupon the Frenchman had 'begged the sailors to stop what they were doing, and they did'.[18] Captain D'Auribeau would conclude: 'I must pay tribute to the very excellent conduct of the crews of the two boats', for there had not been 'the slightest indiscretion committed, although they were sur-rounded by women and enjoying great freedom and familiarity'. 'We saw no sign,' he wrote, 'of jealously on the part of the natives, but it is also true that we carefully avoided giving cause for it.'[19]

Two days later 'a great number' of the Frenchmen from both ships went ashore to 'endeavour to see the savages again'. 'It was not long,' noted Labillardière, 'before some of them came to meet us, giving us tokens of the greatest confidence … and then they took us by the arm and invited us to follow them along the shore.' They had 'scarcely gone a mile' before they found themselves 'in the midst of eight-and-forty of the natives: ten men, fourteen women, and twenty-four children'. If the French were as numerous here as on the previous occasion, there would thus have been about a hundred people present. At first the children were frightened and ran to their mothers, but their fears were soon assuaged and they showed themselves 'very desirous of every thing shining, and were not afraid to come up to us, to endeavour to pull off our buttons'. Labillardière and his colleagues did not fail to decorate them with 'these ornaments'.

At one stage the French threw some gunpowder on to some burning coals. The resultant effect was met with great admiration, and the native people 'entreated us to let them have the pleasure of seeing it several times'. At noon the French observed their hosts preparing 'their repast' and were quite surprised at the 'pains the women take to prepare the food … for their families'. After observing this (which 'continued a long time'), the French 're-embarked to go on board', whereupon, wrote Labillardière, 'these good people followed us with their eyes for some time before they left the shore and … disappeared into the woods'.[20]

Two days later 'a great number' of French again went ashore and met but five native people who appeared 'well pleased' at seeing them. 'It was the first time,' remarked Labillardière, 'that General D'Entrecasteaux had the pleasure of seeing any of the natives.' Joseph Raoul, second pilot on *La Recherche*, specified that there were '150 to 200 people gathered around' the natives, who 'were without fear and showed no distrust at seeing such a large number of us around them'.[21] The inhabitants watched with surprise as the French kindled some eucalypt bark with a burning glass, but their interest may have diminished when one of them, 'desirous of trying the effects of the lens himself, threw the converging rays of the sun upon his thigh'.

'The pain he felt,' noted the botanist, 'took from him all inclination of repeating the experiment.'

On this day, however, one of the natives yielded to solicitations to go on board one of the ships. Such an experience for this man would perhaps be comparable to that of a modern-day Earthling accepting to go on board a spaceship from another planet. The event must have made an impression on the French too, for several of them comment on it at length. 'He went up the side with an air of confidence,' observed Labillardière, 'and examined the inside of the ship with much attention.'[22] 'D'Entrecasteaux himself was present, and stipulates that this encounter … took place on Shrove Tuesday', which, he notes, was 12th February.'[23]

The most comprehensive account of this event, however, is that of D'Hesmivy d'Auribeau, captain of *La Recherche*, the ship honoured with the visit. D'Auribeau confirms Labillardière's observation and wrote that their guest 'exhibited no distress or disquiet upon boarding the frigate', that he was 'very cheerful all the while', and — understandably — 'infinitely surprised and astonished by the great number of new things before him … [and] saw and touched everything with pleasure'. These sentiments were fully shared. 'It was with as much pleasure as surprise,' declared D'Entrecasteaux, 'that I saw this man who had dared to surrender himself on his own and without defence at the mercy of men whose dispositions were unknown to him.' He was invited into D'Entrecasteaux's chamber and then, wrote D'Auribeau, 'he came into my cabin, where he amused us greatly. He sat in an armchair and found himself very comfortable in it. He was delighted when I opened some cupboards for him; there were continual cries of joy and admiration.' He was shown pigs, goats, hens and geese and, recalled D'Entrecasteaux, 'I gave him a rooster, [and] I would have readily given him hens as well, had he not told me that he was going to eat the rooster'.[24] 'Finally,' wrote D'Auribeau, 'when we judged that our new guest's curiosity might be satisfied … I took him back to his fellows. He was extremely joyful during the crossing, joking famously with an officer who was playing tricks on him and on whom he was playing them in return … Thus ended, just as happily as the other, this second meeting ... [with] these good natives.'[25] Better relations could scarcely have been wished for. Indeed, when Labillardière indicated the French intention to set sail the following day, the native people 'seemed to be much grieved at it'.

The next day the French weighed anchor but, the effect of the current being greater than that of the wind, made little progress and went ashore again near Adventure Bay, some 40 kilometres to the north. Here again they encountered some natives, whose 'smiling countenances left us in no doubt that our visit gave them pleasure'. Several others soon came to join them and 'their joy was expressed', wrote Labillardière, 'by loud bursts of laughter'. There were, however, 'no women among them'. One of the natives made it understood that they had seen ships before in Adventure Bay, and the French assumed this to mean Captain Bligh's expedition, which had anchored here in February 1792. Several of Bligh's inscriptions were in fact found on the trees. 'Supposing that their women and children had retired a little way into the woods,' wrote Labillardière, 'we expressed to them our wishes to see them.' For a while the natives allowed the French to accompany them into the woods, but they soon 'expressed their desire to see us return towards our ships, and parted from us'.[26]

The visitors set sail again soon after sunset. They would arrive in New Zealand three weeks later.

Any form of commercial exchange between the French and the indigenous people was soon discovered to be impossible. 'I took with me several articles to give them — not to exchange', wrote D'Auribeau on going ashore in February 1793, 'for their extreme poverty does not permit that.'[27] Poverty it was perhaps for D'Auribeau, but the Indigenous Australians, the French would later observe, seemed to place little value on possessions. Labillardière too would note how 'we made them presents of a great number of things ... but they gave us nothing, for they had brought nothing with them'. The inhabitants, however, were often delighted to receive the gifts offered (although, as mentioned earlier, some — especially clothing — might be quickly discarded). 'They received with great joy,' wrote Labillardière, 'the neck-cloths we offered them', and, on this occasion, 'one of the young native men had the generosity to give me a few small shells ... strung like a necklace'. A few days later the French gave another man a hatchet with which he 'displayed great dexterity' in cutting down a tree. 'He was transported with joy,' noted Labillardière, 'when the tree was felled by his strokes.' The French also 'made them a present of some hand-saws, which they used with great readiness'.[28] D'Auribeau noticed (as Baudin's people will) that the inhabitants seemed to have a predilection for the colour red. 'I showed them,' he wrote, 'some white, blue and red materials, but they very quickly showed their preference for the last colour. They even tried to remove the pieces they could see on the officers' arms, although always with laughter and gaiety.' Perhaps they saw here the colour of the red ochre with which they adorned themselves. Some days later he again offered some lengths of red material, which again 'produced infinite pleasure'.

Some of the gifts brought good fun to all. 'A rather amusing incident occurred in connection with a kid and a monkey,' reported D'Auribeau.[29] Labillardière elaborated further. 'We had taken an ape on shore with us,' he said, 'which afforded much amusement to the savages; and one of the crew took a goat with him ... to which they occasionally spoke, saying "medi" (sit down).'[30] D'Entrecasteaux even surmised quite good-humouredly that, being asked to sit down, the goat may have 'had a better status than the monkey'.[31]

Although they were 'overcome with joy' when offered presents, the Indigenous people rarely endeavoured to keep anything that was only shown to them. 'When I showed them my watch,' said Labillardière, 'it attracted their desire, and one of them in particular expressed his wish to possess it: but he quickly desisted from his request when he found that I was not willing to part with it.' In general, he concluded happily, 'we found ... that they returned to us, without the least reluctance, such things that we could not dispense with for our own use.'[32] D'Entrecasteaux made the same observation. 'Although whatever struck their attention excited their desires, we have not noticed that they are inclined to steal; they never insisted, if whatever they had requested was denied them.'

Perhaps they could not themselves easily 'steal', as the Europeans called it, for they appeared to have little idea of 'property'. They were, wrote D'Entrecasteaux, 'without property other than their wives and children'.[33] La Motte du Portail expressed this observation at greater length. 'The people of New Holland,' he declared, 'lead a wandering life ... Every place is good for them, provided it offers shell-fish. They have no idea of property. They build a hut, and abandon it tomorrow.'[34]

Baudin's expedition, as mentioned in Chapter 1, had been advised by Degérando that 'a community might be gentle and sociable, and yet believe itself in a state of natural war with strangers whose intentions are unknown'. Explorers, he had warned, had usually failed to consider that 'their presence was bound to be a natural source of fear'. If Baudin's people could not introduce themselves 'naturally' with caution, they could nevertheless have heeded their compatriot's well-intended advice.

One eyewitness account of this expedition's first encounter with the indigenous people is that of Baudin himself when arriving in Australia on the west coast (at Géographe Bay) on 4 June 1801. 'Without counting the astronomer and the geographer,' he wrote, 'I had as a travelling companion, Citizens Maugé, Riédlé and Depuch.' The group set out and finally reached the shore after some three hours rowing against the currents. 'As we landed,' he wrote, 'we saw [a native] up to his waist in the water, busy spearing fish. At first he appeared to pay little attention to us ... but when we had landed at about the distance of gunshot from him, he left the water and, without hurrying too much, reached a sand-dune opposite him. I noticed only that, although his step was assured, he frequently looked towards us, no doubt to see if he was being followed.' The Frenchmen eventually caught up with him, and 'Citizen Depuch, who was ahead of everyone, showed him several necklaces of small glass beads ... But, as he continued to advance, the native began to shout violently, signalling to us to go back'. The explorers, however, 'continued to advance' whereupon the man 'went through all sorts of contortions, still yelling, and finally picked up three types of spear and fled precipitately, without having made any offensive movement towards us'.[35]

There is no evidence that the French did anything to harm this person. His fear of these strangers, whose intentions were unknown — and who outnumbered him four to one — may indeed have been very 'natural'. When they arrived at the top of the dune, the man had got such 'a long way ahead of us', wrote Baudin, that 'I gave up the chase'. They did not see him again. However, on arriving back at their boat three hours later, they were told by the helmsman that 'six savages had appeared on the point and that, after considering them for about a quarter of an hour, had gone off into the dunes and disappeared from sight'.[36] Baudin added that, having no weapons, his colleagues 'had thought they were going to be eaten'.[37]

The next day, still at anchor in Géographe Bay, three members of *Le Naturaliste*, Ronsard, Lesueur and St-Cricq, met the pregnant woman described in Chapter 1. In his journal, engineer François-Michel Ronsard tells how the woman's male companion had fled immediately, but she, 'seized with fright', had prostrated herself, her face and body pressed to the sand. 'As this woman showed us sign of life,' wrote Ronsard, 'we left her. We were hardly more than thirty paces from her when we saw her stealing away on hands and knees into the bushes, leaving behind our presents and her stick.'[38] When Péron returned later to this same spot with Lesueur, the woman had disappeared and the gifts still lay on the ground. If Baudin's people had wished to heed Degérando's advice, they thus appear to have failed quite miserably here.

At approximately the same time another group (of five men, among whom were Depuch, Le Bas and Louis de Freycinet) had had a 'long and extraordinary interview with the savages', as Péron termed it.[39] Here we have two eyewitness accounts: that of Le Bas, Baudin's second-in-command, and that of Depuch, a mineralogist.

The two accounts confirm each other and, as the latter is the more complete, it is to this we will refer.

As the group approached the land, 'several natives' kept an eye on them and 'ran about on the shore in every direction, their cries increasing and becoming increasingly loud'. As the Frenchmen approached them, the native people ran away, but Depuch and Freycinet decided to catch up with them and soon heard them calling in the woods to one another. After leaving some gifts 'in obvious places', the two men began to withdraw, but soon noticed, wrote Depuch, 'seven or eight natives, each armed with two *sagaies* and a *patou-patou* [club stick] advancing rapidly to cut off our retreat'. 'They brandished their *sagaies* and threatened us with them and waved their clubs while shouting "Mouye, mouye". Their gestures seemed to invite us to retrace our steps.' The French were thus in a quandary. 'Pressed as we were,' wrote Depuch, 'we either had to fire on them and perhaps kill one to intimidate the others, or retreat in good order. We preferred the latter'. 'The philanthropic sentiments which in this circumstance formed the basis for our conduct,' he reported to Baudin, 'will be approved by you, Citizen Commandant.' Depuch then expressed his opinion as to why explorers never needed to initiate hostilities towards native people. 'The advantage which the superiority of our weapons gives us over these men,' he declared, 'is too considerable for us to be allowed to refuse them ... the first blow.'

Unharmed, the two Frenchmen continued to retreat, 'walking backwards, and facing our enemy [the word is Depuch's] and responding to their menacing gestures with less precipitous ones', and arrived back at their landing place. This, however, was not sufficient to calm their opponents. 'Neither the shouts nor the menaces came to an end,' wrote Depuch. 'The spears threatened our chests and the clubs were waved more violently than ever.' Soon, he noted, 'we were up to our waists in the water ... and then the natives got nearer to us. All our guns were raised and ready to fire [*en joue*] and our safety, for so long so very compromised, was going to put us in the harsh necessity of repelling the blows we were about to receive, when we perceived captains Hamelin and Le Bas, accompanied by the boat's crew, who

had come ... to protect our return.' Before long the French were re-
united, whereupon 'the natives [*naturels*] stopped ... but continued
shouting "Mouye, mouye" and pointing to the way back'. The
French replied by showing again the presents they had brought, but
'nothing appeared to inspire in them the slightest confidence'.

Depuch thus clearly believed that the natives' hostility was inspired
by fear. One of them, 'the youngest and consequently the most audacious', stepped forward and 'taking up a military stance, brandishing a
sagaie with all the strength and suppleness he could muster ... seemed
to invite us to single combat. The others, at first anxious, appeared
however to approve of his actions, and soon even began to applaud'. A
verbal exchange ensued, but with no success. Finally, wrote Depuch,
'in order to try the last means of conciliation, which was our principal
aim, one of us went to the edge of the shore, and put down his weapons in front of the native who watched his movements attentively. He
[the Frenchman] turned towards him bearing a branch in each hand
... and made every sign which he presumed could inspire confidence.
But without success. The native turned away, and his companions re-
joined him, threatening us again'. Again the French offered gifts
(handkerchiefs, looking-glasses and even a snuff box) but these were
all rejected. 'Seeing that it was impossible to gain their confidence,'
wrote the mineralogist, 'and that we might at any moment need to
suppress their ever increasing audacity, we indicated that we were
withdrawing.' 'It is worthy of note,' he concluded, 'that they in no way
tried to impede our retreat. Perhaps that is all they wanted from us.'[40]
The encounter thus ended with no blood shed on either side.

Some two months later (4 August) at Dirk Hartog Island, nearly
1000 kilometres to the north, Saint Cricq had told his colleague
Milius how he had tried to go ashore but had seen 'a dozen savages
walking towards him' who became bolder and seemed to want to oppose his landing. 'They were armed with *sagaies* and wooden sabres
which they waved as if going to throw them', so St Cricq fired one
shot 'to frighten them, which succeeded wonderfully. They all fled
like starlings'.[41]

Conciliatory as they were, the French were clearly not welcome. If in fact they had been any less conciliatory this may have augured ill for the Indigenous people, whose 'audacity', declared Le Bas, 'badly supported by the weapons they possess, would have all too soon made them victims of ours'.[42]

Earlier explorers along this coast had been similarly received. In 1699 near Broome, Dampier had reported one man wounded 'on each side' when encountering '10 or 12 Natives', and in 1705 the Dutch had established only 'unhappy relations'. Depuch, who had suffered this hostility at such close quarters, offered an explanation. 'Like brutes,' he reported to Baudin, 'they live in the depths of the forests and only come out to provide for their most pressing needs ... and especially to prevent any living being getting near it, convinced as they are that people only come to dispute their possession of it.' 'How could they have imagined,' he went on, 'that men could take so much trouble to satisfy the sentiment of curiosity ... They must have thought that, racked with hunger, we were rushing into their forest to fight with them over the few bits of food it can offer.' The mineralogist concluded on an optimistic note. 'I hope,' he said, 'that our gifts will have enlightened them about us, and that the next navigators will benefit from the effects of our moderate conduct towards them.'[43]

On arriving in Tasmania (at today's Great Taylor Bay) on 13 January 1802, Baudin issued careful instructions to five of his colleagues — among them Péron, Lesueur and Henri Freycinet (elder brother of Louis) — who were going ashore. 'Upon leaving the ship,' he wrote, 'you will proceed to the Huon River ... If you should meet any natives, which is very likely, you are absolutely forbidden to commit a single act of hostility towards them, unless the safety of anyone in particular, or all in general, is at stake.' 'According to what is known of their character,' he continued, clearly having D'Entrecasteaux in mind, 'the people of this country do not appear to be savage, except when provoked. Therefore you must influence them in our favour by kind deeds and presents.'[44]

The five men went up the Huon River as far as Port Cygnet (le port des Cygnes) which, Péron declared, 'of all the places I have seen during the course of our long voyage ... is the most picturesque and pleasant'. Both Péron and Freycinet have left eyewitness accounts of their encounters here, and, in their essence, the accounts resemble one another. The party landed at a 'small creek at the bottom of a beautiful valley' and, wrote Péron, 'we had scarcely set foot on shore before two natives appeared' of whom one (a man between twenty-two and twenty-four years of age) 'in the twinkling of an eye was in the midst of us'. His manner, thought Péron, 'displayed at once pleasure and surprise', reactions observed so often by D'Entrecasteaux's people twenty years earlier. 'Mr Freycinet having embraced him, I followed his example, but,' continued Péron, 'the air of indifference with which he received this testimony of good will and friendship made us easily perceive that to him it had no meaning.' The Frenchmen's boat interested this young man greatly, and he examined it in detail, tossing uninterestedly overboard — to the Frenchmen's dismay! — a full bottle of arrack that was offered to him. Péron thought this interest in their boat gave 'the most striking demonstration of attention and reflection we had ever seen among savage nations [*les peuples sauvages*]'. Péron and Freycinet then walked to the top of the valley and there met with 'the second native', an 'old man of above fifty years', who soon signalled to two women, one of whom bore a child, to come and join them. This small 'family', as Péron termed them, only took their leave when the Frenchmen tried to recover a full bottle of arrack which the 'old man' was carrying off with him.[45]

After searching unsuccessfully for fresh water, the explorers were retiring to their boat when they saw the people they had already met on the other side of the bay. Henri Freycinet described this second encounter in his report to Baudin. 'As soon as they saw us,' he wrote, 'they gave cries of joy and hastened to join us. After renewed demonstrations of affection ... we all sat down together round the fire.' This native family that welcomed them 'with such friendship and confidence' consisted of 'an old man and his wife, a young man and his wife, a young girl, two small boys, and two small girls, one of whom was at the breast'. Soon, however, wrote Freycinet, the French returned to their landing place, 'accompanied by these good islanders'.[46]

Péron also speaks of these 'good Diemenese', but presents greater detail of the encounter. He tells how the French were repeatedly invited to sit with their hosts, and how they joined in a shell-fish meal with them, finding their cooking 'succulent and well flavoured'. It was then that the French sang 'the hymn', to which 'at first the savages appeared more affected than surprised but, in a few moments, lent an attentive ear … [and] exclamations of admiration issued from every mouth'. It was then too that the young Henri Freycinet (twenty-four years of age) seems to have become the object of the attention of the 'young lass' Ouré-Ouré. 'M. Freycinet,' noted Péron, 'seemed to be more particularly the object of her regards, and it was easy to perceive in the manners of this innocent pupil of nature, that delicate shade, which gives to the most serious playfulness, a character of serious preference: coquetry itself seemed to be called in to the assistance of the natural attractions of the sex.' On the way back to the boat, 'Freycinet took Ouré-Ouré by the arm', and the young lady spoke to him at length and 'accompanied her discourse with so many winning gestures and gracious smiles that her coquetry was very expressive'. Freycinet himself was more discreet about this apparently romantic moment. 'The young girl', he reported, was 'gay and mischievous'.[47]

Péron's conclusion to this whole encounter resembles that of D'Entrecasteaux. 'The confidence which the inhabitants showed us, the affectionate testimonies of good will, the sincerity of their demonstrations, the frankness of their manners, the affecting ingenuousness of their caresses,' he said, 'all seemed to unite in developing the kindest and most interesting affection and friendship.'[48]

While this group had been at Cygnet, two others, one led by Leschenault and the other by Baudin himself, had gone ashore on Partridge Island (off the southern end of South Bruny Island). Leschenault had seen a 'number of natives' on Bruny of whom two had forded the narrow strait to him, and to whom he had given each 'a necklace of large glass beads and a small knife which, with cries of joy, they immediately showed to the natives who had gathered in large numbers on the other shore'. 'Several of them,' he said, 'then crossed the strait to share in my gifts.'[49] On seeing Baudin's group approaching, 'the natives, no doubt intimidated by our large number', thought Baudin, 'ran off into the wood'. Soon, however, they reappeared and 'came up to us', wrote the Commander, 'without the slightest distrust. We took them by the hand, and embraced them as Mr Leschenault had'. Other native people quickly joined them 'and behaved in a very friendly way'.[50] When the inhabitants forded the sea again to return to Bruny Island, Baudin bade them farewell, preferring to take his boat for this crossing. This initial Tasmanian reception was thus very different from that extended earlier by the West Australians.

The next day, 15 January (or 25 Nivôse, year 10 of the French Revolutionary Calendar), began well. In the morning two boats went ashore and, when one returned, the men reported to Baudin that while they had been busy fishing 'natives had gathered in large numbers' and 'men, women and children and Europeans had all mingled together without any distrust or fear'. There had been no more than six Frenchmen present 'and the natives, all told, numbered more than fifty'. 'A great fire was lit ... and excellent relations continued between them and the oarsmen.' The artist Petit was able to draw portraits of 'several of the natives', although the women and children could not be included 'for they could not stay still for a moment'.[51]

Later the other boat returned with a less happy experience. One of the men, first-class midshipman Maurouard, had joked for a while with the islanders and eventually challenged one of them to an arm wrestle. Although not writing in the first person, Milius seems to have witnessed this event. 'One of our midshipmen,' he wrote, 'wanted to try his strength with one of the most vigorous of these savages. He took his wrist and, without much effort, made it give way. They did several tries, and our man always won. The midshipman, encouraged by this success, took hold of his opponent's body and indicated to him that he was going to wrestle to see who could throw the other.' 'The savage understood wonderfully,' continued Milius, but soon 'fell to the ground beneath our midshipman', which 'made the spectators laugh a lot'.

The native people thereupon took their leave and a few moments later, while reboarding the boat, Maurouard 'was struck by a spear in the side of the neck'. This unexpected attack puzzled the Frenchmen, who tried to explain it in various ways. 'This first hostility,' thought Milius, 'could only be attributed to the struggle which had taken place. A feeling of jealousy or vengeance had doubtless brought these savages to such a condemnable excess. We comported ourselves with moderation as dictated by prudence and as recommended by our instructions.'[52] Lieutenant St Cricq, who, according to Péron (I, p. 236) was 'on shore with Maurouard at the time', wondered if it may not be presumed 'that the New Hollander vanquished by Citizen Maurouard wanted to prove to him that, even if he were superior in strength, he did not thereby equal him in cunning'.[53] Baudin, who was not present, also tried to understand this incident, and appears to ascribe collective responsibility for it. 'It seems likely to me,' he surmised, 'that the natives, upon seeing their comrade defeated by strength, sought later to make it known that they were not weaker in skill and cunning. This, perhaps, is what brought about the throwing of the spear.' Baudin was later advised that 'the doctors do not consider the wound to be dangerous'[54] and St Cricq would consider this 'a small incident' which nevertheless 'served as a profitable lesson for us'.[55]

Several Frenchmen reported on what appeared to be sexual relations that were offered to them this day. 'The women,' observed Hamelin, 'offered their favours to our people quite unambiguously, showing them that which they usually hid with a piece of kangaroo skin.' St Cricq said that this, however, was 'without any provocation from us', and that 'no one came forward to contend with them'.[56] Baudin reported too that 'some of the oarsmen from the *Naturaliste* [had] even affirmed to him that ... the women had entirely voluntarily satisfied their curiosity, but not their desire'.[57] Milius was quite blunt. 'Leur aspect révoltant,' he declared, 'n'était pas fait pour nous inspirer les moindres désirs [their revolting appearance was not made to inspire in us the slightest desires].'[58]

This day was rather singular also because several of the native people went into the *Naturaliste*'s boat and, in Baudin's words, 'stole everything they could lay their hands on, even the chocks from the thwarts'. One child 'had taken a marlin-spike' and 'wept copiously' when reprimanded by an older native, but Baudin could not tell 'whether he was reprimanding the child for having stolen ... or for not having been more adroit'. Bonnefoi gave a woman a small mirror in return for a necklace, of which the locket 'consisted of an English penny and a metal button', but, wrote Baudin, 'nobody could discover where she had acquired them'.[59]

On 16 January Captain Hamelin had tried to go ashore but had encountered about thirty natives who 'thought he was going to land and seemed to want to prevent him'. 'They were all around with spears,' wrote Baudin, 'and several were carrying bundles of them.'

By 29 January the expedition had arrived, after much contrary weather, on the northernmost tip of Bruny Island where that afternoon a dinghy was put ashore, soon to be espied by seven natives. 'Our men were eating their meal under the shelter of a rock,' wrote Baudin, when the seven 'announced themselves by shouts of laughter long before they were seen or their arrival was realised. They were all armed with spears.' After an initial fright, the French offered the natives two bottles, in one of which there was a little rum, but the natives 'emptied it out on the ground' and only kept its containers. 'The friendliness between them and our men became so great,' reported the second-class petty officer who was in the group, 'that they all started dancing together.' Soon tiring of this exercise, all sat down and 'after about two hours together ... they parted the best friends in the world'.

The next day would be full of incident. Commander Baudin and Captain Hamelin were both present (accompanied by the artist Petit and the surgeon L'Haridon), and both have left detailed accounts of an encounter that would leave the French as deeply puzzled as they had been two weeks earlier.

At about ten o'clock in the morning the four men set out to go to the place where the natives (or *Naturels*, to use Baudin's word) had been met the day before. Soon seven natives appeared but, Baudin noticed, 'they retreated as we approached' and 'we were rather surprised at seeing them so distrustful'. After holding up 'one or two necklaces of sparkling beads', Baudin managed to persuade six of the men to come to him, but they kept on 'gesturing all the while' and 'asked us to go back to our boat'. Among the expressions that kept recurring was one, 'Kaoué Kaoué', which Baudin guessed to mean 'Go away'.[60] 'However,' he wrote, 'we took little notice of their "Kaoué" and proceeded inland to look for plants.' The native people followed for a while, but 'made such a fuss' when the French approached some 'fairly dense smoke' that, 'not wanting to damage our good relations', Baudin decided to turn away. Both he and Hamelin thought this must be 'where their women and children were'.

At about two o'clock the Frenchmen were returning to their boat when they met three of the natives seen in the morning. 'We were amazed,' wrote Baudin, 'to see each of them carrying two or three spears.' After some persuasion the men put down their weapons and sat down with the visitors 'and were soon as familiar as if we were very much in the habit of being together ... They went through our pockets — with our consent, however, for we had left nothing in them'. 'During the two hours that we spent with these three natives', wrote the Commander, 'we had plenty of time to observe them at leisure.' During this meeting Captain Hamelin was able to negotiate the exchange of some spears for some buttons from his uniform. Some form of 'commerce' was thus possible on a small and personal level, and calm and harmony seemed to reign.

As they were preparing to depart, however, 'Citizen Petit, who had done a drawing of one of them, had the paper snatched away from him ... but he snatched it back again,' wrote Baudin, 'and we continued towards the shore. We had scarcely reached it when the three natives with whom we had been on such friendly terms and whom we had loaded with presents, began to pick up stones and throw them at us.' To the French eyes such behaviour was clearly as ungrateful as it was incomprehensible. Baudin was the only man to be injured. 'A fairly large stone hit me ... and grazed my hip,' he wrote. 'I immediately aimed at the one who had thrown it, and this action so frightened him that he put his head down and ran for his life.' The native people were thus well acquainted with the effect of guns. The Frenchmen lost no time in returning to their ship. 'We tried to work out the reason for this hostile behaviour but,' confessed Baudin, 'the only explanation we could find was regret at having exchanged their spears with us and the hope of getting them back by this means.'[61] Hamelin's account suggests that the hostilities began when Petit took back his drawing, whereupon one of the natives 'picked up a half-burnt log to throw at him'. As a consequence of this behaviour, the next day Baudin 'expressly forbade' his men to go ashore. Nevertheless, seven Frenchmen on a fishing expedition saw 'about forty natives, including women and children ... assembled on the beach' who 'gestured incessantly' and 'danced around' and made 'all sorts of grimaces' to get them to land. 'But,' noted the Commander, doubtless with satisfaction, 'they did not go.'[62]

The next day, 1st February, would see perhaps the most intense social relations established between these two peoples, and especially between the French and the Aboriginal women. Eyewitness accounts of these are long and detailed. There were in fact two meetings lasting several hours which, in mid-afternoon, would come together as one.

Because, as Baudin put it, 'I wanted to see for myself how the natives behaved', at nine in the morning he, Captain Hamelin and five or six colleagues set off towards the shore. They had barely thrown out their fishing net when 'the natives appeared with loud exclamations' which, he presumed, 'showed their happiness at seeing us'. 'There were sixteen of them, but no more than four were men.' The rest of the group consisted of two women and ten children, aged from about three months to twelve years. The men came towards him without fear, and accepted 'some large glass beads which seemed to please them very much'. The children were then called over, so that 'in half an hour they were familiar with us as if we had been old friends'. Monsieur Petit was then called upon to make portraits of the women and some of the children. 'I asked them to sit down,' said Baudin, 'which they did very obligingly.'

When the fish were eventually pulled in, 'there were no bounds to the delight of the children and even the grown men', but, once again, 'they would accept nothing' from the catch. The French and the native people then 'all sat down on the grass together', but, Baudin noted, 'I always had two men constantly beside me ... because I was the only one carrying a gun ... and I only had to move it to see how much they feared [its] effect'. Meanwhile the children 'were playing very happily' with the sailors and 'their gaiety was most endearing'. They 'ran across, did somersaults and played various other games', while Petit successfully managed to finish his drawings. Baudin thought it 'extraordinary and difficult to explain that the men who were with us were the very ones who, a day earlier,[63] had thrown stones at us as we left'. 'They plainly recognised us,' he said, 'making signs to show that they had seen us before.' He took no action, however, not wanting the inhabitants to 'think we bore them any ill-feeling'.

At three o'clock that afternoon — after some six hours of mingling with the Indigenous people — Baudin noted that three of his colleagues had returned from an expedition to the north of the bay. 'When we saw them,' he noted, 'they were accompanied by a dozen natives, whom we recognised as women as they drew nearer.'[64] The three men concerned were Heirisson, Bellefin and Péron, and it is to Péron's account we refer here.

At first Péron had set off on his own, but had soon 'perceived about twenty savages' coming along the shore 'as if to meet him' and, 'without hesitating a moment' had turned back, 'warmed by the experience of such rencontres'. Then, accompanied by his colleagues, he had returned to the scene and, now more steadfast in spirit, advanced towards the native people who, he discovered, 'were women, and there was not a single male among the party'. One of the oldest of these women invited the Frenchmen to sit down ('calling aloud to us "médi, médi"'), which they all did. Whereupon, wrote the naturalist, 'they asked us a number of questions, seeming often to criticise our appearance, and laughing heartily at our expense'. Perhaps the naked women thought the Frenchmen's clothes bizarre. Bellefin then 'began to sing, at the same time using a great deal of action', whereupon, 'the women immediately kept silent'. At the end of every verse, however, 'some applauded him with loud acclamation, others laughed heartily, while the young women, being more timid, kept silence'. When the doctor had concluded his song, one of the women 'began to mimic his action and the tone of his voice' in what Péron found to be 'a very pleasant and truly original manner'. She then began to dance, and to 'throw herself into divers attitudes, some of which might be thought very indecent', wrote the Frenchman, 'if in this state of society men were not still absolutely strangers to all the delicacy of sentiment and conduct which, among us, is only the consequence of complete civilisation'.[65]

Her dancing finished, 'she came close to me', wrote Péron, 'and, taking from a bag made of rushes … some charcoal which it contained, she crushed it between her hands and … began to apply it on my face'. His colleague Heirisson was soon 'ornamented with a similar mask', after which, noted Péron, 'we seemed to be very much admired by these women'. However, whenever the Frenchmen endeavoured to approach these women, 'who had good will and confidence in us', they 'all sprung up from their position on their heels, and ran away: we were therefore obliged to conform entirely to their wishes, that we might longer enjoy their company'. When the French decided to return to their boat, the 'Diemenese ladies' [*nos Diémenoises*] accompanied them, being 'merry' and playing 'many tricks' and 'many drolleries'. On seeing Baudin and his men, however, 'one of the women … uttered a loud cry of terror, which was repeated by all the rest'. The situation did not improve when 'the husbands [*les maris*] of these poor women' suddenly arrived, looking 'fierce and menacing'. All the unfortunate females who had followed us,' observed Péron, 'seemed quite terrified.'[66] When Baudin finally prepared to leave, he noticed that two of the men 'picked up a bundle of spears, either to be on their guard, or to attack us' and tried to take Hamelin's sword from him as he was getting into the boat.[67] 'Unluckily for him,' Hamelin would say, 'I held onto [it] with my left hand. Judging by the expression on his face … he strongly resented the fact that I did not let him rob me.'[68]

Once again, therefore, the French seem to indicate a deterioration of relations upon departure.

A few days later, however, Péron again met one of the women who had attracted his attention earlier, and discovered that her name was Arra-Maida. 'M. Petit,' he wrote, 'at my request, drew a likeness of her, and which is a very correct resemblance … The last time I met with her, she had a young child at her back.'[69] Petit's drawing appears in the photographic section.

On 5 February, 'all our labours being thus terminated on this part of Diemen's Land', as Péron put it, the ships set sail northward and — after experiencing an 'extraordinary degree of heat … [when] the wind seemed like the heat from a furnace'[70] — arrived in Oyster Bay on Maria Island on 18 February.

At daybreak the following day Baudin dispatched Boullanger,[71] Maurouard and Péron on longboats to tour the island and make a plan of it. Meanwhile the Commander himself went to reconnoitre the Bay, and soon saw 'about twenty natives on the beach'. 'There were men, women and children, most of them armed with a spear,' he wrote, but 'they made no hostile signs when we landed, simply retreating a little from the shore.' The French made 'gestures of friendship' and offered presents which soon 'established mutual confidence'. As with the usual practice, the French and the native people then sat down together, but — again as usual — 'the women and children stayed a little way off. The children, especially, seemed very timid and fearful.' The French exchanged 'some trifles' for spears, 'and the transaction was made very amicably on both sides'. They then left without incident.

Two days later, however, an incident occurred which caused them some alarm — although, of course, the alarm of the inhabitants on being visited by these strange people could have been far greater (Maria Island having received fewer visits than the D'Entrecasteaux Channel). The carpenters from *Le Naturaliste* had gone ashore to seek water, when 'several natives' had gathered around them and 'harassed them a great deal'. One of the men had been 'forcibly led off into the woods' and examined 'from head to foot', but had come to no harm.

When Baudin arrived, the natives at first withdrew but, once again, after 'making signs of friendship ... confidence was soon re-established' and the rest of the day was spent 'most peacefully'.[72]

A day or two later Hamelin recorded in his journal: 'Today Citizens Péron and Petit went to visit the natives ... There was only one sailor [M. Rouget] with them, armed with a gun, so our brothers on Maria Island threatened them from time to time with their lances.'[73] This brief remark covered a host of events recounted by Péron over some ten pages of his original work.[74]

On the south coast of Oyster Bay Péron and his two colleagues had met 'fourteen men who were seated round the fire' and who, thought Péron, 'received us with transport [*avec des transports*], which at the same time seemed to express surprise, admiration and pleasure'. *Médi, médi* ('sit down, sit down') were the first words addressed to us. We seated ourselves and they gathered around us. They were most of them armed with long *sagaies*, others had clubs [*casse-têtes*] which they laid down by their sides.' There the French may have felt themselves hopelessly outnumbered, and cockswain Rouget kept his musket carefully at hand. The two groups then 'mutually surveyed each other for some minutes'.

After a while, Nicolas Petit 'displayed before the natives some feats of sleight of hand, which diverted them very much', and then Rouget 'ran a pin into his flesh, without showing any sense of pain', at which the inhabitants — understandably perhaps — 'regarded each other in silence, as if to impart their mutual astonishment'. Péron does not explain the point of this puzzling exercise. 'Unluckily for me,' he continued, 'among our other presents were some pins ... and one of the natives ... came behind me unawares, and ran one [of them] into the calf of my leg so dexterously and decidedly that I could not help crying out.'

Petit then set about making his sketches, and soon, wrote Péron, 'crowded together among the ashes of their fire, we appeared ... quite satisfied with each other'. Péron believed this a suitable moment to discover whether the inhabitants knew 'the action of embracing'. Failing to get them to understand what he was talking about, he 'approached to embrace them' but 'they all had that look of astonishment which any unknown action occasions in ourselves'. It is worthy of note that none of the French explorers had witnessed such action in Australia — and Péron may have profitably borne in mind that even the French do not embrace complete strangers! Nevertheless, he concluded, 'it appears that ... kisses and tender caresses are entirely unknown among these savage nations'.[75]

While Péron and Petit were engaged in these peaceful pursuits, there arrived from the ships another boat containing several sailors. Upon this, noted Péron with surprise, 'the savages rose precipitately, seized their weapons and, turning their eyes with looks of surprise mingled with ferocity towards the sea, appeared much agitated'. The boats — perhaps fortunately for all concerned — turned away, whereupon 'the fears of the natives seemed to subside a little'. Péron tried to reassure them, but in vain. 'These people seemed to become bolder,' he wrote, and 'they appeared to meditate some violence against us.' One of them wanted the jacket he wore, but he refused. He then suddenly had cause to fear for his life:

> In a moment, when my attention was engaged another way, he seized hold of my jacket and, directing the point of his *sagaie* towards me, brandished it in a threatening manner, and seemed to say 'Give it to me, or I will kill you.' It would have been rash to provoke him, situated as I was, for the wretch [*le misérable*] would certainly have pierced me with his *sagaie*. I affected to take his threats as a joke; but nevertheless took hold of the *sagaie* and, turning the point away, showed him that M. Rouget was pointing his musket at him, and I added one single word of his own language 'Mata' (death). He understood, and laid down his weapon with as much indifference as if he had done nothing to offend me.

After appearing so harmonious, social relations thus suddenly seemed to reach rock-bottom. 'I really believe,' concluded the naturalist, 'that if it had not been for M. Rouget and his musket, M. Petit and myself would have fallen victims to the ferocity of these savage people.' This behaviour rankled sorely with the Frenchman. 'Let us recollect,' he exclaimed, 'that all these men had been loaded with presents by us;

that we had given them looking-glasses, knives, beads, handkerchiefs, snuff-boxes, cups etc. … and had given way to all their fancies and caprices without requiring any return for all our gifts.' In his view these 'savage people' were 'unjust and treacherous [in] their conduct towards us'. He appears thus to have forgotten Degérando's advice regarding 'property', and the indifference with which many of these 'presents' had been received.

As they were about to depart, one of 'the handsomest' of the inhabitants, named Bara Ourou, whom Petit had drawn at his leisure, suddenly menaced the French with his weapons, requiring M. Rouget again to point his musket. Petit's drawing of this young man appears in the photographic section.

'Fearing that these savage people would pelt us with stones or throw their *sagaies* at us in our retreat, as had happened several times before in the [D'Entrecasteaux] channel,' wrote Péron, 'we resolved to retire slowly and with caution. M. Petit and myself walked first, while M. Rouget came behind with his musket. These precautions succeeded, and we gained our boat without any accident.'[76]

On 26 February, 'having nothing more to do on Maria Island', wrote Baudin, 'I gave order to Captain Hamelin to be ready to set sail the following morning'.[77]

During their stay in Tasmania it would appear that on no occasion had the French manifested aggression towards their hosts. They had indeed overtly sought their friendship. If aggressors there were, these were the Indigenous people who, on seeing their visitors arrive in increasing numbers, could become apprehensive and agitated, and then appear aggressive. Several times when returning to their boats, and thus being somewhat vulnerable, the French could find themselves attacked with spears and stones. When playing (what could appear to be rather silly) games with their hosts — such as arm-wrestling or tricks of prestidigitation — it is really not surprising that the Indigenous people should be embarrassed by the behaviour of these strange people, and then react in a quite normal human manner.

While exploring the east coast of Tasmania, Baudin's people created many place-names, most of which still exist today.

At the beginning of his tour of Maria Island on 19 February with Maurouard and Boullanger, Péron noted, perhaps with some pride, 'Soon we reached the most southern cape of this isle, which our geographers have named Cape Péron.'[78] On arriving at the eastern point, they named this 'Cap Maurouard' and, continuing north, they called the next stretch of shore-line 'Baie Riédlé' (thus spelled in the original French), in memory of their naturalist colleague who had died in Timor. Later, at the island's northernmost point, they declared this to be 'Cap Boullanger', and named the small island offshore 'Ilot du Nord'. Travelling south, they went around 'Cap Lesueur' and finally arrived back in Oyster Bay on 21 February. Here they learnt of the death of their colleague, the zoologist René Maugé, whom they buried at a place henceforth known as 'Pointe Maugé'.[79]

Many other place-names created by this expedition are still existent. On the mainland, from south to north (thus in the direction Baudin sailed), we find Cape Bernier (the astronomer on *Le Naturaliste*), Cape Bougainville (in honour of Louis de Bougainville), Point Bailly (mineralogist on *Le Naturaliste*), Cape Tourville and Cape Lodi. Out at sea, in the same direction, we find the Ile des Phoques (acknowledging the large numbers of seals seen here) between Maria and Schouten Island and, on this latter, Cape Sonnerat, Cape Baudin and Cape Faure (marine surveyor on *Le Naturaliste*). On the Freycinet Peninsula (named after Louis de Freycinet) there is Cape Degérando (*en l'honneur*, wrote Péron, *du respectable savant de ce nom*),[80] Cape Forestier, Fleurieu Point and Mount Freycinet. Louis de Freycinet's 1802 map of this area is reproduced in the photographic section.

The next point of significant contact between Baudin's expedition and the Indigenous people was in Western Australia. Here, on 26 February 1803, midshipman Joseph Ransonnet went ashore in King George Sound and, declared Péron, 'this was the first time a European had met the untamed people [*peuples farouches*][81] of this region'. Ransonnet told of his encounter to both Péron and Baudin but, as the former's account is slightly more detailed, it is to this we shall refer.

Scarcely had they landed, reported Ransonnet, than eight natives [*naturels*] came towards them. Three of these were women, who soon departed, leaving the men to help the French disembark. The French ladened them with 'various presents which they received with satisfaction, but which ... they gave back to us with a sort of pleasure'. When Ransonnet again offered these gifts, 'they were abandoned on the ground or on nearby rocks'. He then tried to obtain one of the natives' 'very beautiful and very large dogs' by offering everything that was in his power, but 'their will was unshakeable' and negotiations broke down. These five men did, however, accept to eat some biscuit and salted beef, and to drink some of the French coffee. Nevertheless, noted Ransonnet, 'despite the good understanding that reigned between us, they would never take us to the spot where the others — probably their wives [*leurs femmes*] had gone to hide'.[82] Baudin added that Ransonnet's group 'had forgotten to take the presents I normally had for the natives ... so they gave them just the buttons off their coats, which were greatly prized, some handkerchiefs and a few rough old jackets'. Baudin understood that the two parties had 'spent the greater part of the day together on very good terms'.[83]

Three weeks later (on 17 March) at the Péron Peninsula (over 1000 kilometres to the north) the French experienced the usual hostile reception extended in this region. Two fishing boats were prevented from going ashore by 'a band of natives, all ... armed with spears, clubs and shields'.[84]

A few days later, in the eyes of his commander, François Péron would behave very badly. Baudin and Péron thus recount this event in rather different ways.

On 19 March Baudin sent a party ashore under the command of his sub-lieutenant Bonnefoi 'to try and become acquainted with the natives' and to obtain salt by boiling sea-water in large cauldrons to preserve the fish they had caught. Péron was one of this group, which was instructed to return the following day. That next day came and, by ten o'clock at night, the boat had still not returned. 'I presumed,' wrote Baudin, 'that he [Bonnefoi] had been delayed by the absence of some people, Citizen Péron being unquestionably one of them.' It would not be until one-thirty the next afternoon that the longboat — containing Péron — would finally return. On demanding an explanation, Baudin was told by Bonnefoi (a name meaning 'Good faith') that Citizens Péron, Guichenot and Petit had gone ashore without telling him their plans, and without food and water, and had become inextricably lost. 'Citizen Péron,' declared Baudin, '[was] the most thoughtless and most wanting in foresight of everyone aboard.' He had eventually reached the longboat 'exhausted and weak with hunger and thirst' and, on arriving back on board ship, 'could hardly talk and remain standing'. The commander's patience was wearing thin. 'This is the third escapade of this nature that our learned *naturaliste* has been on,' he wrote, 'but it will also be the last, for he shall not go ashore again unless I myself am in the same boat.'[85] Such a decision would not, of course, enhance Péron's appreciation — already scathing enough — of the expedition leader.

Péron's account tells of his experiences, and of his encounter with the native people. The three men had been walking knee-deep in the water, picking up shells and admiring *diverses troupes de poissons* moving around their feet, when suddenly a large shark came close to M. Petit and frightened him, causing him to fire at 'the animal'. Not doubting that this shot would attract 'the savages', Péron and Guichenault rushed to the shore to gather their clothes and hide in the bush, while 'l'imprudent Petit' laughed at them and stayed in the water. Soon, wrote Péron, 'his indiscretion would give way to horror. Guichenault and I had scarcely finished dressing when we heard a terrible yelling and saw a troop of savages who … rushed down onto the shore. On seeing this, M. Petit, filled with terror, hurriedly seized some of his clothes and ran half-naked to join us'. They then decided how best to prepare their defences. 'Our weapons consisted of only one gun and two pistols,' wrote the naturalist. 'We loaded them … and, after having promised ourselves only to fire as a last resort and at point-blank range, we continued to walk along the shore.' The 'savages' soon caught up with them, 'making terrifying and threatening noises'. Péron continued:

Already they were only 150 paces away, and any further retreat would only have emboldened them. This manoeuvre seemed for a while to disconcert them, and they stopped. One of them came forward alone, making various gestures and addressing us very animatedly in a way which seemed to invite one of us to go forward to speak with him. An interview of this kind ... was precisely what we needed to avoid. Apart from our isolation, we feared the number of savages might increase at any moment and that our means of defence, already so weak, might become completely useless ... So, far from agreeing to divide ourselves, we continued to walk towards them, resolved, if need be, to sell our lives dearly.

The natives [*naturels*] did not wait for us and, although there were fourteen of them, all armed with *sagaies* and waddies like those of New Wales [sic] ... they turned their backs, making off towards the headland whence they had come ... We followed them at a short distance, walking at the same speed as them, without trying to catch them up. In this way we arrived at Cape Guichenault, up which they climbed with admirable promptitude, and stopped at the top. From there, multiplying shouts and gestures, they seemed to insist that one of us go to them. After replying to them for a while with similar shouts and gestures, we bade them a sort of adieu, and continued on our way along the edge of the sea. We had scarcely lost sight of them than we crossed the dunes to go inland and to cross the peninsula.

It was then that Péron and his party got lost, and were eventually found in the state described by Baudin. Péron, however, was scathing about the commanding officer. 'Everyone,' he declared, 'seeing us so weak, felt full of compassion and interest; everyone showed the most tender cares, the most affectionate solicitudes. Only our Commander [*Commandant*] remained for us what he had been till then for all his poor [*misérable*] companions.'[86]

Fifteen years later, on this same Péron Peninsula, Louis de Freycinet returned with his own ships and, in mid-September 1818, sent a party ashore to establish a suitable place for an observatory. Arago was in this party, and described their meetings with some fifteen 'savages'. On this occasion the two peoples were able to negotiate some form of commercial exchange.

'The savages,' wrote Arago, 'had been presented with necklaces of glass beads, looking-glasses and little knives; they had sent clubs and assagays; and this species of barter appeared to please them much.' One of his colleagues, however, had 'made them a present of a pair of drawers: these they tore to pieces, and shared the fragments'. The two peoples clearly valued these goods differently, and put them to different use. The Indigenous people 'obstinately refused to drink some wine and water which was put into a bottle; and rubbed their bodies with a piece of bacon which a sailor had bartered for a small club'. If the French found the native people's reactions puzzling, the latter would no doubt have been equally puzzled to discover the lack of practical use to which the French would put their valuable clubs and spears.

'All of these exchanges were made with a certain mistrust on the part of the savages,' wrote Arago. 'They watched us as dangerous enemies, and were continually pointing to the ship, exclaiming, "ayerkadé", "ayerkadé" (go away, go away).' The desire to see strangers 'go away' seems indeed common to all parts of this continent.

Arago then had what he must have considered an intelligent idea. We have seen (in Chapter 1) how, being 'desirous of knowing whether [the native people] were destitute of fresh water', he had pretended to drink sea-water from his hand and, the inhabitants showing no surprise, he may have thus deduced that the sea was their water source. A few days later he would indeed conclude quite firmly that 'these poor people drink only salt water'.[87] The inhabitants of course did not drink salt water, but doubtless politely assumed that their visitors did.

As the inhabitants were so reticent in coming near them, the French resorted to the usual practice of enticing them with friendly gestures and gifts. Arago noticed that 'the savages ... frequently turned their eyes toward an old man, painted with stripes, who seemed to give them orders', and it was toward this person he directed his attention. 'I had a pair of castanets in my pocket,' he wrote, 'and ... began to rattle them briskly. Judge of my pleasure when the old man rose with astonishment, and ... fell to dancing in such a grotesque

manner that we were ready to die with laughing. Some of the savages
... following his example, danced also; while one of them, sitting on
his heels, beat on an assagay with two little clubs.' The 'old man' then
tried to induce Arago to barter the castanets for 'a little lion-dog [sic],
painted red' which he held, but the Frenchman discreetly declined.[88]
The inhabitants then took their leave.

The next day, fearing his colleagues might oppose his intentions,
Arago went ashore 'without saying a word, armed with a double-bar-
relled gun, a sabre, and a few cartridges, and accompanied by a single
seaman'. 'After an hour's walking,' he wrote, 'I saw a few natives,
armed as before with assagays and clubs ... coming towards me with
loud shouts.' He then made the same decision as Péron had in the
same situation here fifteen years before. 'I put a good face on the matter,' he said, 'and firmly awaited their arrival.' Then, as with Péron, one
of the inhabitants 'came forward alone; and, after a vehement ha-
rangue, pointed to the ship and the two boats, concluding each period
of his speech with the word *ayerakadé*, and a threatening gesture'.

To turn the tables, Arago called out to this man to 'go away', em-
ploying the term of the savages. At the word *ayerkadé*, he wrote, 'I saw
them look at each other with astonishment, repeat it in a low voice,
and deliberate what they should do.' Seeing that they still appeared
disposed 'to attempt a sudden attack', he devised a quick stratagem
with his sailor companion in order to let his protagonists 'know the
terrible power of our weapons'. 'Accordingly,' he continued, 'I assumed a threatening air, turning toward the sailor, and calling to him
again *ayerkadé*, and, as according to our agreement he was to disobey
me, I pointed my gun toward him, and fired over his head. Instantly he
fell: and the savages, terrified at the noise and the fall of my comrade,
took to their heels.' The encounter was thus terminated.

Later that day Arago and two colleagues, Bérard and Requin, again
met some inhabitants with whom 'we made our exchanges, or rather
offered them presents'. On this occasion, Requin 'even undressed
himself' (as one of Dufresne's men had in Tasmania nearly a half-century before), but, observed Arago, 'this mark of courage and confidence led to no result'. The native people offered 'a club badly made,

a very dirty fan, some cassowary's feathers, two bladders painted red filled with very fine down and a assagay of hard wood, six feet long and not over sharp'. After this 'barter' was complete, the native people soon 'disappeared with astonishing swiftness' and, despite extensive searching by the French, could not be found anywhere.[89]

The last expeditions to establish relations with the Aboriginal Australians (apart from in Sydney, which will be presented in a separate chapter) were those of Dumont d'Urville in King George Sound (Western Australia) in 1826 and at Raffles Bay (Northern Territory) in 1839. Here, the Aboriginal people showed interest in the presents offered and, in d'Urville's case, particularly in the food.

On 8 October 1826 in King George Sound 'a savage' approached D'Urville, 'at first fairly resolutely, but as he came nearer', noted the explorer, 'his boldness seemed to leave him [until] I decided to give him a piece of bread'. Far from discarding this, 'he ate it hungrily' and 'in a moment, lost all his suspiciousness' and 'started to dance and sing and call to his comrades'. It is probable that this man had already made acquaintance with bread via the English whalers and sealers here. He readily went on board ship, where 'he lost none of his gaiety and confidence ... and was loaded with presents which sent him into transports of delight'. The man spent the night on board and 'slept like a baby' before being returned to shore in the morning.

That afternoon D'Urville and some colleagues were on shore at Point des Patelles (Wooding Point) when eight 'natives' came to meet them and were 'apparently delighted' to see them. Upon returning to their tent, the Frenchmen met three others who had kept their companions 'constant company since the morning'. 'Their behaviour was peaceful,' noted D'Urville, and 'not one of them attempted the slightest larceny'.[90] Later that day 'the natives ... brought three children to the camp, an infallible proof of their trust in and good intentions towards us'.

The next day, while walking along the beach from Point des Patelles to Oyster Harbour, D'Urville met a native 'carrying a knife made from a piece of quartz stuck in a sort of handle with grass-tree resin'. 'I gave him a real knife, in exchange,' wrote D'Urville, and 'he was delighted with the bargain'.[91]

On several occasions here, as elsewhere, the French noticed that the Indigenous men strove 'to keep their women out of sight'. M. de Sainson, the expedition's artist, noted that 'these natives did not care to let people see their womenfolk. Renewed requests on our own part were put off with a promise for the next day'. When the next day came, however, and 'we reminded them of their undertaking ... they remained silent'. Colleagues Quoy and Gaimard guessed that the women were concealed 'through fear or jealousy'. This fear, they assumed, was caused by the Englishmen 'who have abducted several of them for their own purposes'.[92]

On 11 October D'Urville gave Sainson and three colleagues permission to sleep on shore, and at 6 o'clock that evening they set off with a native guide. After crossing swamp and scrub in total darkness they arrived at their destination, and found themselves 'in the presence of savages'. Sainson's description of this lengthy encounter is worthy of quotation.

> About a dozen men and two boys were standing around a fire; but when they recognized their comrade clothed, and decked out in necklaces and mirrors and the various trinkets that had been given him, their delight knew no bounds. They all started to shout and sing at the same time, and it was a very strange sight to see those thin black figures lit by the reflections from the flames excitedly leaping about and making barking noises ... However, our savage was fêted, caressed and examined by his friends, and each time some new wonder struck their eyes, the transports of delight would recommence even louder and livelier; and he, in response to so much attention, shouted and laughed and energetically joined in the deafening noise of general rejoicing ... Eventually fatigue appeared to put an end to the general frenzy, and we made our way to the tent to prepare our sleeping places for the night.
>
> Seven natives soon detached themselves from the main group and came to settle themselves down not far from our sentry ... When we saw them so close we signalled a desire to increase their circle. This proposal

was eagerly welcomed and they made room for us, then there commenced the most unusual experience for us, rich in new sensations, for the equivalent of which one would seek in vain in the entertainments that civilization has invented for its diversion.

It is a strange destiny that gathers round the same hearth fire such different inhabitants of our globe. We were involuntarily reflecting thus and would have continued in the same vein had our hosts not diverted us from it. Being little preoccupied with philosophical ideas, they were obedient to whatever physical impressions were influencing them at that moment. Their bright expressive eyes observed us with curiosity and rolled over us. Their hard thin hands alternately touched our clothing and our skin and every word we uttered amazed them and provoked laughter.

We soon understood that our hosts wanted to exchange their names for ours. This custom that travellers have found to be widespread among the archipelagos of the Southern Ocean certainly amazed us among these poor human beings who seemed to us so little endowed with intelligence. It is the mark of an already advanced society, and we could not have expected to find it established among a nomadic troop in this wild country. Whatever the case, the exchange of names took place to their great satisfaction and several of them, to mark the occasion, sang songs in which we were able to recognise our own names. One young man of the group seemed to enjoy some renown as a poet among his comrades, for when he started to sing everyone fell silent and from time to time a flattering murmur seemed to applaud him. The monotonous and rather melancholy chanting begins with high notes and gradually falls into a solemn low tone which imperceptibly dies away and finishes in a long humming in which all join in unison. M. Guilbert and I sang then a very lively duet, and we had reason to be proud of our success, for not only did they observe complete silence, but at the end of the song they deigned to applaud us with shouts and handclapping. This latter method of expressing pleasure, also in use in our Europe, was yet another cause of astonishment for us among this miserable people ...

The evening wore on, and the merriment gave way little by little to the need for sleep. We rose to go back to the tent without any native attempting to follow us.

Towards the middle of the night, while we were resting on the sails

spread out in the tent, we once more heard the melancholy and monotonous chanting of a man and the child Yalepouol. By 2 am everything was
asleep; the savages crouching down with their chins on their knees were
huddled one against the other to keep out the cold, and in this position
they took up only very little space. The fire gave out no more than a dull
glow, and the silence which reigned along the whole shore at this late
hour contrasted with the happy noise that made these solitudes echo a
few hours earlier ...

 We spent the day in the forests, and met there three natives who kept us
company for quite some time. We had no luck with our hunting, we only
saw one very tall cassowary which we pursued without catching it. At 5
pm we went back on board.[93]

D'Urville's final encounter with the Aboriginal Australians would be
at Raffles Bay in March 1839. After examining the ruins of the English settlement there ('a piece of wall still standing' and 'some graves
with simple wooden fences'), the French returned to their boats,
where they discovered 'seven natives gathered'. 'On seeing us,' noted
D'Urville, 'they showed neither fear nor surprise; they are quite sin-
gle-minded, they want from us some biscuit to satisfy their hunger.
And in fact they approach us for the sole purpose of begging.' He distributed some hard tack to them, which they 'gobbled down' before
stretching out under a casuarina tree. On his return, D'Urville took
two of the natives on board *L'Astrolabe*, where they were soon joined
by three others in a 'poor looking canoe', all carrying 'little woven
baskets to receive all the gifts expected from our largesse'. All they
wanted, however, was to satisfy their hunger, and 'several slabs of
weevilly and worm-eaten hard tack were greedily devoured'. When
they later saw the crew's meal brought on deck, 'they quickly went to
prowl around the sailors' food to pounce on anything that was left
over'. One of them 'started to perform a ridiculous and pointless
dance to arouse the sailors' interest to get more from them'. In vain
D'Urville tried to communicate with them, but 'to all my questions
they only responded with pantomime gestures by which they were
trying to convey to us they were still hungry'.[94]

Two days later — still in Raffles Bay — Lieutenant Demas

accompanied by Lafarge and Goupil set off early to seek water and hunt kangaroo. After walking several miles they 'fell in with a group of fifteen to twenty natives [who] were crouching round a fire on which there was a big lizard and some shellfish'. Demas noted that 'there were two women among them, or rather two she-animals, who seemed very forthcoming: for a slab of ship's biscuit there were no favours they would not have granted us'. The group followed the French for some time, but soon, seeing that they could not get anything from them, left them alone.

After hunting all day, 'laden with parrots and doves', Demas and his colleagues were returning to the ship when Lafarge thought he saw something move in the long grass, and took aim. Instead of a kangaroo looming before him, however, he saw 'two long black figures who cleared out as fast as their legs would carry them, shouting ... "Wattaloo! Welleton!" [Waterloo, Wellington]'. 'Some recommendation!' exclaimed Demas, 'but the poor devils mean no malice; these were the names the English had given them'.

Arriving at the shore, there was no boat awaiting them. 'Luckily,' wrote Demas, 'we found a savage with a little bark canoe. He had a basket on his back; I dropped a note in it and pointed to *Astrolabe*. This chap understood me with an intelligence I wouldn't have expected. He paddled out to *Astrolabe*, handed my note to the first sailor he saw on deck, and soon they came to fetch us.'[95]

French perception of Aboriginal character and language

Perceptions of the Aboriginal Australians' character or temperament evolved considerably between D'Entrecasteaux's expedition (Marion Dufresne's people made little mention of this) and those of Dumont d'Urville half a century later.

D'Entrecasteaux himself appears at first to have been a romantic, and, although we do not know for certain that he had read Rousseau, he was at the outset certainly well imbibed with the spirit of his work.

D'Entrecasteaux spoke of the people he met in Tasmania in 1793 as being 'close to nature', and 'whose candour and kindness contrast so much with the vices of civilisation'. On one occasion Labillardière and three companions spent the night ashore and, while asleep, had been seen by the *naturels*. D'Entrecasteaux believed his colleagues 'would have been the victims of the ferociousness of these savages, had they been as perverse as they seemed to M. Marion in 1772'. He declared the Aboriginal Tasmanians to be 'kind and without mistrust', and even exclaimed, 'Oh! How much would those civilised people who boast about the extent of their knowledge learn from this school of nature!'

After some three weeks in Tasmania and several long encounters with the inhabitants, he would conclude that 'they are interesting men in every respect, with whom I would have liked to spend all the time we have been ... at anchorage'. His enthusiasm for the good nature of these *naturels* appeared boundless. 'This tribe [*peuplade*],' he declared, 'seems to offer the most perfect image of pristine society, in which men have not yet been stirred by passions, or corrupted by the vices caused by civilisation ... Their open and smiling expression reveals a happiness that has never been troubled by intrusive thoughts and unattainable desires.' D'Entrecasteaux would end on a comparative note. 'Although their civilisation is less advanced than the people of New Zealand, they do not possess a ferocious temper. The hatreds that divide the inhabitants of that island seem to be unknown to those of this part of New Holland.'[96] D'Entrecasteaux was thus deeply impressed with Tasmania and Tasmanians.

His subsequent travels would delude and disappoint him, however, as to the pristine innocence of the 'noble savage'. In New Caledonia in April 1793 he would declare the inhabitants 'a frightful people', and in Santa Cruz the next month they would be 'generally disagreeable and sinister'. In Tongatabou the islanders would plunder his supplies, thus creating open hostility. A similar situation would arise in the Solomon Islands, causing him to declare that this confirmed 'the opinion that ... travellers have given of the treacherousness of the inhabitants'.[97]

Among D'Entrecasteaux's companions, Labillardière did not

explicitly express an opinion about the inhabitants. The others, however, were quite loquacious and, *grosso modo*, reflected the sentiments of their leader.

At the time of the first meeting in February 1793, D'Auribeau had found the eight indigenous men there 'without any sign of defiance or fear, but with that openness and lack of apprehension which indicate a perfect tranquillity and a nature as good as it is trusting'. Later that day, when women and children were also present, he found them to be 'all extremely contented and very cheerful', possessing 'complete confidence and natural goodness' and, he felt, 'they know no evil, and do not think that anyone could do them harm'. After a second meeting he would speak of 'their boundless trust and their quietness'. D'Auribeau, indeed, did not have a bad word to say about his hosts.

La Motte du Portail's attitude was similar. He was not present at the first two encounters and, he declared, 'to give an account of these people I will wait until I am able to judge for myself'. He was present at the third encounter — with no less than forty-eight 'natives'. 'The kindness and gentleness ... of their character,' he wrote, 'gave to our meetings rather the air of a reunion of friends than a meeting of individuals who were quite different in every way ... This people, undoubtedly the closest to the primitive state of nature, seemed to enjoy all the good fortune associated with it ... From our first meeting there had been a basis of confidence which they had always maintained.' After spending a long day with them, he would conclude that 'most perfect harmony seemed to reign among these natives' and would mention Jean-Jacques Rousseau explicitly. 'One would have difficulty,' he considered, 'in finding a people who are less far from the primitive state of nature and, seen at first hand ... they offer strong proof in support of the idea which the immortal J.J. Rousseau has developed in his discourse on the origin of inequality of conditions.'[98]

If La Motte du Portail was thus well acquainted with Rousseau's work, one may suppose that he was not alone among his companions to be so. Here, as Voltaire could have said (in his *Candide* in 1759), all seemed for the best in this the best of all possible worlds.

★ ★

Nicolas Baudin's expedition — although supposedly the best ever planned — would have a generally different impression.

These Frenchmen's feelings about West Australians were, like their reception there, rather mixed. Milius believed the inhabitants were neither 'ill-intentioned or to be feared', but thought he and his colleagues may, reciprocally, not have inspired them 'with a great idea of our courage'.[99] Henri de Freycinet believed 'a character of timidity and fear' was their predominant feature, but that they could also be 'bold and sometimes even audacious'.[100] Depuch declared (after his unpleasant experience described earlier) that, 'among all those who do not yet know the benefits of civilisation', these *naturels* were 'the closest to the primordial state, [and] to the state of nature'.[101]

Péron considered the native people's hostile reception was a 'peculiarity of character, so different from the eager solicitude with which all the nations of the Pacific Ocean meet and receive Europeans who visit their shores for the first time'.[102]

Their opinions concerning the Tasmanians seem to be more circumspect.

On the first encounter (in the D'Entrecasteaux Channel) Baudin's response resembled that of his earlier compatriot. 'The natives ... appeared to us to be of a gentle, peaceful nature',[103] he wrote. Péron agreed whole-heartedly and spoke twice at Port Cygnet about 'our good Diemenese'.[104] Louis de Freycinet was already more cautious, however. 'Most [of them] seemed to us ill-intentioned [*méchans*], suspicious and fearful', he thought, although there were 'a few individuals who looked gentle and affable'. But, he warned, 'we have not stayed long enough in the same spot to be able to trace in a precise and definitive manner the moral character of these people'.[105]

Freycinet was right. These happy expectations — and indeed realisations — were soon to be doomed to disappointment. But one must wonder to what extent the French themselves were to blame for this.

We have seen how midshipman Maurouard had initiated arm-wrestling and then full-body wrestling with one of his hosts, and the subsequent spear and stone throwing. Milius would then declare that 'these people ... appeared to us in every circumstance to be very cunning [*rusés*].'[106] Baudin himself would speak of the 'inconstancy and instability of their character', and would even go so far as to question the judgement of 'Citizen Labillardière' (although he probably meant here D'Entrecasteaux). 'I do not doubt,' he wrote, 'that in the resources of his fertile imagination, Citizen Labillardière would have found a suitable reason for excusing their behaviour in these two incidents.' 'Personally,' he continued, confessing his confusion, 'I honestly admit that I am unable to form an opinion of their character.'[107]

His companion, botanist Leschenault de la Tour (who mentions the Maurouard incident) would find that 'the faces of the [Tasmanian] men reflected wickedness and treachery' and, in his turn, would question the idea of 'the noble savage'. 'I confess I am surprised,' he wrote in his journal, 'that after so many incidents of treachery and cruelty reported in the accounts of all [sic] the voyages of discovery, reasonable people still say that natural men are not wicked, that one can trust them and that they are only aggressive when provoked to take revenge. Unfortunately, many travellers have fallen victim to these false arguments, and personally I think that one cannot be too much on one's guard against men whose character has not been softened by civilisation.'[108]

On Maria Island Baudin's men would experience further disappointment. The *naturels* here, thought Freycinet, were 'as distrustful and perfidious [*défians et perfides*] as those in the D'Entrecasteaux Channel'. Péron would echo resoundingly the opinion expressed earlier by his companion Leschenault. 'I have noticed before,' he wrote (speaking of the Channel), 'the changeableness of the character of these ferocious people.' On Maria Island his opinion would be confirmed, and he expressed himself in no uncertain terms:

> Certainly no one ever was more disposed, both from character and principle, to conciliate and oblige these men, and to submit to their caprices; but I must declare frankly, that the whole tenor of their conduct shewed a treacherous disposition, and a degree of ferocity that disgusted both me and my companions. In comparing what we had now seen with what had

before happened in the Gut [*le canal*] to several of our ship-mates, we derived this inference, that it is not prudent to go among these people without sufficient means of defence against their attacks; and farther, that this principle does not only apply to the people whom we have just described, but may with equal propriety be applied to all savage or un-civilised nations, as may be easily proved by reading the accounts of voyagers.

In those very places, where the inhabitants are said to possess the greatest gentleness and mildness of character, unprotected Europeans have experienced many great dangers, and very often have fallen victims to their own generous confidence.

Péron almost seems to excuse himself for writing at such length, but, he concluded, he did this so 'that the reader may be the better enabled to judge how many difficulties and dangers are experienced by voyagers in their communication with the people belonging to savage nations, and how impossible it is to conquer the natural ferocity of their character'.[109]

We are far, it would appear, from the gentle optimism engendered by the experiences of D'Entrecasteaux and his colleagues, and also from the philanthropic ideals expressed by the untravelled Degérando.

Neither Arago nor D'Urville formed very favourable opinions of the Aboriginal Australians, although they found that nature itself did not treat them very kindly.

Speaking of the West Australians he met on the Péron Peninsula in 1919, Arago wrote that 'little dependence was to be placed on the engagements which they appeared to contract', and that 'several of our people had been deceived by their empty promises'. He was not lacking in sympathy for them, however. 'When I consider the resources of these unfortunate beings,' he said, 'their mode of existence appears to me quite a problem.'[110]

In King George Sound in 1826 D'Urville would express similar feelings. 'The tribes of King George Sound,' he wrote, 'living in an arid, infertile country, like many of the tribes of New Holland, must be considered one of the most miserable people on earth.' In Raffles Bay, nearly thirteen years later, he again declared his sympathy for these Australians generally. 'In a country like New Holland,' he wrote, 'where you do not find any of the fruit trees or food plants that grow wild in tropical lands … life must be difficult for the Australians; these unfortunate people must turn to the coasts, for it is there that they most easily find food.'[111]

Such was the French perception of the Aboriginal people. In her book *Risdon Cove: From the Dreamtime to Now,* Tasmanian Aboriginal historian Kaye McPherson tries to imagine, in turn, how her Aboriginal ascendants may have perceived the Europeans.

'How can any European interpretation of an Aboriginal past,' she asks, 'offer a description which explains why the people came over the hill?' She then goes on to try to answer her question. 'If the Ancestors had written their own version of what happened, it might have gone like this.' The beauty of her opening paragraph would doubtless have delighted Rousseau and his followers; and her whole description is worth presenting at length.

With the sun shining out of a sky the colour of sun orchids, and the rustling whisper of the wind like the movement of waves on the sand. The walking path crossing over a place of gentle rolling hills swaying like waves in an ocean as the wind rippled through the long grass almost as tall as a child before adulthood. The air alive with the raucous call of the crow and parrot interwoven with the song of the magpie, and combined with the musical tones of the small birds as they flittered about in the trees and grass in the vicinity of the people. The smells of the bush pungent with the fragrance of the oil from gum trees, blended with the sweet odour of the grass and the flowers in bloom. The smell of kangaroos, Tasmanian tigers, and other animals mingling to make the familiar bush smell called home. Upward of a thousand people of all ages, from babies in fur lined slings, to grannies, all laughing and singing the walking song as they made their way to the eating place.

In the distance faint sounds which do not belong begin to form a rhythm which is out of sync with the land. The dominant sound is a pounding combined with blurs of noise that have no meaning. They come through the valley overshadowed by the tall mountain range ... Dark oily smoke can be seen smudging the skyline telling them of the intruders making camp.

Suddenly there is an acrid smell on the breeze, a smell that burns the nostrils and causes the people to pull faces of despair at the now familiar sour smell known to belong to the new people who are now visiting the coasts ... It is a smell ... from rotting dead things left to decay in the open air rather than burnt in the cleansing fire. It was a smell becoming associated with knowing where the visitors had been or were presently visiting. It usually meant having to fire the area to cleanse it before it could be visited or used by the people ...

The people could not understand why the visitors failed to clean the mess of living with a fire before they left on their ships. Their ships carried even worse odours than their land places, but the smells and the noise always gave a warning as to where they were, allowing the place to be avoided if necessary ... The people knew to hide their revulsion at the smells which affronted both them and the land, the people knew from experience that overtures of friendship were always well received. At the last big meeting it was discussed how the visitors had funny customs and failed to understand the correct way to do things, but the people were sure with time the new visiting ones would learn the correct methods when they came in their season.

As the large body of people moved forward towards the sheltered cove where they were to eat, they flushed the sleepy kangaroos and wallabies out of their warm sunny beds in the long grass, causing them to casually hop in front of their onward movement. The children were laughing and joking as they played chasings with the bounding animals, who showed no fear only a desire to move out of the way. The adults had more caution and were wary about the visitor people being near their destination. They had already learnt in very recent times that these new people caused sudden death by putting holes in the people in attempts to remove their spirit. Death given for no reason from the thundersticks they pointed at those people they apparently did not like. It was hoped that when these visitors saw the women and children they would realise that they came in peace and friendship.

Already it was known that there were different groups that visited, some were friendly and others were not.[112]

* *

'The first means to the proper knowledge of the Savages,' Degérando had suggested to Baudin's expedition, 'is by learning their language.'[113] After spending two months in Tasmanian waters, D'Entrecasteaux had declared: 'We have stayed for a very short time among the people we have met in Van Diemen's Land, and have obtained only a very imperfect knowledge of their language.'[114] Baudin would stay for only a month, and Dufresne (in 1772) only a week. Let us therefore examine this linguistic experience in Tasmania.

Dufresne's people mention language only incidentally. When the Frenchmen's third boat tried to land, the inhabitants opposed this strongly. 'They all shouted "gola gola",' wrote Jean Roux, 'the cry was repeated by all, and that moment they let fly their shafts.' Lieutenant Le Dez would comment that generally 'they speak with a singular vivacity' and 'we were unable to distinguish any other sounds than these: "la-ga — la-ga".'

Julien Crozet, Dufresne's second-in-command on *Le Mascarin*, considered that 'their language seemed very harsh, and they appeared to draw their sounds from the bottom of their throat'.[115]

Although D'Entrecasteaux did not stay in exactly this spot, neither of the above words appears in his or Labillardière's vocabulary list. Chaplain Ventenat, however, voiced the same opinion as Crozet and Le Dez when he said that the inhabitants (of the D'Entrecasteaux Channel) 'articulate in the throat and speak very rapidly'. He would also notice how there were 'few consonants' in their language, and how 'the sounds T and F are unknown, it being difficult for them to pronounce them'. 'They have never,' he wrote, 'been able to repeat the word "Français", but they repeated quite easily the word "Paris"'. D'Auribeau noted too that they were 'unable to articulate the F, and that they substituted the P for it. For the rest, there is nothing disagreeable in their pronunciation: it is crisp and lively.'

One of the happier expressions learnt from the Tasmanians was their invitation to sit down: 'médi, médi'. This was noted by both the D'Entrecasteaux and Baudin expeditions. When Labillardière was walking with his hosts one day, after half an hour 'they asked us to sit

Bara Ourou: pencil and charcoal drawing by Nicolas Petit, Maria Island, February 1802. 'The handsomest fellow of the whole company' — Péron, A Voyage …, p. 223. (Source: Bonnemains, *Baudin in Australian Waters*, p. 150)

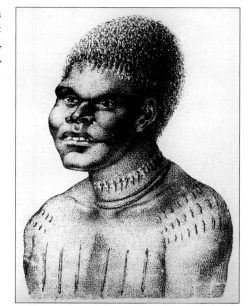

Arra-Maida, gouache by Nicolas Petit. 'In the features may be discovered that expression of courage and superiority, which so eminently distinguished her from her companions.' F. Péron, A Voyage …, p. 200. (Source: Bonnemains, *Baudin in Australian Waters*, p. 138)

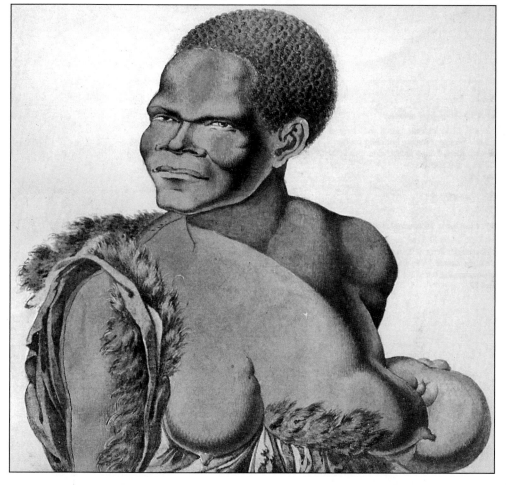

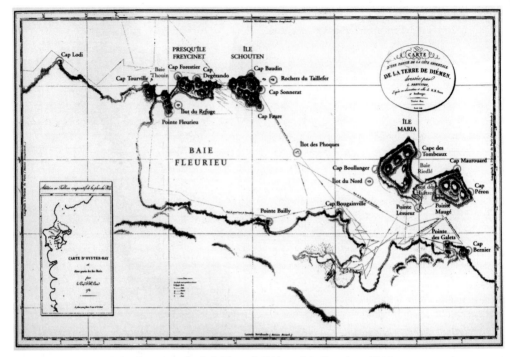

'Carte d'une partie de la côte orientale de la Terre de Diémen', L. Freycinet, 1802.

'Le Serpent Noir', from J. Arago, *Souvenirs d'un aveugle* …, 1839, opp. p. 53.

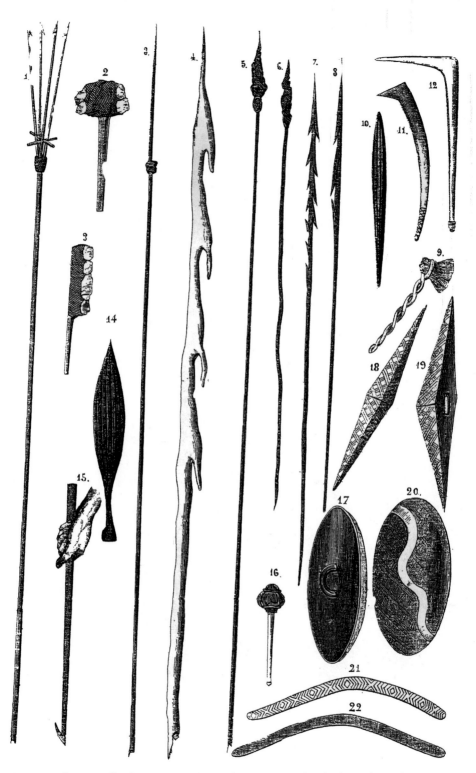

Weapons of New-Holland. (Source: Eugène Delessert, *Voyages dans les deux océans, Atlantique et Pacifique, 1844–1847*, Paris, 1848, p. 132)

Source: J. Arago, *Narrative of a Voyage round the World*, vol. II, opp. p 172

Source: Port Jackson, Nlle Hollande. Cérémonie préliminaire d'un mariage. Louis de Freycinet, *Reflections on New South Wales*, 1788–1839, Hordern Press, 2001 (opp. p. 162).

Tombs of Aborigines on Maria Island, 1802. (Source: Bonnemains, *Baudin in Australian Waters*, p. 125)

Aboriginal tombs on Maria Island (detail). (Source: Bonnemains, *Baudin in Australian Waters*, p. 126)

'Sauvages des environs de Sydney'. Top row (from left): Nani and Abinghou. Centre: Taran.
Bottom row: Broten and Timbéré. State Library of New South Wales. (Source: Louis de Freycinet,
Reflections on New South Wales, 1788–1839, opp. p. 306)

KING BUNGAREE

CHIEF OF THE BROKEN-BAY TRIBE N.S.WALES.

DIED 1832.

Drawn from Life 1831. and on Stone 1834. by Cha.ˢ Rodius.

Printed by I.G.Austin. 15. Phillip Sᵗ Sydney.

'King Bungaree, Chief of the Broken-Bay Tribe, New South Wales. Died 1832'. (State Library of New South Wales)

'Savage climbing a tree'. (Source: Arago, *Souvenirs d'un aveugle: Voyage autour du monde,* opp. p. 79)

down, saying to us "Médi" [and] we immediately stopped'. D'Entre-casteaux himself remarked that when he gave the Indigenous people a goat 'they invited it to sit down, repeating the word "médi" (sit down)', and, he declared, 'this word is so familiar to us that we cannot have been mistaken'. Perhaps the 'D' in this word resembled the French 'R', for La Motte noted that 'the word "meri-meri" was the preliminary for all conversation. This word meant "sit down", and, he noted, 'these people do not like it when we stand up'. Ventenat too believed that this sound could best be represented as 'meri-meri'.[116]

A decade later, again in the D'Entrecasteaux Channel, François Péron would receive this same invitation. At Port Cygnet he and Freycinet (aged 27 and 23 respectively) met an 'old man' (as Péron thought him) who took them to a hut with his family. 'Fire was lighted in an instant,' wrote the young Frenchman, 'and after repeat-ing several times "médi, médi" (sit down, sit down), these savages themselves squatted down on their heels, and began to eat the pro-duce of their fishery.' A few days later, when walking on Bruny Island, Péron and two colleagues came upon a group of women, one of whom 'made signs to us to stay where we were, and to sit down, call-ing aloud to us "médi, médi" (sit down, sit down)'. Later, on Maria Is-land, the French were again invited to sit — and the fact that this is so often mentioned indicates perhaps how remarkable the French felt it to be. Upon landing at Oyster Bay, Péron and his colleagues met 'fourteen natives, who were seated round the fire … [and] 'Médi, médi' (sit down, sit down) were the first words addressed to us. We seated ourselves, and they gathered round us'. Thus in three different places (Port Cygnet, Bruny Island and Maria Island), all separated by the sea, this same invitation and expression was encountered.

At this last encounter Péron managed to learn several words of the islanders' language. 'I seized this opportunity,' he reported, 'to ask them numerous questions … [and] I successively obtained an answer to the words yawning, laughing, weeping, whistling, blowing, tying, untying, burning, spitting, making water, going to stool, breaking wind, striking a blow, wrestling, tearing, strangling etc.' The inhabitants doubtless found him an interesting spectacle! He must have done well for, he continued, 'in general they appeared to understand me easily and ... they soon conceived the meaning of my gestures and, indeed, in a good-natured manner repeated those words which I had at first pronounced wrong'. Earlier (in the Channel) the zoologist had remarked that 'these people speak with such quickness and volubility that it is impossible ... to distinguish their pronunciation with any degree of precision', so his task could not have been an easy one. Their language, he said, 'is a sort of rolling sound, for which our European languages do not furnish any expression of comparison or analogy'.[117]

Vocabulary lists were made by D'Entrecasteaux and several of his people, including Labillardière. D'Entrecasteaux's and Labillardière's lists resemble one another closely, and it is the latter's which is presented here. As will be seen, Labillardière believed that 'lia' placed at the end of a word indicated 'the plural number'. D'Entrecasteaux looked upon this 'fact', however, as 'being very doubtful'.[118]

Labillardière's 'Vocabulary of the Language of the Savages of Diemen's Land'

A	
Arms (the)	Gouna lia
B	
Beard	Conguiné
Branch of the eucalypts with its leaves	Poroqui
Bark of a tree	Toline
Bird	Mouta mouta
Basket	Terre
Breast of a man	Ladiné
— of a woman	Heré
Here, as in many other instances, lia placed at the end of a word indicates the plural number.	
C	
Charcoal, reduced to powder, with which they cover their bodies	Loira
Cut (to)	Rogueri, toidi
Crown of shells	Canlaride
Chin	Onaba

D	
Drink (to)	Laina
Death, to die	Mata
Distance (at a)	Renaué
E	
Eat (I will)	Madé guera
Ears	Cuegni lia
Eyes (the)	Nubru nubéré
F	
Fingers	Lori lori
Family (my)	Tagari lia
Fire	Une
Fly (a)	Oéllé
Fish (small) of the species of gadus	Pounerala
G	
Go and eat	Mat guera
Give me	Noki
Grease (the hair)	Lane poeré
Grass	Poéné
H	
Hair	Pelilogueni
Hands	Riz lia
I	
I will go	Ronda
K	
Knees	Ragua lia
Kernel of the eucalyptus refinifera	Manouadra
Kangarou's skin	Boira
L	
Let us go	Tangari
Lobster	Nuélé
Lips	Mogudé lia
M	
Me	Mana
Me (for)	Paouai
Mortal (that is)	Mata enigo
Muscle (sea)	Miré

N	
Nose	Muguiz
Name of a man	Mara
Name (another) for a man	Mera
Navel (the)	Lué
No	Neudi
Nails of the toes	Peré lia
— of the fingers	Toni lia
O	
Oyster–shell	Louba
Ochre	Mallaué
P	
Posteriors	Nuné
Pillow (a small) on which the men lean	Roéré
Parrot	Mola
Plunge (to)	Bugure
Polishing (the act of) with a shell	Rina
S	
Sit down	Medi
Sleep (to)	Malougna
Sclerya (a species of very large)	Leni
Sun (the)	Panuméré
Stone (a)	Loïne
Sea weed, (a species of) fucus ciliatus	Roman inou
See (I)	Quendera
T	
That belongs to me	Patourana
Tree of the species eucalyptus	Tangara
That	Averé
Teeth	Pegui
Throw (to)	Pegara
Tongue	Méné
Tattooing	Paléré
Trunk of the eucalyptus	Perébé
This way	Lomi
W	
Woman	Quani

Will you come	Quangloa
Y	
You	Nina [119]

Another means of communication was of course by sign language, used either on its own or as a supplement to the verbal language.

The story Labillardière tells of the incident that occurred during his first night on Tasmanian soil had been recounted to him by an inhabitant solely in sign language. (As we have seen, D'Entrecasteaux thought his colleague was lucky to escape with his life.) 'One of the savages,' wrote Labillardière, 'expressed to us, by unequivocal signs, that he had come to reconnoitre us during the night. In order to make us comprehend that he had seen us asleep, he put his right hand on one side of his head, which he inclined, at the same time shutting his eyes to express sleep. With the other hand he showed us the place where we had passed the night. He then indicated to us, by signs no less expressive, that he had all the time kept on the other side of the rivulet, whence he had watched us.'[120]

A few days later Labillardière and his hosts made an appointment, at a given place and time, by sign language alone. 'To signify to us that they should in two days perform this journey [to the ships' new anchorage],' he wrote, 'they described with their hands the diurnal motion of the sun, taking care to indicate the number 'two' by holding up as many fingers.' When the appointed time arrived, the botanist noted with pleasure that 'the savages ... had been as good as their word'.[121]

Here again, but a decade later, Baudin will admit frankly that 'we could make nothing of their long speeches, but their signs were much more intelligible and we understood them perfectly'.[122]

Needless to say, the French also used sign language and, when Joseph Raoul (with D'Entrecasteaux) had wished to know if the inhabitants ate kangaroo flesh, he 'asked them by means of signs if they had eaten what was in the skin [of the kangaroo], and they signified that [he] had thought correctly'.[123]

In the Northern Territory, Western Australia and New South Wales there is less evidence of the languages heard.

At Raffles Bay in 1839, M. Desgraz (D'Urville's secretary) will say of the few 'natives' they had met that their language 'is very hard to get to know: the words have strange consonants and confused pronunciation'. 'Often,' he said, 'one hears a gobbling noise rather than the sound of the human voice. Of the ten natives we have seen, half have two different ways of naming the same things.'[124]

In Western Australia (at Péron Peninsula in 1818), Arago had not been confused at all when he heard repeatedly the native people shouting to him 'ayerkadé' (go away) accompanied by the appropriate gestures.[125] In the conclusion of his *Narrative of a Voyage round the World* he spoke of 'some of the people, whether half civilized or perfectly savage' whom he had visited, and noted that generally 'above all things, they delighted in teaching us their language'. However, he wrote, 'on the western coast of New Holland, we had so little communication with the fifteen or eighteen Savages who shewed themselves, that we were unable … to learn any more than this one word: "Go away — Ayerkadé"'.[126]

It was here too, one recalls, that Baudin's people had met with a similar reception, although then (in June 1801) they had heard repeatedly the word 'Mouye'.[127]

Further south, in King George Sound, D'Urville's people would be more fortunate (in 1826). Here, sitting round the 'hearth fire' one evening with several natives, the artist Sainson and some colleagues started up a conversation with their hosts. 'One of the most natural ways to start a conversation,' he wrote, 'was to tell them our names and to learn theirs.' Sainson noticed that 'they seemed particularly incapable of pronouncing the S and R' and thus distorted the Frenchmen's names.[128] Among the natives' names they learnt 'Mokoré', 'Patêt' and his son 'Yalepouol'. Later that evening the Indigenous people examined with curiosity the Frenchmen's clothing, repeating the word 'kingarou'. 'This word,' thought Sainson, 'probably expressed a logical sequence of ideas for them … since the quadruped they mentioned furnishes them with their only item of clothing.'

Generally speaking, the French found the language of the Indigenous people at King George Sound to be 'very soft'. 'It is a sort of twittering,' wrote Quoy and Gaimard, 'produced by the concourse of vowels.'[129]

On the other side of the continent, in Sydney, René Lesson would find the inhabitants' language less soft. 'The idiom of the Australians of New South Wales is very difficult to grasp because of the guttural sounds [*sons gutturaux*] with which it abounds,' he wrote. And, he declared, 'there is not the least analogy between the languages spoken on the north, south and west coasts of New Holland'.[130] Even in and around Sydney itself the native languages varied considerably, as the following table indicates. Included in the table are words for parts of the body noted by Lesson in Port Jackson and at Lachlan River in 1824, by David Collins in Sydney in 1798[131] and by Labillardière in Tasmania in 1793. (René Lesson's complete vocabulary list is reproduced in Appendix 2.)

English word	Lesson		Collins Sydney	Labillardière Tasmania
	Lachlan River	Port Jackson		
Hair	Bulla–Yega	Gue-Dan	De-war-ra	Peligoueni
Arms	Bargar	Dalan	Tar-rang (arm)	Gouna Lia
Nose	Mo-ro	Nougourou	Nogro, or Nogurro	Muguiz
Teeth	Erra	Nandarra	Dara	Pegui
Chin	–	Oualou	Wãl-lo	Onaba
Beard	Ana-ny	Ira-me	Yarrin	Conguiné
Hand	–	Iamerai	Tam-mir-ra	Riz Lia (hands)
Lips	–	upper: Date-Oui-line	Wil-ling	Mogudé Lia
	–	lower: Kiss		
Eye	Mill-a	Gousbri	Mi	Nubru Nubéré (eyes)
Ears	Whada	Donna-baie	Go-ray (ear)	Cuegni Lia
Woman	–	Gowe	Din	Quani
Man	–	Mem-àa	Mul-lã	Mera

The Aboriginal Australians as anthropologists

The Aboriginal Australians were, like the explorers, often keen anthropologists and, quite naturally, took a lively and curious interest in their visitors. Few (if any) of these visitors, however — the French

included — appear to recognise the reciprocality of this phenomenon, that the Aboriginal people too were, in their own way, explorers.

If the European explorers found the Aboriginal Australians to be
'uncivilised' or 'savage', these latter could have found the Europeans
also to be lacking in a certain civilisation, and indeed that their ignorance of some elements of this (such as surviving in the apparent
'desert') could bring about death from starvation in a very short
while. The Europeans' treatment of the environment too could have
appeared to them to be quite savage, or at least insensitive.

The only documental records we possess of this Aboriginal anthropological interest, however, are those of the Europeans. Here,
therefore, we can only see through the eyes of the French what their
Aboriginal hosts may have seen or thought.

Everything, of course, about these strange visitors was of interest.
Many of the objects (mirrors, bottles, coins etc.) left behind as gifts
would become white-man artefacts and used in practical ways or as
ornaments for many years. But the white men themselves, their colour and their singular sex in particular, were of special interest.

When Marion Dufresne was preparing to land in Tasmania (the
first European to do so), he asked two of his men to undress and to
precede him 'to evidence', recorded Jean Roux, 'that we wanted to
be friends'. 'As soon as these men were ashore the natives uttered loud
cries, obviously of joy … An old man came forward first, after which
all the others came and surrounded our men. They looked with astonishment. They seemed to doubt that we were the same species as
them; our colour was so strange that they could not stop staring and
inspecting.'

Describing the same event, Chevillard de Montesson wrote: 'Once
ashore, our people were surrounded by savages who caressed them
and touched them all over the body, and they seemed very surprised
to see they were the same shape as they were themselves, yet of a different colour.'[132] Their surprise should not have been unexpected.
The only white men these inhabitants could have heard of may have
been those of Tasman's expedition, glimpsed at a distance, back in
1642.

In the D'Entrecasteaux Channel in 1793 D'Entrecasteaux's people had the same experience when, wrote Joseph Raoul, the natives 'looked us over at leisure, touching all parts of our bodies, and undressing some. They seemed very astonished that we had the same sort of body, only differing in the colour'.[133] When Péron and Freycinet landed at Port Cygnet in 1802, they were both examined intensively by a young man who had come to investigate them. 'What appeared at first to interest him most,' observed Péron, 'was the whiteness of our skin and, doubtless wishing to ascertain whether the rest of our bodies were of the same colour, he successively opened our jackets and shirts, and expressed his astonishment by loud exclamations of surprise and by very quick motions of his feet.'[134] The Frenchmen's arms and legs seemed to provoke special amazement. D'Entrecasteaux himself noted, for example, how the Tasmanians' 'arms and legs are very thin; and the shape of ours surprised them enormously, and they would feel in disbelief the calves of those within reach'.

Great astonishment was also expressed when the French divested themselves of parts of their clothing. Not having seen clothes before, the Aborigines naturally assumed that these were an integral part of their visitors' bodies. Flesh and clothing could be readily confused, which could be horrifying for the Aborigines. In Tasmania one day in 1802 François Péron was 'among the savages, occupied in observing them', when one of the young women 'showed some evident marks of astonishment, of which the cause', wrote Péron, 'was frivolous enough, but which I ought not to pass over in silence'. The cause, however, was scarcely 'frivolous' for the woman. Péron continued with the story:

> One of our sailors wore a pair of fur gloves which, on approaching the fire, he drew from his hands and put in his pocket. The young woman, on seeing this, uttered such a great scream that we were at first alarmed, but we were not long at loss to recognize the cause of her fright, and we could not doubt from her gestures but that she had taken the gloves for real hands, or at least for a sort of live skin, which he could take off and put into his pocket or replace at pleasure. We laughed heartily at this mistake.[135]

That this was not an isolated incident is borne witness to by the fact that, even some forty years later, these reactions were still occurring. In his *The Other Side of the Frontier* Henry Reynolds presents three examples of this, of which the following is one. When the Europeans arrived at Cardwell (in today's north Queensland) they threw clothes and blankets towards the black people. When one of the white men took off his shirt and trousers, the inhabitants, recounted one of them, 'thought this man was changing his skin' and that 'he has been peel himself like a snake'. The Aboriginal people then picked up the shirt with a stick, 'because they was too frightened to pick it up with a hand because in our custom it might be very dangerous witchcraft'.[136] The French visitors in 1802 were not aware of this possible explanation for the woman's fright, and it is hoped that their laughter was more sympathetic than offensive.

What surprised the explorers themselves most, however, was the desire of many Aboriginal Australians — men and women — to investigate the contents of the front of their trousers. Accounts abound of this quite unbecoming behaviour (for the Europeans), and several of them — inevitably — recount the same event, but with slightly different emphasis.

D'Entrecasteaux soon guessed the reason for this curiosity. 'Since they believed that such a large number of men could not be without women,' he declared, 'they probably believed that the same garments confused the sexes. Thus, all those with a youthful or an agreeable face bearing some resemblance to the feminine sex had to submit to a very exacting inspection.'[137]

Such was the interest aroused that, on occasion, the native women could be called upon to delve into this subject. Thus, La Motte du Portail explained how the Tasmanian women in February 1793 had examined 'with the utmost attention the ones among us chosen by their husbands to be the object of some exploration from a bold and inquisitive hand, to learn the sex that our clothes concealed'. He continued: 'That search was mainly addressed to the ones whose beardless faces seemed more promising, but they remained unavailing, and this seemed to be a major cause for amazement. However, it was said that if they had explored, in the same way, the steward ... on *La Recherche*, they would have come across what they wished to find.'[138] It was rumoured indeed that a woman had sneaked herself on board before the ship left France. This rumour would be justified, for some months later, reported botanist Louis-Auguste Deschamps on *La Recherche*, 'this courageous woman died in the Strait of Sunda of the effects of illness caught at Batavia and, on dying, she recommended her two children to Captain Rossel'.[139]

The Indigenous people's curiosity was, a decade later, extended to members of Baudin's expedition. During their meeting with three native men in the D'Entrecasteaux Channel on 30 January 1802 Baudin and his companions had allowed themselves to be inspected quite thoroughly. 'In order to humour them in everything,' wrote the commander, 'we showed them our chests ... but only the doctor's [Heirisson] gave rise to astonishment. Being hairless, it caused great exclamations and even greater shouts of laughter. After satisfying themselves in this region, they passed on to our legs, and ... they would very much have liked to see something else, but we did not think it advisable to show them.' Hamelin, who was also inspected, wondered if the native men laughed simply because the doctor's chest was hairless, 'or because they thought they had discovered a woman'. At a meeting the next day, one of the women took Dr Heirisson 'off amongst the trees' and, noted Baudin, 'might have completely satisfied her curiosity'.

On Maria Island three weeks later one other young Frenchman was similarly taken aside by 'several natives' and 'forcibly led off into the wood'. 'They contented themselves,' wrote Baudin, clearly quite relieved, 'with examining him from head to foot without doing him any harm.'[140] Midshipman Breton gave more details. 'It is certain,' he wrote, 'that the natives took the young carpenter for a woman. It must have seemed surprising to them to see men without women, and so at our meetings they never failed to feel in the trousers of those who had no beards. To be left alone by them it was necessary to show oneself without trousers.' Captain Hamelin had a similar view of this incident. He thought the natives, because the young carpenter (named Buron) had 'a pretty face', 'mistook him for a woman' and later 'released him with great roars of laughter when they saw he was a man'.[141]

It was here on Maria Island that François Péron finally allowed the natives' curiosity to be satisfied officially. Sitting together round the fire at Oyster Bay, the hosts happily examined the colour of the Frenchmen's skin. 'Presently, however,' noted Péron, 'they wished to pursue their researches somewhat further: perhaps they might doubt whether we were formed like themselves, or perhaps they might wish to satisfy themselves of our sex.' After much insistence and gentle refusal, the native people, continued Péron, 'pursued their inquiry with one of our young sailors who … being without a beard, seemed to be the more proper object for verifying their conjectures. This youth having, at my solicitation, consented to give them the satisfaction they required, the savages seemed transported with pleasure; but scarcely were they convinced that he was formed like themselves, than they set up a cry of joy and acclamation that perfectly stunned us.'[142]

In King George Sound (Western Australia) in 1826 the inhabitants there asked D'Urville's colleagues if they 'were all really of the same sex'. 'Our affirmative reply,' wrote the artist Sainson, 'did not seem to convince them … Our youth and clean-shaven chins made us the object of this lusty curiosity. As for M. Gaimard, who sports a bushy moustache and sideburns, his masculine dignity went unchallenged.'[143]

What the Aboriginal Australians really thought of all this we do not know. Perhaps, however, they were quite astonished themselves and perplexed to discover that, among all these strange white people from out of the sea, there was not one woman to be found.

Appendix 1

Péron's vocabulary list in the D'Entrecasteaux Channel
Source: F. Péron and L. Freycinet, *Voyage de découvertes ...*, vol. 2, pp. 126–9, Paris, 1824, 2nd edition.

Amounga	Diodon, ostracion, and perhaps all fish able to inflate themselves
Ahri	Three
Boura	Thunder
Boura (Uné)	Lightning
Bourdougnia	Rain, to rain
Bourai	Two
Cagoulé	The cheeks
Couani	Spouse
Couarâ	Bark with which they cover their huts
Cuegi	Head
Drué	Leaf of a tree
Drohi	To laugh
Erré	Yes, it's all right
Gagoui	To warm oneself
Gouanarana	What do you call that?
Gouanera	To kneel
Goui	Wood
Gouaragrâ	To jump
Cuirgra	Parrot
Gune	Sand
Gouna (Moïdo)	To take a fall in wrestling
Gana (Nourè)	To kill lice with one's nails
Iné	Fly-catcher
Kangourou	Kangaroo
Laïdoga	Heel
Ledrâni	To sing
Ledreïe	To dance
Linè nuberé	Eyebrows
Logomangari	Lines of tattooing on the upper arms
Lonî	To call someone
Lôna	Neck
Loubaudia	Oyster

Lubada	Fruit (species indet.)
Lué	To cut wood with a knife
Lupari	Tree
Lurè	Calf of the leg
Laguana	To burn oneself
Leganě	To yawn
Louga	Bottle
Lê	Waddy
Leuni	To untie
Loda Meredé	To have pain in the belly
Mata	Dead, to die
Midougnia	To fall down
Mingoui	To piss
Moroueni	Tattooing, the circle which they have behind the shoulder
Médelo	Sit you down
Médi	Sit down all
Maïgouèré	To strangle
Méregui	To have an erection
Manenna	Moss
Meûné	To whistle
Maraï	One
Nidego	I don't know / understand
Nuberè	Sun
Neuga	French dinghy
Nimené	To make a knot
Nouré	Lice
Noeni	To slap the face
Oueri	Starfish
Ouié	To pierce, prick someone
Ouré	To tear off
Pas	Day
Pereledé	Necklace of little beads
Pî	Spear
Poura	To blow
Ranga	The knees
Reigoua	*Fucus palmatus*
Rinouari	Crab
Tiné	To fart
Tara	To cry

Togué	Hand
Trini	To put wood on the fire
Taé	To defecate
Veré	To kick

Appendix 2

René Lesson's vocabularly list in New South Wales

Source: R. Lesson, *Voyage autour du monde …*, Paris, 1838, vol. II, pp. 296–7.

'The idiom of the Australians of New South Wales, very difficult to grasp because of the guttural sounds with which it abounds, varies according to the tribes. There is not the least analogy between the languages spoken on the northern, southern and western coasts of New-Holland. One noun alone in forty conserves one root analogy: this is the word "eye". Thus I have chosen a certain number of these nouns designating parts of the body (the least variable of the nouns, for they belong to the primitive terms) in order to compare them with words borrowed from the language of the natives visited by Mr Oxley. The reader can thus gather an idea of this singular language, still almost unknown in the lexicons of savage peoples [*peuples sauvages*].

Français	Naturels de la Nouvelle Galles (Port Jackson)	Naturels de la Rivière Lachlan et de Lewis Creek (M. Oxley)
Head	Ti-a-kas	Ulan-gar
Eye	Gousbri	Mill-a
Nose	Nou-gou-ro	Mo-ro
Eye brows	Méderé	Mh-air
Forehead	Mou-a-ra	>>
Hair	Gue-dan	Bulla-yega
Ears	Dona-baie	Whada
Nose	Nougouro	Morro
Mouth	>>	Chu-ang

Français	Naturels de la Nouvelle Galles (Port Jackson)	Naturels de la Rivière Lachlan et de Lewis Creek (M. Oxley)
Cheeks	Oualou	>>
Upper lip	Date-oui-line	>>
Lower lip	Kiss	>>
Teeth	Nandara	Erra
Gums	Beguéré	>>
Tongue	Dalan	>>
Chin	Oualou	>>
Beard	Ira-me	Ana-ny
Neck (front of)	Ca-le-a	Oro
Nape of neck	Ou-ro	>>
Shoulders	Me-li-an	>>
Arm	Dalan	Bargar
Fist	Malmal	>>
Forearm	Ma-ta-ra	>>
Hand	Iamerai	>>
Nails	Tei-lé	>>
Tummy	Doneboule	Bur-bing
Chest	Beren	Ben-ing
Nipple	Aban	>>
Armpit	Ké-li-an	>>
Back	Karé-ba	Dhua
Navel	Ouillai-ouillai	>>
Penis	Godon-Godon	>>
Penis hairs	Dadaé	>>
Vagina	Kala	>>
Thigh	Darra	Dha-na
Leg	Ko-lomb	>>
Calf	Don-dai	>>
Foot	De-na-ban	Dhee-nany
Knee	>>	Wolm-ga
Heel	Mo-non	>>
Toes	Tanga-ne-bène	>>
Small of back	>>	Mille-aar
Indigenous man	Mem-àa	>>
Woman	Gowe	>>

Français	Naturels de la Nouvelle Galles (Port Jackson)	Naturels de la Rivière Lachlan et de Lewis Creek (M. Oxley)
Bone worn in the nose	Mor-raya	>>
Skin they cover themselves with	Mada	>>
Skin made to adorn the body	Wamb-aur	>>
Belt (around the body)	Gum-ill	>>
Night	Un-clenar	>>
King hornet's nest, which they eat	Wam- àa	>>
Fire	Warenur	>>
Wood, trees	Curr-eli	>>
Thistle, of which they eat the roots	Galu-nur	>>
Moon	Gulura	>>
Sleep	Yandu	>>
Stone axes	Galen-gar	>>
	Ori-al	>>
	Tawi-uth	>>

CHAPTER 3

Relations between the Aboriginal Australians themselves

THE way Aboriginal Australians related among themselves was, as seen in the first two chapters, of primary interest to many French explorers.

This chapter examines first how the French saw the Indigenous children being born, and then the relationships between them and their parents. The relations between the men and the women are then discussed, including the subjects of courtship and marriage. Lastly the Indigenous people's weapons and the way they fought among themselves and punished their crimes are looked at, and their attitudes to dying and death are presented.

Only one of the French explorers appears to have been present at the birth of an Aboriginal child. In Sydney in 1819, 'by the side of the river and near the house of Mr Piper',[1] Jacques Arago came upon a group of Aboriginal people near the shore. Upon hearing 'loud cries, or rather fearful yells', he decided 'to advance cautiously'. There he saw 'a score of savages were dancing, leaping, brandishing their spears and clapping their hands … round a woman hideously ugly, who was crouching on some kangaroo skins'. He went on:

As soon as I made my appearance, he whom I took for the Chief of the party ... came to me and pressed me to advance. He spoke to his companions, who soon came eagerly round me, offering me their hands. The cries of the woman put a stop to their entreaties; they resumed their posts; and howled their best. At length the woman was delivered, uttering a few deep sighs, and the hurly-burly was at its height. What was my astonishment at seeing the poor creature with difficulty rise up, carry in her arms the little infant just born, enter a canoe, and dip the child several times into the water! ... I approached in my turn, and gave the poor mother my handkerchief and cravat, which she accepted without the least sign of acknowledgement, to cover the new-born babe.[2]

Elsewhere Arago suggest that the reason the woman's colleagues made so much noise was 'to convince themselves that the woman was not suffering because they could not hear her'.[3]

The relations between the Aboriginal parents and their children were frequently the subject of French interest. It was seen in Chapter I how the women carried their young children on their backs, and how (in the illustration by Piron) the men also took close physical care of their youngsters. Generally, it was felt that the parents loved their children dearly, and would take great pains to protect them.

'The pains taken by one of the mothers to quiet her infant, yet at the breast, who cried at first sight of us,' wrote Labillardière in Tasmania, 'appeared to us very engaging. She could not pacify him, till she covered his eyes with her hand, that he might not see us.' Soon, however, noted the Frenchman, 'their confidence in us was so great, that one of the woman, who was suckling a child, was not afraid to entrust it to several of us'. Two days later, among a larger gathering, this experience was repeated. At first the children, 'frightened at the sight of such a number of Europeans, immediately took refuge in the arms of their mothers, who lavished on them marks of the greatest affection. The fears of the children were soon removed' and some moments later, these same children, 'very desirous of everything shining, were not afraid to come up to us to pull off our buttons. Their mothers held them to us, that we might decorate them with the ornaments we had intended for themselves'. If a child misbehaved, however, he could quickly receive a correction. 'I shall not pass over in silence,' wrote

Labillardière, 'the correction a father gave one of his children, for having thrown a stone at the back of another younger than himself: it was
merely a light slap on the shoulder, which made him shed tears, and
prevented him from doing so again.'[4]

In Sydney Arago also observed how 'the maternal tenderness' of
the Indigenous women 'can be compared to the most heated and violent of human passions'. 'We see the greatest care at all times,' he
wrote. 'Should a shout of attack ring out the mother quickly gathers
up her child, hangs it on her back with a kangaroo skin … and makes
sure she will only be wounded from the front.' However, continued
Arago, using the rather romantic language of his day, 'if in the bloody
mêlée [*sanglante mêlée*] her child is killed, oh! then there must be victims to her rage; oh! then there will be blood and corpses around her.
The lioness from whom one has taken away the young is not more
terrifying, [and] it is rare that, after losing her suckling child in a
mêlée, one does not find after the carnage [*le carnage*] two corpses laying on the ground, the one protecting the other from the tooth of
their victor'.[5]

In King George Sound Dumont d'Urville expressed himself in
more measured terms. 'Paternal love,' he thought, 'seems fairly well
developed among them, as we saw from our friend Patêt; this good
Australian took great care of his son Yalepouol, who accompanied
him everywhere.' Yalepouol was 'a child of twelve or thirteen' years,[6]
and a sketch of him and his father by Louis de Sainson appears in the
photographic section.

Only Cyrille Laplace seems to add an unhappy note to these par-
ent-child relations. In New South Wales he appears particularly harsh.
'Maternal love,' he declared, 'seems to be banished here … On occasion, little children, deprived of care, die of illnesses caused by rapid
variations in the atmosphere or else, looked after carelessly, roll at
night into the fires around which their parents sleep.' Here again,
should hard times befall, 'the mothers, extenuated by hunger and no
longer able to carry them [their children], leave them to die in the
woods'. If the mother should die 'before the child is strong enough to
live without her', he continued, then 'it is put with her into the same

grave, and … the first stones, cast by the father himself, quickly cover up its cries and moans with the silence of death [*le silence de la mort*]'. Laplace, however, does not say he actually saw this, nor does he give a source for this information.[7]

The relations between the men and the women in Aboriginal society were not always easy to observe at first, because often, as soon as the French approached, the Aboriginal men, as Crozet discovered as early as 1772 in Tasmania, 'sent their women and children into the woods.'[8] In King George Sound in 1803 Baudin noted too that 'the natives would not allow anyone near where they had put their wives'[9] and, as seen in Chapter 2, D'Urville had this same experience there in 1826.

Family life indeed appeared to be 'patriarchal' or 'paternal'. After his first meeting with the native Tasmanians, François Péron wrote that 'the kind of patriarchal life we had witnessed had strongly affected our feelings', but, he continued, 'I was at the time far from conjecturing the many privations and miseries to which such a state is liable'.[10] Ventenat also noted how 'the savages live a free life' and how 'they are under paternal government'. 'Each head of family,' he wrote, 'is master of his children.' 'Their only chiefs,' D'Entrecasteaux thought, 'are those appointed by nature, that is, the fathers of families and the elderly.'[11] Labillardière elaborated on these simple statements. 'We observed in the children,' he wrote, 'the greatest subordination to their parents, and in the women the same to their husbands. It appeared that the women were careful to avoid giving their husbands any cause for jealousy.'[12]

Later, Péron would have occasion to witness the consequences of this apparent jealousy. After he, Bellefin and Heirisson had entertained some of the women on their own for a while, they had met up with the men. 'At this unexpected rencontre,' he observed, 'all the unfortunate females who had followed us seemed greatly terrified; and their savage husbands gave them such looks of rage and anger, as were not at all likely to reassure them … These humiliated wives placed themselves in a group behind their husbands … and here, during the rest of our stay, these unfortunate women did not dare to speak, or even smile, or even lift up their eyes from the ground.'[13] Perhaps the most unpleasant experience of these inter-gender relations was that of Barrallier in the Blue Mountains in November 1802 when in the company of an Aborigine, Gogy, and his wife. 'I had given to Gogy's child,' wrote the Frenchman, 'a few morsels of kangaroo … which he had taken to his mother's hut to eat. Unfortunately, this woman started eating a portion of this meat which she took from the child, who complained to his father, shouting and crying … Gogy then took his club and struck his wife's head such a blow that she fell to the ground unconscious. My people having tried to appease him, he went out of the hut, dropped his club, and started abusing his wife … After dinner, seeing that nobody was taking any notice of him, he got infuriated and again struck his wife on the head with his club, and left her on the ground nearly dying.' At dusk that day, wrote Barrallier, 'fearing lest Gogy should commit some act of violence, I had a sentry told to follow all his movements.'[14] Speaking more generally, Milius concluded that 'the inhabitants of the W.N.W. coast of New Holland and those of the D'Entrecasteaux Canal in Diemen's Land and Maria Island remind us of the barbaric state of Europe before civilisation' and that the Aboriginal women, who were 'condemned to the most painful tasks', were also 'often the victims of the brutality of their tyrants'.[15]

Perhaps the most painful of these tasks was the procurement of food for the family, and among these the need to collect lobsters and shellfish by plunging for long periods into the cold seas of southern Tasmania. Several of D'Entrecasteaux's people (including D'Entrecasteaux himself, Labillardière, Ventenat and La Motte du Portail) give detailed accounts of this activity, all of which resemble one other, and confirm the Frenchmen's concern for the women involved and their surprise at the apparent laziness of the men. La Motte du Portail's account will suffice here.

Lunch time was approaching, and we were curious to see them make their meal. The women, to whom this whole task was left, went to take their fishing gear from the bush where they had hidden it. This consisted in a basket made out of reeds ... of which the strings were arranged in such a way that the head and left hand could be passed. In addition to the basket there was a piece of wood whose shape was like our toilet knife [sic], and which was carried between the teeth. So arrayed, they would go to the sea and dive several times and eventually fill up their basket with crayfish, abalones and oysters that they would remove from the bottom with their little piece of wood.

Elsewhere La Motte du Portail, along with colleagues Labillardière and Ventenat, also noted that the women brought up several lobsters. La Motte du Portail continued: 'Chilled to the bone [and this in mid-summer!], they would come out of the water and then each would light a fire, around which the family would gather, and she would cook the catch ... Soon afterwards, a distribution was made: first the children, and then the husband who had been waiting for this moment with the greatest patience without, however, having made the slightest move to help ... A second fishing followed this meal. They do so as many times as necessary.'

The French were 'amazed at seeing how women were reduced to so tiring a task', and tried to discover why. One of the native men 'made us clearly understand', wrote La Motte du Portail, 'that the work we had seen the women do, would be fatal for him and his companions'. The Frenchman's own conclusion was clear. 'I thought it might be the result of some prejudice having been turned into a religious be-lief,' he declared, 'but its source might be just found in laziness and the privilege of the strongest.'[16]

In New South Wales, some forty years later, Laplace would note how, in order to catch fish or shellfish, the women 'spent whole days and often even nights plunging amidst the foam of the waves, or fish-ing out at sea on makeshift rafts with crude nets made from the bark of trees'.[17]

When travelling, it was also the Aboriginal woman's task to carry everything, whether in Tasmania or on the mainland. This, indeed, may have been a reason for the French finding so many discarded gifts! 'It is the women,' wrote Ventenat in Tasmania, 'who undertake the duty of carrying the bundles. I felt truly sorry for them as I saw their riches increased, but they made a point of getting rid of them very quickly by throwing them away when we were no longer there.'[18] In the Blue Mountains, Barrallier would be quite outspoken. 'During their marches,' he wrote, 'the women are obliged to carry the children, and have in addition a net in the form of a sack hanging on their back in which they have to carry opossums, and all tools necessary to their husbands … They are in everything their husbands' beasts of burden.'[19] In Sydney, Arago would be quite upset when he saw a man 'throw on his wife's shoulders a little bag [and] … ordered her to walk a little faster, and even assisted her with a few kicks that made her advance more speedily than she wished. Indignant at the brutality of this man, I followed him, well disposed to put a stop to his ill treatment'.[20]

This apparent uneven distribution of labour would lead Laplace to present an interesting claim. 'So much barbarity,' he thought, 'towards a sex for whom revenge is not always without charms, necessarily brings about some reprisals. It is claimed at least that poison … avenges only too often the wife for the cruelties of her husband.'[21] D'Urville's people would also claim that, in view of the way Aboriginal women were 'ill-treated by their husbands', 'they can only find pleasant the lives they lead with the Europeans who treat them far better'.[22] The extent to which these two claims are based in conjecture is not clear, but the ill-treatment of the woman certainly appeared such as to give rise to them.

Courtship itself appears to have been an early initiation into this future way of life, for the women then were often beaten with clubs.

Milius interpreted this as follows. 'A very polite way,' he wrote, 'of courting a lady [*une dame*] in New Holland is to bash her with a club. It is by the force of the blows that the women judge of the love felt for them. We never tried such methods, so we never obtained any favours. Such a treatment makes the women very faithful to their husbands. They love them to the point of being very jealous of them.'[23]

René Lesson expressed this differently and offered greater detail. 'Rarely do the natives [*naturels*] buy their spouses by paying a certain sum to the father,' he wrote. 'They prefer to have recourse to kidnapping. A native watches for the moment when a marriageable girl [*une fille nubile*] from a neighbouring tribe is separate from her people, in order to jump on her and drag her away to his camp after having stunned her with blows from his waddy [*casse-tête*]. There he triumphs over her [*il en triomphe*] more brutally again and the girl, having become his property by this savage abduction, becomes a faithful and submissive wife.'[24] An illustration of a 'ceremony preliminary to a marriage', after an original by Nicolas Petit, may be seen in the photographic section.

Jacques Arago actually attended a marriage ceremony during his stay in Sydney. The bride and her party were walking along a path just behind 'the magnificent garden of the Governor of Sydney' when Arago joined them. He wrote:

> The joyful horde stopped on a lawn where there were a few graceful casuarina trees. After several minutes' rest, the fiancé stood up, took his timid beauty by the hand, placed her standing in front of him in the middle of a circle formed by his kneeling comrades, and muttered a few guttural sounds which, for the spouse, must have been some guarantees of future happiness.
>
>   When this was done, the husband shook himself violently, spat into the face of the happy loved one … then, with the thumb and the index finger of his right hand, took some red powder and traced a few wide lines on the forehead, nose, and down to the navel of the one he was going to possess, and continued his work with the help of new spit and a white powder … The girl, all glorious [*toute glorieuse*] walked around the assembly and showed herself off, adorned with her beautiful decorations.[25]

In New South Wales Lesson had thought that polygamy was 'the prerogative of the chiefs'.[26] Views as to the existence of this practise in Tasmania were less decided, however. D'Entrecasteaux summed up the situation of his colleagues when he wrote that some 'thought one thing and were convinced of it, others took a different view'. The problem lay in the fact that their only means of communication was by sign language, and different people interpreted this differently. D'Entrecasteaux himself was uncertain. After the Frenchmen's second meeting, with forty-eight natives in February 1793, he 'thought we had noticed that it was the two most robust men who had each an extra woman', but this, he considered, 'could only be determined if we had spent a longer time among them'.

Two of D'Entrecasteaux's colleagues believed they saw no polygamy. D'Auribeau asked 'several officers ... to study the matter carefully'. 'We made the most expressive gestures to make ourselves understood,' he wrote, 'and I believe that we succeeded ... Most of the observers saw no sign at all of polygamy', although, he conceded, 'I am far from wishing to settle this matter absolutely.' La Motte du Portail thought these signs were 'mistakenly interpreted' and that there were 'better ways of observing this'. 'Thus, for example, the close relation between the number of men and the number of women. The former numbered ten,' he wrote, 'while there were fourteen of the others; but, taking away three girls from this number, one will then see that it is impossible for the men to have two women.'

Two other colleagues felt quite differently. Labillardière had few doubts on the matter. 'Two of the stoutest [men],' he noted, 'were seated in the middle of their children, and had each of them at their side two wives; they expressed to us, by signs, that these belonged to them; which gave us another proof that polygamy is established among this people.' Chaplain Ventenat also took a keen interest in this subject, and agreed wholeheartedly with his botanist colleague. 'There was not the least doubt,' he calculated, 'that there were seven married women and five men of whom two had each two wives. Polygamy is therefore an established state among these natives.'

He readily admitted, however, that not everyone agreed with him. One of his (un-named) colleagues, he said, had 'wished to destroy' his 'painstaking observations' which, he thought, must have been 'invariably true' because of their 'exact identity with those of Messrs. La Billardière [sic] and Riche'. The objections put to him were these:

firstly, that 'polygamy stands apart from simple nature'; secondly, that 'polygamy was unheard of among savages'; and lastly, that 'a man cannot satisfy equally several women' and that 'if he loves one of them in preference then there would be trouble'. Moreover, he was told, 'if this custom had an established place the population would be much greater'. Ventenat believed, however, that it was 'quite natural that the strongest [men] have preference' and that, in the group of people they had met, 'where there are thirteen married women and eleven men, the two most robust of the latter have each two women'. 'Without entering into deep thought,' he continued, 'to prove that polygamy is a consequence of the state of nature, I will say no more than that there are only eleven men and thirteen women. There it is!' He refuted bluntly the contention that 'polygamy was unheard of among savages', and the third objection (that one man could not satisfy equally several women) the chaplain declared to be 'a shameful comment'. He similarly dismissed the objections concerning lack of population growth. 'Everyone,' he said, 'knows that a people who are not agriculturalists, [and] who die of hunger as a result for two-thirds of the year, cannot increase much.'[27]

The weapons used by the men to inflict such heavy blows upon the women were, of course, also used (with others) for duels, inter-tribal warfare, and for punishing people who had committed offences. Louis de Freycinet presented the Indigenous people's main weapons when he wrote: 'they have different kinds of spears [*sagaies*], clubs [*casse-têtes*], shields, and a wooden instrument, very dangerous, in the shape of a blade of a curved sabre [*sabre courbé*] which they throw with much skill'.[28] No Australian, of course, will fail to recognise this last 'instrument' as the boomerang.

Spears were seen in Western Australia by D'Urville's expedition in King George Sound where they were described as 'long, slim straight javelins, hardened in the fire and pointed at one end'.[29] No other weapons were seen. On the mid-west coast, Baudin's people simply had time to note that the inhabitants were armed with 'spears, clubs and shields'.[30] In Tasmania and New South Wales, however, greater detail was observed.

In Tasmania in 1772 one of Dufresne's colleagues (Le Dez) had described these spears (which had, of course, been used against them) as 'nothing other than sticks about six feet long, pointed at the thick end. They are not poisoned at all … because the man who was wounded by one experienced no pain at all the next day and there was not even inflammation'.[31] Twenty years later, in a less hostile situation, Labillardère was shown the use of these weapons. One of the natives, he wrote, 'seized hold of one of [the spears] nearly about the middle; then raising it as high as his head, and still holding it in a horizontal position, drew it back towards him three times in succession with a jerk, occasioning a very evident quivering at both its extremities; he then threw it near a hundred yards'. 'This weapon … flew upwards of three-fourths of that distance nearly in a horizontal direction. The tremulous motion,' he thought, 'doubtless contributed to accelerate its progressive motion, and to support it longer in the air.' This man then accepted Labillardiére's invitation to demonstrate his skills further, whereupon he aimed at a mark which was indicated to him and 'at each throw he came sufficiently near it to give us a great idea of his dexterity'. The man then showed how the spear was used to kill kangaroos. 'They throw it with sufficient force,' declared the Frenchman, 'to pierce the animal through and through.'[32]

In 1802 on Maria Island Baudin found the native people 'did not show great dexterity' and that 'only one spear hit the target aimed at, 15 to 20 paces away'. He was shown, however, how the spear heads were sharpened. 'Firstly,' he wrote, 'they use a stone, as we would a piece of glass, and then for polishing them, they use an oyster shell that they have sharpened on one side.'[33] Milius noted that the spear heads were 'garnished with pieces of shell or glass to render the wound more fatal'.[34]

In New South Wales René Lesson would declare that 'the weapon universally used … is the *sagaie*, which they throw with the help of an instrument called "méara"'. These spears were 'long and very sharp' and made from 'a very hard wood'.[35] Both the Dufresne and the

Baudin expeditions discovered spears alongside deceased people or upon their graves. In Tasmania, when Jean Roux came across the young man his colleagues had shot, he noted that 'near the dead man was a large number of lances … broken in several places', and that this was 'probably an honour rendered to those who are killed in war'.[36] In King George Sound in Western Australia Baudin found 'two rather peculiar and interesting monuments erected by the natives' for which he could not discover the reason. The first was surrounded by eleven 'finely-tapered spears painted red at the tip' and the second, with the same number of similar spears, was close-by across a stream. These latter, he conjectured, 'seemed to be guarding the passage to the right bank from the left, as those on the left seemed to be guarding it from the right'. 'Several people,' he said, 'thought that the spears had been painted red with blood', but, after examination, they 'realised that this colour had been achieved with eucalyptus resin'. Baudin's opinion was that these were 'graves in which lie two warriors of different tribes … seeming still to defy one another after death'. He gave orders that no one should 'defile these graves nor remove the spears that decorated them'.[37]

Waddies (a form of club) were also used as aggressive weapons. In Tasmania Milius noted that the men 'carry a club made of very hard and heavy wood', and also bore 'shields which protect them from their enemies' blows'.[38] Baudin too would report here that 'the only manifestations of industry we saw were their spears and a not very dangerous club'. In Western Australia (near Dirk Hartog's Island), he described how the men were 'all armed with spears, clubs and shields'.[39] Simply throwing stones could inspire fear and cause damage — as Dufresne and his colleagues had discovered when 'a hail of stones' was thrown at them, hitting both the captain and Duclesmeur.[40] Also in Tasmania, Milius remarked how, while the Indigenous people had no knowledge of the bow, they did 'cast stones very skilfully with a sling'.[41]

Freycinet was not alone in observing the boomerang. In February 1824, on the north shore of Sydney Harbour, an Indigenous man gave D'Urville a demonstration of this weapon. D'Urville reported:

I knew nothing of this implement and, on my asking him, the savage hurled it four or five times. Thrown horizontally at first, this projectile, which looks like a wooden sabre bent in the middle on two different planes, quickly rises, turning from right to left to an extraordinary height and well away ahead of the person throwing it. I estimate at almost 45° the angle under which it slowly rises and at 150 feet at least, the distance it reaches. After describing pirouettes and undulations for this tremendous distance, it turns back on its tracks with the same movement and comes back to fall near the thrower; so that anyone beside him at first does not know what to do to avoid the boomerang; but he soon works out the direction of its trajectory and then it becomes easy to get out of its way. The savage in question never failed to bring it back right to his feet, and to do that you need a lot of practice.[42]

Another weapon the Indigenous people could use in time of need was of course their bare hands. In his *Souvenirs d'un aveugle*, Arago describes how, with John Oxley in the country near Sydney, he had been approached by a 'savage' begging for food. Suddenly 'an enormous black snake' appeared, and Arago pulled out his sword and put a bullet in his pistol. 'The savage, however,' he recalled, 'made me understand that these preparations were a pure waste of time.' The Frenchman was then asked for his handkerchief. Arago withdrew a few paces, and watched in awe. 'The savage,' he wrote, 'wrapped his fingers and part of his wrist with my handkerchief ... and advanced with the greatest prudence towards the formidable "hisso".' The native man then seized the snake strongly by the tail. As soon as it was 'ready to bite and to kill', continued the onlooker, 'my intrepid savage moves his arms and swings the snake as if he were swinging a sling-shot. After having swung the reptile for at least two or three minutes, and especially after seeing that its resistance to the rotation movement was nullified, the savage approached a felled eucalyptus tree and, with a last and vigorous effort, hit the snake's head against it.' As it was still not dead, the man then asked Arago for his knife and, placing his foot on the snake's head, soon 'separated this from the body with three quick cuts'.[43] An illustration from Arago's original work of this incident is reproduced in the photographic section.

In his *Voyages dans les deux océans*, Eugène Delessert describes the weapons used by the Aboriginal people in Sydney where he stayed for some eight months in 1845. During that time he managed, with great difficulty, to make a collection of these weapons. His illustration is reproduced in the photographic section, and the following is a translation of his descriptions.

The lance (number one), called the 'mo-ting', is usually employed for fishing. At one end it has four prongs whose extremities are fitted with sharpened kanguroo bones. These prongs may be brought closer together or further apart by using the little cross-pieces fixed against the cord, which ties the prongs to the lance. The lance itself is about eight feet long. At the other end there is an indentation into which fits the hook on a stick (number 15) called the 'wom-mur-mur', which helps to throw the 'mo-ting'. I have often witnessed the skill with which they harpoon fish several feet under water and which I could hardly see.

The 'ta-win' (number 2) is a club made of very hard wood, about a foot and a half long. On each side, large pieces of sharp silex are fixed which create a double edge (and take the place of iron, the use of which is known only a short distance from the sea). The pieces of silex are attached with hard and resistant resin. This very primitive weapon is today only used by tribes in the interior.

The 'wa-rai' (numbers 3 and 5) is a lance made of light wood with a piece of iron or silex at the end. The same name is given to a weapon made of wood of iron [sic],[44] which has knots and hooks or teeth (number 4).

The 'tolos' (numbers 6, 7 and 8), or javelins, come in several shapes. They are made of wood of iron [sic], and armed with either kanguroo teeth, pieces of silex, or hooks. These javelins, which the natives throw great distances without using the 'wom-mur-rur' [sic], are five to six feet long.

The 'mogo' or 'bai-bai' (number 9) is a sort of axe consisting of a sharpened stone held by a shaft of braided cane. Again, this is one of those primitive instruments no longer seen near places occupied by Europeans.

The 'waddy' (numbers 10 and 14) and the 'nulla-nulla' (number 16) are the most common weapons. They are all small clubs. The waddy is quite long; the nulla–nulla is made of ebony and has one end which is heavy, rounded and carved. The indigenous people [*indigènes*] rarely walk about without carrying one or the other of these weapons, and use them to settle their various disputes. When this occurs, each of the combatants lowers his head in turn to receive his adversary's blow, until one of them falls down. Avoiding a blow is considered cowardly.

Other weapons of various shapes and sizes are to be seen, and are always made of wood and more or less roughly carved. The ones the natives call 'mal-ga' (numbers 11 and 12) are head-breakers.[45] One has a long sharpened point at right angles to the shaft which is straight; the other, whose shaft is somewhat curved, forms two sharp angles. These are terrible weapons in the hands of the natives, and it is all the more difficult to protect oneself from them because one cannot see whether the blow will come from the point or the back of the instrument.

The 'muri-muri' (number 13) takes the place of the knife and, like the ta-win, is made of blades of silex set in hard and non-flaky resin. It seems that bows and arrows are not known in New-Holland; at least I have never seen any, and I don't think they've ever been mentioned in any travellers' accounts.

The aborigines ['*aborigènes*] have two kinds of shields or 'koreils' (numbers 17 and 20). One is narrow, thick and triangular, and just over two feet long, and they use it very skilfully by whirling it around. The other is oval-shaped, and protects the carrier against blows from lances or javelins. These shields are usually carefully sculpted, and daubed with red and white colours.

Like Freycinet and D'Urville before him, Delessert was most impressed by the boomerang. 'The most remarkable weapon by far,' he declared, 'is the boomereng [sic], called 'tur-ra-ma' (numbers 21 and 22) by the aborigines'.

It is a projectile made of a piece of very hard wood, about two feet two inches long[46] and slightly curved. It weighs about 9 to 9½ ounces.[47] One side is slightly convex and clad with inlaid ornamentation, while the other is flat and smooth. When ready to be thrown the boomereng is held horizontally and, as a rotation movement is imparted to it when thrown, the air presents so much resistance to the flat side and so little to the convex and cutting edge while it cleaves through the air, that on its long journey it does not seem to submit to the usual effects of gravitation. This weapon, so simple and strange, would pose complicated problems to learned people who would like to explain why, when thrown to the right, it comes back at two or three hundred paces to the left; and why, after having been thrown out of sight and as far as a gunshot, it comes back after cleaving the air for several minutes [sic] to fall at the feet of him who threw it.

The use of the boomereng requires lengthy practice. I have often tried, but have never managed to throw it further than any ordinary stick. The aborigines do the most surprising things with it. If they wish to kill an enemy two or three hundred paces away they successfully throw one or two boomerengs, one to the right and the other to the left, and the unfortunate fellow who is their target rarely escapes this terrible projectile. If the first weapon misses him, the second inevitably hits him. One can only dodge these by using great skill, and a very special shield.

There are two kinds of boomereng. One (number 21) is less long and more curved, and comes back to the thrower's feet. The other (number 22) does not come back, but travels further. In his book on New South Wales, Major Mitchell says one can achieve incredible feats with this weapon, as for example, sending it over the top of a tree to hit something behind it … When cast amidst a flock of wild ducks it creates the most frightful carnage, and it is used mainly for this. It can skim just above the ground or rise to great heights, according to the wish of the thrower.[48]

Delessert was not the only Frenchman to observe the awe-inspiring duels fought between the Indigenous men. In Sydney in 1824 Lesson had also witnessed such combat. He reported:

I was witness to a veritable duel between two individuals. All the men gathered around in a circle, and the two champions walked towards one another, each armed with a club [*casse-tête*]. The plaintiff made the first blows and thumped vigorously his wooden club down onto his antagonist's skull. The latter stumbled, but steadying himself, took his revenge, and his club spun around with the speed of a lightning flash upon his motionless enemy. What can be the strength of these people's skulls which can withstand blows that would break, like a fragile glass, the head of any

European! With the Australians it is each one his turn, and true courage is to be able to resist the blow that would smash the skull of an ox.[49]

In Sydney a few years earlier, Arago had witnessed a similar scene, but with a very different ending. On this occasion the men had been drinking: 'the vapours had taken hold of their brains'. After testing their skills in a club–throwing contest, two men faced each other. Arago described the scene:

> The loser stands facing his enemy, lowers his head, and raises his eyes a lit-tle in order to study the movements of his opponent whose hand holds the fatal weapon, ready to strike and open up his skull. If he misses, it's then the first man's turn to try, and so on until one of the two falls dead. After the duel, the men and women take up the corpse, load it on their shoulders and throw it away either far from town, into the waves, or into a two-foot grave upon which brothers and sisters kick the earth to level the ground.

A few pages later Arago offered some advice to anyone who might be challenged by 'four or five of these individuals without weapons and ready to fight'. 'Do not run away,' he insisted, 'but go towards them and with one punch you are sure to knock over the one you can reach.' Arago himself claims he did this on one occasion against no fewer than three men, and, he wrote, 'I had no trouble in knocking them all to the ground, although I've never been considered a very vigorous athlete'.[50]

Intoxication, Arago observed, could also lead to more generalised combats.

> A few bottles of spirits produce a surprising affect on these poor crea-tures. Scarcely do the intoxicating fumes get into their heads, when they breathe nothing but battle and shout forth their war cries. Impatient for murder, they seek antagonists … They find all too readily the opportuni-ties they provoke; and their war-whoop is answered by whoopings no less terrible. Then the combatants, drawn up in two lines perhaps twenty paces from each other, threaten mutually with their long and pointed spears, launch them at their adversaries with wonderful strength and dex-terity, and finally attack each other with ponderous and formidable clubs.

Limbs are fractured, bones smashed, skulls laid open: no exclamation of pain escapes from these ferocious brutes. The air resounds only with frightful vociferations.

Having described these physical manifestations of the struggles, the Frenchman then endeavoured to examine the protagonists' motivations. 'He who falls without having found a victim,' he conjectured, 'dies rather of despair, than from the hurts he has received; and the warrior who has laid low a few enemies soon expires without regretting the loss of life.' Arago drew a picture of one of these 'savages' after such a battle, and this is reproduced in the photographic section.[51]

Intoxication, however, was not always a necessary component of hostilities. On the north shore of Sydney Harbour one day, Arago and two of his colleagues were witnesses and participants in a struggle in which their lives at one moment appeared at risk. While exploring the area, they came upon a clearing where 'about twenty natives were standing, very excited and shouting, and seeming to deliberate upon some perilous enterprise'. When this group moved on, Arago and his friends decided to follow them, and a quarter of an hour later saw them join up with another group, before they all moved off together. 'I wanted very much to turn back,' declared Arago, 'but my curiosity got the better of me, and we followed their footsteps.' After climbing to the brow of a hill, he heard this group shout loudly into the air, whereupon a second shout was heard replying in the distance. At this moment 'weapons were waved furiously, clubs flew about, and the wild horde [*horde farouche*] crouched down in readiness for bloody action'. The Frenchmen were then 'only a few score paces away', and Arago described what he saw when the 'enemy' appeared.

In the valley below, the opposing horde stopped and sent forward a woman. When half-way up the hill, she shouted and came to a halt. A woman from the first group went towards her and, both armed with clubs, they spoke in lowered voices, then shouted again together, whereupon the natives on our side went down into the valley.

The two armies marched one upon the other and stopped when separated only by a few metres. The one which had just arrived had a few more warriors than the other, but these withdrew after a sort of inspection, and each one of the savages could then choose himself an opponent.

First of all there was leaping and jumping, then wild cries followed by blows struck upon the weapons, and then a general mêlée ensued.

The battle had begun.

Vigorously thrown spears hurtled through the air; but no combatant fell. The champions then approached one another, whereupon there was fury, rage, frenzy and delirium all worthy of hell itself. Bodies fell and rose again, resuscitated by the desire for revenge. Blood flowed, skulls were opened, ribs were broken, and even teeth played a destructive role in this horrible scene of carnage.

Seeing that one side appeared to be losing, the three Frenchmen considered entering the battle to help them. 'Upon reflection however,' wrote Arago, perhaps thus saving their lives, 'drawing my pistol from my belt, I fired it into the air. At that very instant the battle ceased, the warriors separated and upon a second shot they fled into the depth of the wood.'[52]

The Indigenous people's ways of punishing those who had committed offences often resembled battles in the eyes of the French.

On 29 February 1824 Dumont d'Urville and his colleague René Lesson, at the invitation of the native chief Bungari, attended 'a great gathering near Sydney to punish several natives accused of various crimes'. While D'Urville is not precise about the location of this gathering, Lesson says it was 'in a field between *la route de Botany-bay et Brich-Field* [sic]'. In their journals both Lesson and D'Urville recount their experiences, but it is to D'Urville that we will refer principally here.[53]

When D'Urville arrived at about 10 o'clock that morning, 'several tribes were already camped around in the bush'. He then went on to describe in detail what he saw.

At a general signal all the tribes got up and went to the arena in groups of fifteen to twenty men, all armed with spears, shields, clubs and boomerangs. Already there were the people from Parramatta, Kissing Point,

Sydney, Liverpool, Windsor, Emu Plains, Broken Bay, Five Islands, Botany Bay and even from Hunter River etc. etc. All were distinguished by the designs of their body paintings, black, red or white; but there were only five or six complete tribes, and others had merely sent representatives who had gathered under allied chiefs ...

To start with, six women were placed in a semicircle in the arena, each armed with a long stick for support and at the same time to ward off the blows they were going to receive; while two men were stood up a short distance away in the same line, and only defended by the long narrow wooden shield they call a *heloman*.

From as much as we could understand of their language, they were accusing these various individuals of having caused the death of a man from the Windsor tribe, which was allied with the Liverpool tribe commanded by Cogai, and all were to receive punishment for their crime. For the women it consisted of withstanding a number of blows from clubs wielded with some force, and the men from powerfully thrown spears. Cogai and his warriors were to mete out this vengeance.

Some natives made speeches, then the executions began. First one man approached the women to strike them, but they had only to present their sticks transversely and he merely hit them; however, at the fifth woman, instead of directing his blow at the stick, he bashed her right in the throat. The unfortunate woman immediately fell to the ground, but lost no time in getting up again to endure the rest of her punishment. The sixth one was treated like the first four. Several men and women who had followed did the same, and I noticed that each of them set upon the one who had already been so knocked about; nevertheless only two assailants, a man and a woman, were still cruel enough to hit her with their clubs, one to the chest and the other on top of her head. At each blow she fell and immediately got up again supporting herself with her stick.[54]

The men's turn having come, about fifteen savages stepped forward and hurled their spears in turn, which the condemned men parried with amazing dexterity, and lucky for them, for, of these shafts, some dug into the earth about thirty feet beyond them and the others penetrated an inch or two into the helo-man [sic]. One man was gathering up the spears and sending them back to their owners. Often the natives being punished threw them back themselves, challenging their enemies and mocking them for their lack of skill.

While this was going on, they returned from time to time to the punishment of the women, and occasionally the savages made their boomer-
angs curl and whine all around them; anyway this instrument is more
suited to frightening someone than actually causing harm. Finally, when
the two men had endured what was almost a barrage of about sixty spears
each, they were set free, as were the women, and no further notice was
taken of them. Only the unfortunate woman that I indicated seemed
overwhelmed by the blows she had received; she could hardly stand up
and was dragged off into the bush by the women of her tribe. The reason
for this excessive severity was another crime, separate from the one that
was shared in common with her accomplices whom they had merely ter-
rorised and publicly humiliated.

The ceremony had begun at 10 o'clock and the punishment of the
culprits had lasted about half an hour. A few minutes later several warriors entered the arena and were followed in turn by others, so that general fighting started with about twenty men against an equal number;
moreover, the spears were thrown from each side with admirable order
and precision, and this fight resembled rather an organised tournament
than a confused free-for-all. The savages fought with laudable serious-
ness, coolness and courage; all the thrusts were awaited and parried without flinching, while the women ran through the ranks to stir up the men.
I watched one of them; she was stark naked and the grace and beauty of
her figure made a perfect whole. She approached one warrior who
bowed his head before her while she hit him twice with a club in a deliberate and dignified manner; she returned two or three times to the fray,
and then she disappeared from the gathering and I could not be sure if her
face matched the beauty of her form.

While the spears were flying in almost equal numbers from all sides, I
noticed a young man from the Five Islands against whom all the shafts
from the opposing side seemed to be concentrated, and who seemed to
be deprived of the right of retaliation, for he appeared to attempt it only
two or three times. Bidgi-Bidgi, the chief from Kissing Point, seemed
particularly set against him and urged his warriors to vengeance. As the
two parties changed position continually, and in consequence the spears
their direction, to avoid being hit the spectators had to move pretty
smartly, and nobody waited to be asked to shift. The force with which the
spears penetrated the shields showed us what would have happened if we

took the risk of being hit. Furthermore, the combatants took not the slightest notice of the Europeans surrounding them; only the chiefs of the tribes who were not involved in the fighting took the trouble to warn us and to get us to keep a wary eye out. For about fifteen to twenty minutes this fight went on without any remarkable incident. I decided to take myself round the battlefield and visit the few groups of women and children in the surrounding bush.

Upon his return, D'Urville saw that the young man from Five Islands had been badly wounded and was being helped from the field. The Frenchman continued his account.

I came nearer and saw that turning aside to avoid a shaft had caused him to be struck in the lumbar region where the spear had penetrated quite deeply. One of his friends was supporting him in his arms; the spear had been withdrawn and the blood had been sucked from the wound, after which it had been bandaged. The poor fellow, however, although pale and weak from loss of blood, made no sound and even attempted to walk by leaning on his spear. I then learned that this young man, who had more regular and attractive features than most of his companions and was a native of the Five Islands as were the other guilty persons, was accused by Bidgi-Bidgi of having strangled his nephew at the Parramatta school to get possession of his clothes.[55]

What is odd is that while there was, it is true, a strong presumption of his guilt, the most convincing alleged proof for condemning him rested on a dream of one of the chiefs. That was why he had been sentenced to receive so many spear thrusts without the right to return them; those who fought alongside him, all his friends and relatives, did it as a point of honour or out of self-esteem rather than from any very strong urge for vengeance. In fact, as soon as he was wounded, the fight was much less willing, lasting scarcely eight to ten minutes longer, and was without any further incident. Probably it was enough for the aggrieved tribe to have spilt the blood of the guilty person, whose allies were not keen to purse the matter any further. A few natives made speeches again, women wailed and fresh warriors made threatening gestures with spears and boomer-angs, but it all quickly subsided; at 11.45 everyone returned through the bush to his own side.[56]

While clash and clamour were customary, and broken bones the general rule, death was not an inevitable outcome of these impressive struggles. 'During my stay in Sydney,' wrote Milius, 'I was witness to several combats between the savages … They rarely die as a result of their wounds, although they are often such as to leave them little hope. I have seen some of them allow a spear to be pulled out of them without showing the least pain, and they heal themselves with herbs which are unknown to us.'[57]

If the French saw few people die, they did, however, observe some of the ways in which respect was paid to those who had died.

As mentioned earlier, in Tasmania in 1772 and then in Western Australia in 1803, spears appeared to be used to honour the dead. In 1802, however, François Péron made an even more extensive discovery, on Maria Island (in Tasmania), when he came across 'a monument whose construction excited a considerable degree of curiosity'.

He went on to describe this monument in detail, and even asked two of his colleagues to assist him with their artistic abilities. 'The drawing of this tomb,' he explained, 'done with great precision by Mr Petit and finished by Mr Lesueur, leaves nothing to be desired for the details of the monument and for the pleasant view from the hilltop on which he is seated.'[58] This drawing (which presumably shows Péron examining his discovery) is reproduced in the photographic section facing page xx. Another drawing, by Lesueur and presenting detail of the monument's interior, is also reproduced.[59]

Péron described the interior of these constructions. 'All the upper part,' he noted, 'was unoccupied; but at the bottom was a large flattened cone, made of fine soft herbage, disposed with much care in concentric layers of considerable depth.' His investigation of the tomb would prove to be the most important of any French expedition. He continued:

I had no sooner taken off some of the upper layers of verdure than I perceived a large heap of white ashes, which seemed to have been gathered together with great care. I put my hand into the middle of these, and felt something of more substance, which I drew forth — it was the jaw-bone of a man, to which there yet adhered some remains of flesh … I shuddered with a sensation of horror … Nevertheless, on reflecting a few moments on all I had observed in the construction of this monument, I soon began to experience sensations of a different kind: this verdure, these flowers, these protecting trees, this thick bed of green herbage, which so carefully had covered these ashes — all united to convince me that I had discovered a place of burial.

As I removed some of the ashes, I perceived a black coal, friable and light, which I soon ascertained to be animal coal: as I found some that still shewed remains of flesh, in which might be distinguished parts of the large blood vessels full of calcined blood. I next found parts of the bones that were easily known to belong to the vertebrae, the shoulder, the leg. &c. All were much changed by the fire, and some of them easily crumbled into powder. These bones were not, as I had at first thought, laid simply on the surface of the earth; they were all collected together in the bottom of a circular hole of sixteen or eighteen inches diameter, and eight or ten inches in depth: we shall prove that these observations are of some consequence.

Péron then allowed himself 'a few minutes' to indulge in 'reflections' and 'meditations', words which presage well the Rousseauesque expressions that ensued. Noting that this monument was 'at the foot of a hillock' whereby 'ran a stream of fresh water, cool and limpid', he endeavoured to interpret the Indigenous people's actions. 'Among these terrific rocks,' he proclaimed, 'in the depths of these venerable forests, nature has yet preserved some of her rights, since the first monument which we discover of the uninformed and savage race who inhabit them, was consecrated by Nature herself.' Observing too that near this spot 'shell fish was to be found in greater plenty', he concluded 'that the same principle which dedicates these monuments also raises them in situations that are most interesting and dear to those who visit these places, impelled by their daily wants, and where they must experience in a greater degree the sentiments of gratitude and attachment'.

On the more practical question of why a body was burnt rather than buried, Péron was more down to earth. 'To bury it,' he assumed, 'is a labour so such more difficult as the soil is generally hard and flinty, and the absolute want of every kind of tool makes it almost impossible for them to dig any kind of grave.'[60]

At this same time, again on Maria Island, Leschenault de la Tour discovered another tomb which, he declared, 'was very little different' from the one found by Péron.[61] Baudin himself was most impressed with these discoveries. 'The tombs are the most skilfully and carefully-made things that we have seen,' he concluded. 'They are infinitely superior to anything else that we know of belonging to the natives, and one may say that they are more concerned to preserve the meaning of their dead relations or friends than they are to think of their own preservation.'[62]

In New South Wales the French were also witness to customs regarding the dead. In 1819 Arago made the following observations:

As soon as a man has breathed his last, his friends and relations … gather around the cadaver [*le cadavre*], probe him one by one to ensure that he is beyond any further help and then, painlessly — or at least tearlessly — each one busies himself with his task. One, with the aid of his waddy, his spears and finger-nails digs a hole in the earth. Another goes to search for small branches from trees, and a third pulls up grass and weeds. Then all return to the cadaver. They make a bed for him with the materials I have described, and lay him on it before half surrounding him with leaves and grasses. He is then bound with cords or pieces of skin, and his waddy and spears are laid beside him. Everything is then cast into the hole, which is then covered with earth before the troop [*la troupe*] jumps up and down on it to level it. Then nothing remains of the absent man: not even the memory.[63]

In 1824 Lesson presented a succinct account of these final moments. 'They burn the cadaver,' he wrote, 'and, placing the ashes under a mound after enveloping them in foliage, they engrave hieroglyphic epitaphs on the bark of the trees nearby.'[64]

Both these observers surmised as to the role of religion in the Indigenous communities.

Arago was not at all impressed and had no hesitation in sharing his thoughts.

> These fine people [*ces braves gens*] have never bothered themselves with what happens after death and, if they have a religion, which I doubt very much, it teaches them nothing about this. A few philosophers, studying the ways of man in the dreams of their imagination, have not feared to propose ... that all primitive people had a God, and that it was only as one advanced in civilisation that doubts began to appear. The natives of New South Wales give the lie to this opinion ... One must assume men need a certain intelligence to create a God, but the people of whom I speak here have little more than brutish instinct.[65]

Lesson was more gentle in his interpretation.

> We do not know exactly what ideas they have about divinity. They never ostensibly practice religious enactments. We only know that they believe first of all in the existence of a bad spirit which they must intercede with so it cannot send them any evil, or oppose their plans for abduction, hunting, fishing or travel. However the tombs they honour, the burial places to which they devote mysterious ceremonies, the dead to whom they accredit the power to come back in the form of shadows: all seem to prove they have an idea of another life and of a spiritual being whose power rules the march of the elements. The funeral rites they practise, when one of their family of friends dies, allows us better to assess their beliefs, about which they will obstinately say nothing ... They render to the dead the religious cult of remembrance and grief. Some tombs have three furrows cut into them, and placed in semi-circles.

Lesson also concluded in a more positive manner than his compatriot. 'The brutish Australians [*les Australiens brutaux*],' he wrote, 'thus have a vague instinct of fine art, since they know, with signs, how to represent the memory of one of their loved ones for the consideration and respect of generations to come.'[66]

Eugène Delessert would add another dimension to this subject. He wrote:

The aborigines appear to have no idea at all of religion, and I do not know that, anywhere in the land, anything has been found resembling an idol. However, they are not strangers to all sorts of superstitions ... They believe that those who die go to another land, are there transformed into white men, and come back later to inhabit their country ... This doctrine, which reminds one of metempsychosis, is engraved so deeply in their imagination that every time they believe they see a resemblance between a white man and one of their dead friends, they are absolutely convinced as to the identity of these two persons.[67]

CHAPTER 4

Relations between the Aboriginal Australians and the British

THE town of Sydney, although only fourteen years of age in 1802, was then already a source of admiration for François Péron who stayed there from June until November that year. 'Upon arrival at Port Jackson,' he wrote, 'we were completely astonished at the flourishing state in which we found this singular and distant establishment.' He went on to speak of the excellent facilities (the hospital, the docks, the store-house, the armoury, the public school, the barracks, the prison, 'the governor's house built in the Italian style') and the kind and generous people he met, including the Governor, Philip Gidley King.[1]

Seventeen years later, Jacques Arago was similarly impressed on approaching 'the spacious harbour of Port Jackson'. There he saw 'a novel and vigorous vegetation intermixed with small houses, the European architecture of which strikes our eyes, and excites our admiration ... We are scarcely arrived, and ask how many years this colony has existed'. He was struck by the 'magnificent light-house' and, further on, glimpsed 'country houses that remind us of the elegant seats in the environs of Bordeaux'. Later, in Sydney itself, he would note how, under the guidance of 'a judicious, impartial and rigid Governor [Macquarie] ... on the very spot where savages formerly engaged in bloody combats ... a town arises — a colony is formed — Sydney becomes a flourishing city'.[2] During his stay he and his colleagues were introduced to all 'the principal officers of government'. 'General Macquarrie [sic]', he wrote, 'governor of all the English possessions in New Holland, received us with extreme kindness, and assured us that whatever the country afforded was at our service.' Macquarie's improvements to the town did not escape his attention. 'Magnificent hotels, majestic mansions, houses of extraordinary taste and elegance, fountains ornamented with sculptures ... spacious and airy apartments, rich furniture, horses, carriages and one-horse chaises of the greatest elegance, immense storehouses — would you expect to find these four thousand leagues from Europe? I fancied myself transported into one of our handsomest cities.' When he returned aboard ship that evening he carried with him 'an eager desire to land again, and again to enjoy the same spectacle'. His praise for the new colony appeared to know no bounds.

The Aboriginal inhabitants of this land, however, may not have shared his enthusiasm. The Europeans' gain here was surely their loss.

> When the sun is setting, and the observer from the top of a lofty building turns his eyes towards the country, he enjoys a prospect truly interesting. From the midst of those deep forests that lately were trodden by the feet of savages alone, arise immense columns of smoke, amid which burns a bright flame, illuminating the distant horizon. All the new grants are cleared by burning ... The proprietor of a piece of ground [referring to the newly-arrived Europeans] begins by circumscribing with the axe the space he means to cultivate. The fire, arriving at this boundary, as it ceases to find aliment, stops, dies away, and its beneficent ashes give life to the land it has thus cleared.[3]

The number of Europeans in this fine town had also flourished handsomely. 'Today,' wrote Lesson in 1824, 'Sydney is more than a mile and a half in length, although they say there are only 10 000 inhabitants.' He then presented details showing the growth of this population since 1815.[4] The numbers appear almost to double.

Extract from Lesson's table of the general population of New South Wales

Year	Sydney	Parramatta	Windsor	Liverpool	Newcastle
1815	5688	2566	2749	1167	344
1816	5882	3581	3164	1550	413
1817	7409	4257	4257	1922	553
1824	10 000				

The French visitors suspected, however, that the Aboriginal populations were in decline. 'You may hire horses that will carry you beyond the Blue Mountains,' wrote Arago, 'and return to Sydney ... after having seen those savage hordes, which are gradually disappearing from this fifth [sic] quarter of the globe.'[5] Speaking of the colony in general, he declared: 'The race of these men is extinguishing itself little by little, and in twenty years time the eastern part of New-Holland will be totally bereft of them.'[6]

The reasons for this were not difficult to discern. 'Not long ago,' wrote Laplace, 'one encountered plentiful tribes of nations around Sidney [sic]; today one scarcely discovers but a few families, and soon the immoderate consumption of strong alcohol and epidemic illness brought from the Old World will have wiped them out.'[7] His compatriot Lesson had expressed a similar opinion. 'These natives,' he said, 'are exposed to a great number of chronic illnesses ... Most have lingering catarrhs; some women are consumptive, and others are eaten into by large gangrenous and syphilitic ulcers, skin sores, etc.'[8] Bougainville proposed that 'everybody knows with what ardour most of the savages who live near European settlements indulge their penchant for strong liquor, and the natives of Australia are not exempt from this deadly passion'.[9]

Yet another reason for this decline was put forward by an Englishman, 'Mr Field, a wealthy planter', whom Arago had befriended during his stay in Sydney in 1819. When Arago had returned to Sydney after witnessing the two native 'armies' combating each other on the north shore, Field had exclaimed: 'You can see well enough then, that we don't need to chase away these wild animals [*bêtes fauves*], because they are destroying each other, and very soon you will only be able to find them beyond the Blue Mountains.'[10] The Indigenous people had clearly not been 'destroying each other' before the arrival of the British, then only three decades earlier.

The nakedness of the Aboriginal people in Sydney, from the early years to as late as 1845, never ceased to amaze the French. 'I cannot comprehend,' exclaimed Arago, 'how the government of Sydney … can permit savages from the interior to reside in the capital. For the purpose of concealing from women and young girls the disgusting spectacle of hideous nakedness, it ought to confine all those wretches who wear no kind of clothing to a separate quarter; or … oblige the savages to conceal at least certain parts with the skin of a kangaroo, or some other covering.'[11]

Five years later Lesson would note that 'the chiefs of each community have received from the English administration great copper plaques which they wear about their neck … They and their wives are somewhat voluntarily half-clad 'à l'européenne'. He continued:

> The rest of the islanders [i.e. Indigenous Australians] go about in the most complete nudity, unless a few individuals may have obtained a jacket from a convict, or a hat. The strangest spectacle is without contradiction the encounter I have often had, in the streets of Sydney, with these austral Negroes [*nègres austraux*] in the most absolute undress, walking about in the midst of the crowd, bumping elbows with the fresh and prim young ladies, whose mother's wing, in the full light of day, could not protect them from the strangeness of this intimate costume.[12]

Some twenty years later this same 'costume' was still no less 'allowed'. 'The English,' wrote Eugène Delessert, who stayed in Sydney for eight months in 1845, 'have perhaps still not done everything they should to raise this barbaric race of aborigines [*cette race barbare des aborigènes*] of New South Wales. They persist in allowing them to wander almost naked about the streets of the town, when it would be easy to require them to dress, at least every time they came into places inhabited by Europeans. One could believe they would quickly conform to this requirement if it were imposed upon them.'[13]

One of the best known personalities among the Aboriginal people in Sydney was a man named Bungaree (spelled in a variety of ways by different people). As a young man he had sailed to Bribie Island with Matthew Flinders in the *Norfolk* in 1799 and then, two years later, had circumnavigated Australia, again with Flinders, in the *Investigator*. In the 1820s he became quite friendly with some of the French visitors.

Lesson saw him in the centre of Sydney in 1824. 'He showed me his skull, he recalled, 'all cracked by numerous waddy blows which would have felled a strong animal. One of his arms had also been broken by the same weapon, and the two extremities of the fractured humerus, rubbing incessantly against each other, had created a false articulation. Despite this Bongarri used his arm skilfully, either to row his boat or to wield his weapons.'

Lesson had been advised that Bungaree had been 'a great warrior' and that the neighbouring tribes admired him greatly. However, wrote the Frenchman, 'we had difficulty in discerning this hero in the arrant drunkard and tenacious beggar who called every day to harass us for liquor and tobacco. Bowing and scraping, his grotesque way of dressing made him look even more ridiculous. He wore an old dragoon's helmet, and around his chest flapped a toggled greatcoat left to him by the last Russian expedition.'

On the day Lesson saw him, Bungaree was 'escorted by his two wives, the most striking, the most ugly and the most disgusting creatures I have ever seen', thought the Frenchman. 'One of these women, however,' was mother of a little white creature.' How could this be explained? 'Bongarri,' he conjectured, 'like a true practical philosopher, replied to the jests of those who questioned him: 'My wife loves white bread, and has eaten a lot of it, so it's not surprising her child is white.'[14] Lesson may have been reminded here of the story told about the Queen of France at the Court of Versailles just a century before. Louis XIV's wife, Marie-Thérèse, had given birth to a black baby girl shortly after receiving 'a nice little blackamoor as a toy and pet'. According to Madame de Montespan, one of Louis XIV's mistresses, 'the Queen admitted that, one day, soon after becoming pregnant, he [the blackamoor] had hidden behind a piece of furniture, and had suddenly jumped out to give her a fright'.[15]

In 1815 Governor Macquaire had decorated Bungaree with a brass plate inscribed 'Bungaree, King of the Blacks'.[16] In July 1825 Bougainville would speak at length about 'the famous King Boongaree' (as he called and spelled him) who often came to visit him on board his frigate *Le Thétis* 'along with his family in order to drink our health and a few glasses of brandy by which he put great store'. On these visits Bungaree was dressed 'in a black cloak three-quarters worn out, an old military hat adorned with ribbons' and sometimes, continued Bougainville, 'decorations made of golden or coloured paper would complete His Majesty's city suit'.[17]

Bungaree's broken arm, observed earlier by Lesson, may have in fact served more purposes than just rowing a boat or wielding weapons. When Bougainville could not find one of his crewmen after an expedition to North Head, he requested the assistance of Bungaree to search for him. Supplied with adequate provisions of brandy, the Aboriginal leader set forth. Shortly after his departure, the Frenchman was found by two Englishmen and brought back on board. Bungaree returned some forty-eight hours later, and revealed his broken arm to Bougainville, who tells the tale as it was told to him. 'Boongaree said it was an accident,' wrote the Frenchman, 'which had happened while he was busy looking for our man, and he seemed to be suffering greatly from it. Distressed by this event, I was wondering what compensation to offer him, when I learnt from our chief surgeon, who had been summoned, that the arm had been broken three years before.' Bougainville went on to confirm what Lesson had been told the previous year. 'Because this master scoundrel had never rested it, it had formed what the doctor called a false articulation. A singular aspect of this, which explains why I had not until then noticed Boongaree's infirmity, was that he could still use his hand, the muscles having kept all their elasticity.'[18]

The 'little white creature' seen by Lesson may also have been seen — then rather less 'little' — by Bougainville. 'In Boongaree's retinue,' he noted, 'there was a young girl whose hair was almost blond and whose white skin and face betrayed her European origins.' 'Later on,' he continued, 'at the house of Mr Macarthur, I also met a half-caste who was handsome and well-built. Although he was the son of a white man, he had chosen the free and nomadic existence of his native ancestors. All this goes to show that, contrary to the reports of travellers, Aborigines do not always put to death children of a union between one of them and a European.'[19]

Bungaree appears to have died in 1832, according to a portrait of him by Rodius (presented in the photographic section), but a notice in *The Sydney Gazette* on 27.11.1830 shows he died on 24.11.1830.

While Bungaree clearly lacked for neither food nor drink, this was certainly not always the case for his compatriots.

In 1802, only four years after the colonisation of Port Jackson, Louis de Freycinet noted the alimentary problems of the Aboriginal people. In such early days, it may appear difficult to apportion blame for this to the English. 'Their existence is extremely miserable,' wrote Freycinet. 'When winter comes and the fish become scarce ... they migrate northward to seek more plentiful food. Despite this precaution, these unfortunate people are often exposed to cruel famines. Should a whale be washed up on the shore, this would be a gift from heaven. I have seen them fight each other tooth and nail over such a disgusting quarry.'[20]

Seventeen years later, however, the English themselves seemed to accept some responsibility for these problems. John Oxley, the surveyor-general and explorer (who, in 1823, would explore Moreton Bay and the Brisbane River), was quite explicit on this subject when speaking with Jacques Arago, who was staying with him at his property at 'Kirkham' in December 1819. Oxley told the Frenchman:

> I don't want you to leave my home without making some acquaintance with the men who roam these solitudes, and who are disappearing little by little, especially since our fire-arms deprive them of resources they used to have before our conquest [*notre conquête*]. Everything is not gain

in the victory of civilisation, and the conquered people who wish to remain free from our laws have everything to fear from their resistance. You
see, the savage inhabitants [*les sauvages habitants*] of this part of the world
scarcely frequent any more the shores where we have our settlements,
preferring hunger and the solitude of the forests rather than the plentiful
food and ways of life we would like to give them.[21]

In his *Narrative of a Voyage round the World* Arago gives a vivid description of the condition of the native people who had been thus
deprived. 'As the frequent shooting parties [of the English] have
destroyed the greater part of the game that served for food for these
wandering tribes,' he wrote, 'the latter, in consequence of the famines
to which they are exposed, have been compelled to approach the
European settlements ... These poor creatures, uncertain of the
future, and terrified by remembrance of the past, wander like spectres
in the depths of the forests and search the ungrateful soil for the means
of life it refuses ... What people ever dragged out a more deplorable
existence?'

Arago was aware, however, that these problems of food supply were
not caused solely by the arrival of the English, for he quotes David
Collins, who arrived with the First Fleet in 1788. 'We have seen, says
Mr Collins,' wrote Arago, 'the unhappy natives of New South Wales,
in times of great scarcity, reduced to such extreme leanness that you
would take them for so many skeletons, and whole tribes have per-
ished for want of food.'

Arago then went on to describe how the native people consumed
all kinds of creatures quite unpalatable to the European. 'These
unhappy beings,' he wrote, 'after having carried on a war of extermi-
nation against frogs, toads, snakes, lizards and different species of caterpillars ... have pursued in their fearful rage the most hideous spiders
and devoured them greedily; and then had recourse to the earth, and
attacked in their dwellings those formidable ants that burrow in the
ground and lay it waste.'[22]

At Kirkham Falls on one occasion, he was present at — and almost
shared in — a feast of these ants. 'Eleven savages', he observed, 'skinny
as skeletons', had set light to an ant-hill. He then described in detail

what he saw. 'Three spears, thrown with great vigour, pierced the besieged mound and, from the holes made by these weapons, fled enormous ants which the fire quickly made turn back into their home. The waddy then joined the spears … and soon the mound was but a pile of ruins, and the fire continued still. An hour later the work was done.' Then, as he watched, 'the horde rose … and grabbed an enormous ball of agglomerated corpses, forming a kind of black mastic, upon which they threw themselves with sickening gluttony'. 'I even thought for a moment,' he wrote, 'that these miserable famished people seemed to fear that I would ask them for a share in their hideous repast.' He did not, and this was perhaps fortunate for the Indigenous people because, he noticed, 'when I drew away from this spectacle of horror, each of the guests hastened less to devour his pittance'.[23]

In the centre of Sydney, and indeed on the harbour itself, life could appear less onerous for the Aboriginal Australians. 'During the last fortnight of July and the early days of August,' wrote Bougainville, 'my crew caught such a large number of mackerel with fishing-rods that we were able to salt thousands of them. This catch … attracted to our neighbourhood several boats crowded with natives who, each day at noon, headed towards Sydney to sell their catch or to receive their pay from the boats' owners. The men wore straw hats and were dressed like sailors, in wide trousers and round jackets, and the women were draped in rough striped blankets, serving alternately as overcoats or skirts.' Nevertheless, he continued, 'nothing could be more hideous and disgusting than these poor creatures, whose skinny bodies rutted with scars [*cicatrices*] bore witness to a wretched existence and barbaric customs'. 'It was not a new spectacle for us,' he said, 'to see these unfortunate indigenous people condemned to drag out their existence as beggars about Sydney.'[24]

The Aboriginal people's plight was indeed often such that they were reduced to begging, and examples of this abound. On the day that Arago had witnessed the ant feast, he had earlier been accosted by 'an absolutely naked savage [*un sauvage absolument nu*] looking pitiful and fearful … and nearly falling from inanition who asked for food'.

'I told him not to move,' said the Frenchman, 'and brought him in a serviette a few pieces of fowl, two *côtelettes* and a large chunk of bread.'[25] In 1831 Cyrille Laplace had a similar experience near this same place. 'In a valley on the left bank of the Nepean,' he recalled, 'about 12 miles from Regentville … we received the visit of a savage, accompanied by his wife and children … The man threw himself gluttonously on the remains of the meal left for him by our boatmen and, without the precaution we took of subtracting some bits from his voracity in order to gratify his companion, this unfortunate woman would have had nothing.'[26] No mention is made of the children.

By 1845 the situation seems to have changed but little, if at all. Eugène Delessert observed that 'it is rare to meet in Sydney more than twenty or thirty Aborigines [*aborigènes*] at one time, unless this is at the beginning of the year when the Government distributes blankets to them'. He noted that sometimes, 'when they want to make long journeys along the coast, they come on board the steam-boats, where they are given free passage'. 'One traveller,' he continued (without naming the person), 'has portrayed these men as tenacious and even insolent beggars, but I have never met a single black man [*un seul noir*] who answers this description.'

> They are not in the habit of annoying anyone, unless people seem to take pleasure in ogling them, which sometimes happens. How, indeed, can one prevent oneself from staring with curiosity at these men, clad in the most grotesque of costumes, be it in a suit without trousers, a waist-coat without a shirt, or simply a pair of under-pants. Sometimes just a kangaroo skin will serve the purpose! Soon, noticing the attention being given to them, they take advantage of it to ask for a few pence which they use to buy tobacco, and their request is always accompanied by grand salutations. They are generally quite well received in the shops, where they rarely leave without being given a little something. If they need a fish-hook, for example, they go to a hardware store, and they often obtain the object they desire as a gift. Charitable families put aside for them left-overs from dinner, and put them up in some part of their house. These men, it should be said, do not lack a sense of gratitude: they seek quite willingly to be of service to the people who have helped them. In

this way they will help the servants chop wood, or look after fetching water.

Outside Sydney the Aboriginal inhabitants, deprived of their food supplies, could be tempted into what the white people would perceive as theft. Delessert wrote:

> One can understand that men, reduced to such an abject situation and forced to obtain food by every means possible, experience a certain temptation at the sight of a large flock of sheep (which they no longer fear), and that the desire gets hold of them to seize a few of these animals. But this act is often punished by a rifle shot, for the whites [*les blancs*] put no store on the life of these miserable beings. I am far from approving such brutality towards creatures who, after all, are men. I also do not approve of the whites needlessly killing kangaroos when they come upon them, just to have their skins, when they know very well that these animals, unique to New-Holland, form a major part of the Aborigines' food. A native said on this subject already some years ago: 'White fellow come come [sic], kangaroo all gone'.[27]

Louis de Freycinet summed up the general situation of the Aboriginal people as he saw it in Sydney in November and December 1819: 'A drawing [reproduced in the photographic section] will,' he said, 'give an idea of the degraded appearance of the natives of the Sydney region when the "Uranie" was moored in these parts. Debased by the use of strong liquor, they have abandoned themselves to their naturally indolent natures as well as to the slothful habits that have been induced in them, and they do nothing but wander about all over the place, like vagabonds with neither aim nor ambition.'

He then turned his European eye to their role as mendicants.

> They are not, strictly speaking, beggars, but they nevertheless readily accept scraps of meat and table leavings which are given to them in exchange for the oysters and fish they bring into town.
>
> Should they manage to extract a little money from this sort of barter, it is unusual for them not to hie off straight to a tavern where they drink until they are lying dead drunk in the street. At other times they can be seen hawking news around Sydney, or lounging about on the wharves

with nothing to do. They know everybody, and know about the work that everyone does, although they themselves want nothing to do with any sort of heavy work.[28]

Such was the overall interpretation and judgement of the French, and indeed of the Europeans generally.

It was clear to the French that some attempt was being made by the British to assimilate the Aboriginal Australians into European ways.

The question of lack of clothing, as we have seen, appeared important to the French. In Tasmania they had been concerned to clothe the native people in order to help protect them from the cold. In Sydney, however, the intention may have been more 'civilising'.

'A certain Banedou,' wrote Baudin's colleague Milius, 'was sent to England where he resided for several years before returning to his homeland. Scarcely had he set foot on land, discarding all his clothes, than he returned among the savages, his dear compatriots. He came to see me several times,' recalled Milius, 'and it must be said that, all the times he came to see me, he would put on some sort of clothing, which he would get rid of very quickly upon leaving me.'[29]

As we have seen, Arago was quite upset in Sydney by Aboriginal nakedness juxtaposed with the elegant clothing of the colonists. Such was his indignation that, on one occasion, he personally attempted to clothe one of the native people. The gift he would receive for his trouble, however, would not be to his taste at all! He wrote:

During a week I spent at Mr Field's delightful country house, I tried to clothe the chief of a band of unfortunate natives [*malheureux indigènes*], who came prowling around the house like famished dogs, and draped him with clothing made from an old shirt and a jacket which I myself put around the wild native [*farouche naturel*], who did nothing but grumble about my charitable kindness. There were no leaps and jumps his comrades didn't do when they saw thus clad the man whose body had never been sullied by any kind of clothing! However, he was more grateful than I could have suspected, and he came back four days later, with his clothes all in tatters, offering me with a certain joy the head of an enemy he had cut off in his last foray. I must have appeared ungrateful and ridiculous to this man when I refused with disgust his hideous and bloody offering. Mr Field was much amused at my frank generosity, and assured me that the gratitude of such beings was only ever expressed with such gifts.[30]

Five years later, again in Sydney, compatriot René Lesson would feel just as strongly.

The stubbornness of this race in rejecting even the narrow loin-cloth … would deeply astonish the moralist,' he declared. 'The apathetic indifference in public places of these [Aboriginal] men, who unceasingly see about them customs which should awaken them to their own ideas, slips by without leaving the least trace of its passage. What is worse is that there are some of these Australians [i.e. the Indigenous people] who have sailed on English ships … and who return to their rocks and woods, quickly casting off the clothing in which they had been dressed. They especially hate clothes for the lower part of the body, for they are less fussy about those which cover the back or the head.[31]

This of course was unfortunate, for it was this lower part of the body which concerned the Europeans most.

These persistent endeavours by the Europeans may have indeed been for protective or 'civilising' reasons, but the British may also have had commercial motives. Reflecting on his stay in Sydney in 1819, Louis de Freycinet thought that 'what shocked the English above all was to see that the Australians, with very few exceptions, refused to wear clothes, and were therefore unlikely to increase the consumption of British goods'. 'But,' he continued more philanthropically, 'had these poor Aborigines not the right to think, in turn, that the intelligence of the settlers must be very limited, when they failed to understand, after passing so many years in their midst, that clothes were superfluous in a mild and healthy climate?'[32]

The British also tried to encourage the Aboriginal people to live in houses. Barron Field appears to have had some limited success at his country home. 'In this delightful residence, built *à l'européenne* and perfectly surrounded by gardens,' enthused Arago, 'the noble planter had built a vast hangar for the natives' benefit, who came along in crowds when the stormy weather approached.' Arago may have feared for the Fields' safety with such numbers, but 'he assured us', he continued, 'that so near town one need fear nothing from the native ferocity of these men, and that he had never need to reproach them for any theft of any kind'.[33]

By 1825 all hopes of the British that the Indigenous people could be persuaded to live in houses or 'villages' appeared to be dashed. In 1824 Lesson had observed that 'a few Governors have tried to soften their lot by ... giving them permanent housing', but, he noted, 'the houses built for them, by bringing them into sorts of villages, have been deserted, for they only breathe at ease under the vault of the open skies'.[34] Lesson may have been thinking especially of Governor Macquarie who had done much in this way and in 1815, for example, had offered Bungaree a farm on the outskirts of Sydney. By 1825, however, Bougainville would recount how Bungaree and his tribe would 'retire in the evenings into the woods on the north coast of the harbour and there, men and women taking off all their clothes, lay pêle-mêle on the ground, after having lit fires to windward to keep off the humidity and insects'.[35]

Louis de Freycinet again seemed to understand the Aborigines' point of view. 'As for houses erected on a fixed site,' he wrote, 'they are merely repressive and vexatious to people for whom the nomadic life holds so many attractions. No Aborigine would be tempted to build a brick or stone house.'[36]

On occasion, however, the British appeared less to assimilate their unhappy hosts than to alienate them by using them for entertainment. One evening Arago witnessed, in the 'court' of 'one of the richest and most respectable merchants' in Sydney, 'girls from fifteen to eighteen years old encouraging in their savage sports, men and women absolutely naked'. He recalled the scene:

> These persons, covered with old scars, and armed with spears and clubs, had already received as rewards for their capers and grimaces, some pieces of bread, which they still held in their arm-pits, and a few glasses of wine or brandy ... Their gestures soon became violent, and their language

more loud: all spoke at once, all shook with a ferocious air their murder-
ous weapons. Attracted by the noise, the master and mistress of the house
hastened to the place with their guests and invited me to wait the issue of
the disturbance. I yielded with a good grace, persuaded that their excesses
would not be carried to any greater height, and that the ladies would
leave us to *enjoy* the spectacle alone. In this expectation I was disappointed; and their soft voices, on the contrary, excited the courage, or
rather the ferocity of the actors … These unfortunate men whose gaiety
at first appeared so peaceable, struck each other with repeated blows; two
of them were stretched on the ground dangerously wounded, and a third
received a mortal blow. Their companions, who had hitherto taken no
part in the action … then rose, quietly carried off the victims who were
perhaps their fathers or brothers, and disappeared with their burdens.

This scene took place in the midst of a civilised city; the spectators
were respectable merchants, and elegant and accomplished young ladies.

A few days earlier, reported Arago, he had seen 'a similar spectacle in
the yard of a public-house, where also one savage fell a victim to the
cruelty of another'.[37]

Five years later, René Lesson would remark how often he had seen
'natives' in the streets of Sydney, 'drunk, in the centre of circles of
people, urging them on by promising them gin, and hitting one
another with waddies until one of the champions asked for grace or
fell'. One of the unhappiest scenes Lesson witnessed was 'the women
of Port Jackson who prostituted themselves to the convicts for a glass
of brandy'.[38]

Other forms of entertainment could also place the Indigenous
people's lives in some danger, but involved no combat.

When Arago was visiting John Oxley at 'Kirkham', his host had
spoken of the Indigenous people. 'Don't they look hideous and
skinny! [*Quelles formes hideuses et mesquines!*]' he had exclaimed.
'Monkeys are infinitely superior to them for grace and intelligence.
And yet, you shall see.' Arago then described the scene presented to
him.

Mr Oxley blew a whistle, and I saw coming out of a hangar an absolutely
naked savage [*un sauvage absolument nu*], armed with several sagaies, two

waddies curved like hussard's sabres, and a small axe … This man came towards us. He was a chief, a king, anything you like: he commanded other men built like him, brutish like him, wild like him. Why was he in charge? I don't know, and Mr Oxley didn't know any more than I. A few words were said to him, and a few signs. He ran away, leaving behind his weapons, which could have hindered his speed of movement. After half an hour he returned with five of his most disgusting subjects, although they were less so than the girl who accompanied them and whose breasts flopped against her lower belly …

'You are going to witness a curious spectacle,', Mr Oxley said to me. 'Look! Here is a eucalyptus tree, very tall, straight and smooth. Arms cannot grasp it, for its diameter is too great. Do you think one of these men, in five or six minutes, could be capable of reaching the top?'

'That appears to me unbelievable,' I replied.

'Well, it is!'

'When I have seen it, I shall still doubt it.'

'I was only convinced myself,' replied Oxley, 'after the hundredth time I saw it.'

Mr Oxley then had one of the youngest-looking natives brought to him, and showed him a handkerchief which he placed on the ground saying it was his if in five minutes the tree was climbed. The savage uttered a cry of joy, threw himself to the ground, got up, seized the small axe I have mentioned, placed himself against the trunk of the eucalyptus, looked it up and down with a sort of disdain, uttered another cry, and got on with the job. With three chops, a notch was made two feet from the ground … A second notch two feet higher was made in the same way and, after climbing these stages, the savage with a vigorous blow planted the axe in the tree-trunk above his head.

Arago then tried, in one breathtaking sentence, to match the speed of his description with that of the climbing man:

Vertical against the tree, he stretched out his right arm, seized the instrument's handle as a fixed point, heaved himself up, clung against the tree with the help of the folds and bumps of his belly and chest like a lizard or snail would, steadied himself as if suspended for a moment, made more notches like the first ones, fixed one foot in one, then the other, replanted the little axe, thrust himself upward once again — and all this with more rapidity perhaps than I can tell it to you — went up, still stuck close to the tree as if it and he were one, and reached the top branches by using the same means in four and a half minutes.

'My word,' exclaimed Mr Oxley, 'he put some pride into that! Can you interpret or explain what you understand of this, now you have just seen it?'

'I shall try,' I replied.

'No one will believe you.'

'I shall invite the non-believers to undertake the voyage here. This alone is worth the trouble.'

'Now see this man come down,' continued Mr Oxley, 'and then feel his chest.'

A second blast on the whistle pierced the air. The savage placed himself upright against the trunk, let himself slide down, all the while looking to the left or the right, stopping at intervals as if to soften the pain of the friction and, in no time at all, was standing alongside us. I added a handkerchief of my own to the one he had just won, and the native bounded away like a deer. The skin of his rough chest bore no marks or any cuts.

Arago's illustration of this event is presented in the photographic section.

The other men then asked the Europeans if they wished them also to demonstrate their skills.

'Let us not spoil them,' said Mr Oxley, 'Unless you wish to see that the woman is no less agile and skilful than the men?'

'Two tries would not be too many to convince me,' I replied.

The woman thus began climbing and, in six minutes minus a few seconds, the feat was accomplished.'

Oxley then invited Arago to witness a contest between two men throwing boomerangs (or 'little curved waddies', as Arago called them). Like other explorers, the Frenchman tried in vain to understand the workings of this instrument, but, unlike them, he became himself quite expert at it. 'I acquired in a few days,' he declared, 'such a great skill that no savage in the country would have been able to take me on.'

It appears, therefore, that all classes of society, from the surveyor-general to the people in the public-houses, were prepared to use the Aboriginal inhabitants in some way for their entertainment. This use — or abuse — may have made assimilation of these people into European ways all the more difficult.

French attitudes to, and assessments of, these assimilation attempts varied over the forty years of their visits, but were generally similar in tone. In 1802 Pierre Milius was already quite pessimistic. 'It is impossible,' he declared after observing Banedou's experience, 'to hope to bring the savages of this country to any ideas of civilisation. They are veritable brutish animals [*de véritables bêtes brutes*] who must be left to live in their ways.'[39] His colleague, Louis de Freycinet, was less pessimistic. 'The English colonists,' he considered, 'live with these savages in very good harmony. They do not seek to enslave them, [and] leave them every liberty to follow their tastes and ways … Although these people are naturally enemies of work, one can hope that, with care and patience, they will be brought to this. A few colonists have tried the experiment and have obtained happy results. It's true that they have taken these savages very young into their homes, but with their full agreement and without using force or violence.'[40]

Seventeen years later, when again in Sydney but with his own expedition, Louis appears more philosophical about what he saw. 'Some educated English,' he wrote, 'when they cast their eyes on this degenerate and degraded race, are not loathe to deliver themselves of the opinion that these people, being too lazy to serve and not sufficiently intelligent to be masters, would never have a place in an industrious colony, and that perhaps it would be better if they died out completely.' One seems, indeed to be evolving here from assimilation to alienation, and even to possible annihilation. Freycinet's own view was, however, rather hopeful.

Every race doubtless has particular qualities and failings which are characteristic, but it is the slow and steady progress of time … that can be hoped to modify these people eventually, and finally draw them from their forests and civilise them …

Whatever success the future may hold, it is obvious that what has been done hitherto has produced only inconsequential results as far as civilising the Aborigines is concerned … Must we not fear that the unhappy Australian race is moving further away from the centres of colonisation which are pressing in on it? — and that those tribes which are already weak in number will now dwindle further?[41]

His colleague, Jacques Arago, was more outspoken, and perhaps even outraged, at what he saw on this same visit. After witnessing the deadly duels fought between the Aboriginal people of Sydney, he exclaimed: 'What can be the aim of the English in permitting, and even encouraging and provoking these hideous struggles? Can they be doing to these men what they do to aggressive dogs? Do they wish, in their culpable lack of concern, to let this race annihilate itself? Do they want them to destroy one another? I understand their contempt, I can understand their disgust. But does not humanity also have its duties, and should such scenes be allowed in the midst of a beautiful city, flourishing and well policed?'[42] His questions remained rhetorical, but his answers were perhaps clear enough.

Five years later, Dumont d'Urville was even more emphatic that hope for the Aborigines had been abandoned. 'As for the possibility of bringing the natives of New South Wales to a state of civilisation or even to a condition less savage and less nomadic … that is a hope which the English appear to have completely abandoned … In spite of the rapid growth in the number of Europeans on this foreign soil, this strange race pursues its sad existence almost in the same way as at the time when its members were the sole owners of it. In fact, the English administration does not in any way harass them. Provided they do not transgress the police laws of the colony, it can be stated clearly that they still enjoy full and complete freedom.'[43]

D'Urville's colleague on this expedition, René Lesson, had a similar impression. 'The Negro race [*la race nègre*], spread out upon the austral continent,' he wrote, 'has constantly showed itself to be enveloped in a thick skin of savagery, resistant enough to prevent civilisation from ever breaking into it … Examined from the point of view of our civilisation, one can only concede to these people a profound moral mindlessness [*abrutissement*]. The present-day English authorities treat the wretched remains of these numerous tribes with great gentleness, and oppose as much as they can the cruel game which the navigators play of sending them off their ships, where they go to beg, dead-drunk from alcohol.'[44]

In 1825 Bougainville expressed himself at length on the question of 'civilising' the Aboriginal people, and of their possible future annihilation. Again, his sentiments resemble those of his earlier compatriots, although one may detect here a small note of what he may have considered optimism.

> The Australians, being firmly anchored in their customs, faithful to their traditions … and perhaps only possessing the degree of intelligence appropriate to the life they lead, will probably never yield to the forms of civilisations which, not having managed to subjugate them, will end up, according to all appearances, by annihilating their race.
>
> It is still not demonstrated … that the Australians are entirely incapable of civilisation. The small number of unfruitful attempts carried out to date are far from sufficient to provide proof! because the English, too occupied by their own affairs, have not been able to give them attention … Whatever the case about their intelligence — whether it be at its highest point or capable of greater development (which I am disposed to believe) — it is still true that the indigenous people of New-Holland have remained absolutely the same since Europeans set foot here.

This inability or unwillingness to adapt to 'anything which could upset their customs or undermine their independence', thought Bougainville, 'has necessarily greatly cooled the interest they had at first inspired'.[45]

In the early 1830s Laplace too would note this lack of success. 'The government of Sidney [sic],' he wrote, 'has done everything possible to … incubate the first notions of agriculture in order to ensure [the Indigenous people's] existence, but these attempts have not succeeded. It even appears that the proximity of the habitations … makes them even more lazy.' 'Thus,' he continued, looking at the positive side (for the Europeans at least), 'it is rare that they degrade the plantations. They even pander to the desires of the colonists in order to obtain food, woollen blankets and especially rum and tobacco. They bring back deserting convicts and lost cattle … and serve as guides in the forests.'[46]

The observations of Eugène Delessert in 1845 seem to indicate little or no progress over the previous fifteen — or indeed fifty — years. Like Laplace and others, he saw how in Sydney the Aborigines could be trustworthy and helpful to their now unquestionably permanent visitors. 'If they are sent fishing,' he noted, 'they faithfully bring back their entire catch to those whom they regard as their masters [*leurs maîtres*] … Sometimes people are not afraid to confide them rifles, and they set out to hunt game without even having the idea of fleeing with these weapons which, for them, would be a fortune.'

'The natives who live around Sydney,' he continued, 'are half civilised and speak English quite well. Their language is all the more difficult to understand because it is not at all generalised, each tribe having almost its own dialect … As a consequence one finds few whites [*blancs*] who can say a few words and make themselves understood by the indigenous people. There exists, however, a grammar book of the language of the natives of Hunter's-River [sic] and the Macquarie River, written by Mr Threlkeld, which I have looked at. I have thus got to know and memorised several words and phrases of this language, which have been useful to me on a few occasions.'[47]

The Aborigines were not only helpful for fishing. 'The young sportsmen of Sydney,' said Delessert, 'seek out the strongest and handsomest men whom they employ to beat the undergrowth when they go shooting. These men are of great help to them for they know better than the whites where the game is most plentiful.' Later that year Delessert would indeed receive a letter from 'Mr Shustleworth, secretary of the sportsmen-club [sic]' in Sydney inviting him to be their guest of honour at a formal dinner on 14 July where, he noted, on arrival 'there was a large tricolour flag made of silk which adorned, with the flag of the colony, the two corners of the tent'.[48]

Delessert, however, was not optimistic about the overall 'improvement' of the native people about him. 'Doubtless,' he concluded, 'the charm which these people, who are not alien to the enjoyments of life and society, find in a wandering vagabond life will always present some obstacle to civilising them. Perhaps, however, more could be done than has been attempted till now. Schools had been established for the natives, where they learnt to read and write. These schools have been closed, and I do not know what caused this. A project has just been adopted by the Legislative Chamber aiming to improve the lot of these men, who cannot be repelled for ever, and of whom,' concluded the French visitor, 'it is not impossible to soften the ways of life, and to master the savage instincts.'[49]

In Tasmania the problem was far more acute, for here open warfare had occurred with considerable numbers of casualties on both sides. For Dumont d'Urville, as early as 1827, the fate of the Aboriginal people here seemed already foreseeable. 'The savages,' he wrote in Hobart, 'shun all communication with the English. The depleted tribes which still exist have fled to the most mountainous and inaccessible parts. As a consequence of on-going aggression between these people and the settlers, the number of natives has rapidly decreased, and … it is probable that within forty or fifty years this whole race will have completely disappeared … Every indication is that the Tasmanian and later the Australian, being uncivilisable, will finally die out altogether.'[50]

By December 1839, when D'Urville's second expedition stayed in Hobart, the situation was even clearer. 'Tasmania proper,' observed ensign Tardy de Montravel, 'no longer contains a single one of its original inhabitants, that the English have eliminated by hunting them down like wild beasts.' 'One tribe … was brought to bay,' he declared, 'at the sea coast on the north of the island. The government then forced it to leave its native soil and transported it to Flinders Island in the Bass Strait … Before long, this miserable transplanted remnant will have entirely disappeared.' During their stay in Hobart the French had seen only one Aborigine, 'a child of nine or ten that the government is raising probably to take to England as an interesting animal'.[51] The Flinder's Island Aboriginal Establishment had in fact been organised by George Augustus Robinson in 1832 and, after accommodating many Aborigines from various tribes in lamentable conditions, had finally been abandoned in 1848. Truganini, sometimes referred to as the 'last' Aboriginal person in Tasmania, died in 1876.

Only a few people (of whom Louis de Freycinet was one) appear to have endeavoured to envisage the situation from the Aboriginal point of view. Perhaps one of the most understanding and humane outlooks on this whole question, indeed, was that expressed by Captain Nicolas Baudin in his letter to Governor King from King Island (as it would be called), just halfway between Tasmania and the mainland, on 23 December 1802. Baudin had only recently spent five months at Port Jackson and, earlier that year, had spent some weeks in Tasmania which at that time had still not been settled by the British.[52] Baudin could thus have been expressing his opinion regarding the whole of Australia in his letter, which is worthy of quotation at length.

'I now write to you,' said Baudin, 'as Mr King, my friend', but, he underlined, 'nothing in the whole of this letter will relate to the policy of Governments'. He then went on to make his position quite clear regarding the Europeans and the Aboriginal Australians.

> To my thinking, I have never been able to conceive that there was justice and equity on the part of the Europeans in seizing, in the name of their Governments, a land seen for the first time, when it is inhabited by men who have not always deserved the title of savages or cannibals which has been given them, whilst they were but children of nature just as little civilised as are now your Scotch Highlanders or our peasants in Brittany … From this it appears to me that it would be infinitely more glorious for your nation, as for mine, to mould for society the inhabitants of their respective countries over whom they have rights, instead of wishing to occupy themselves with the education of those who are very far removed from it by beginning with the seizure of the soil which belongs to them and which saw their birth … It follows therefore that not only have you to reproach yourselves with an injustice in seizing their land, but also in

transporting on to a soil where the crimes and diseases of Europeans were unknown all that could retard the progress of civilisation, which has served as a pretext to your Government. etc.

If you will reflect upon the conduct of the natives since the beginning of your establishment upon their territory, you will perceive that their aversion for you, and also for your customs, has been occasioned by the idea which they have formed of those who wished to live amongst them. Notwithstanding your precautions and the punishments undergone by those among your people who have ill-treated them, they have been enabled to see through your projects for the future; but being too feeble to resist you, the fear of your arms has made them emigrate, so that the hope of seeing them mix with you is lost, and you will presently remain the peaceful possessors of their heritage, as the small number of those surrounding you will not long exist.[53]

Notes

A note on vocabulary

1. *Le Petit Larousse illustré*, 2001, p. 920 (translation by present author).
2. *The Oxford English Dictionary*, Oxford, 1989, p. 523.
3. 'A Discourse on the Origin and Foundation of the Inequality of Mankind', in *The Social Contract and Discourses by Jean-Jacques Rousseau*, translated by G. D. H. Cole, London, 1913, pp. 181 and 182.
4. Diderot, *Oeuvres complètes*, 'De la poésie dramatique', Paris, 1875, tome 7, p. 312 (translation by present author).
5. Jean-Jacques Rousseau, *Emile for Today*, translated by W. Boyd, London, 1956, p. 11.
6. J. J. Rousseau, *Rousseau, Judge of Jean-Jacques*, University of New England Press, Hanover, NH, 1990, vol. I, p. 213.
7. *Dictionnaire historique de la langue française*, Robert, Paris, 1992, pp. 1885–6 (translated by present author).
8. E. Littré, *Dictionnaire de la langue française*, Paris, 1885, pp. 696–7, quoting Buffon *Oeuvres*, t. I, p. 320.
9. *Le Petit Larousse illustré*, 2001, p. 688.
10. H. de Bougainville, *Journal de la navigation autour du globe*, Paris, 1837, vol. I, p. 486.
11. R. Lesson, *Voyage autour du monde …* Paris, 1838, vol. II, p. 286.
12. Cyrille Laplace, *Voyage autour du monde …*, Paris, 1833–35, vol. III, p. 257 (translation by present author).
13. Ernest Scott, *The Life of Matthew Flinders*, Angus and Robertson, Sydney, 1914, p. 1. Scott also dedicates a whole chapter to 'The Naming of Australia' (chapter XXX, p. 420).

14. Reproduced in *The French Exploration of Australia*, L. A. Triebel, Hobart, 1957, in the illustrations between pp. 32 and 33.

15. For our purposes here we will refer to him generally as Louis de Freycinet.

The Expeditions

1. Abel Tasman, *Journal of a voyage to the Unknown Southland in the Year 1642*, presented in E. Duyker, *The Discovery of Tasmania*, St David's Park Publishing, Hobart, 1992, p. 15.

2. Julien Crozet, *New Voyage to the South Sea* ..., Jean Roux, *Journal of the Voyage made on the King's ship 'the Mascarin'* ..., and A. Duclesmeur, *An Account of a voyage in the South Seas and the Pacific* ..., quoted in *The Discovery* ..., pp. 24, 42 and 22. Details of Dufresne's death may be found in Edward Duyker's *An Officer of the Blue*, Melbourne University Press, 1994, pp. 137–63.

3. In a manuscript letter reproduced in *Voyage de Lapérouse*, Paris, 1831, opposite p. xviii.

4. Paul de Rossel, *Voyage de Dentrecasteaux à la recherche de Lapérouse*, Paris, 1808, 2 vols.

5. Translated in 1800 as Jacques de Labillardière, *Voyage in Search of La Pérouse*, Stockdale, London, 2 vols.

6. Rossel, French original, vol. 1, p. XLI (translation by present author).

7. *A Voyage round the World, in the Years 1785, 1786, 1787 and 1788, by J.F.G. de La Pérouse*, edited by M. L. A. Milet-Mureau (translated from the French), 3 vols, London, 1798, vol. I, pp. 105–9.

8. John Kenny, *Before the First Fleet: Europeans in Australia, 1606–1777*, Kangaroo Press, Sydney, 1995, p. 105.

9. La Pérouse, *A Voyage round the World* ..., vol. III, pp. 406, 412, 413 and 414.

10. Hesmivy d'Auribeau, quoted in N. Plomley, *The General*, Queen Victoria Museum, Launceston, 1993, p. 282.

11. M. Labillardière, *Voyage in Search of La Pérouse*, vol. 1, p. xix.

12. *The Journal of Post-Captain Nicolas Baudin*, translated by Christine Cornell, Libraries Board of South Australia, Adelaide, 1974, pp. 1 and 6.

13. The Société was formed in 1799 and disbanded in late 1804.

14. François Péron, *Voyage de découvertes aux terres australes*, Paris, 1807, vol. I, p. 9 (translated by present author).

15. Joseph-Marie Degérando, *The Observation of Savage Peoples*, 1800, translated by F. C. T. Moore, London, 1969, 123 pages, pp. 64, 70, 94 and 67 respectively. The original French title was *Considérations sur les méthodes à suivre dans l'observation des Peuples Sauvages.*

16. Quoted in John Kenny, *Bennelong, First Notable Aboriginal*, Royal Australian Historical Society, Sydney, 1973, p. 9.

17. Degérando, pp. 100–1 and 104.

18. Péron, *Voyage de découvertes*, vol. I, pp. 340–1.

19. Péron, *Voyage de découvertes*, vol. I, pp. 377–8.

20. Commodore Baudin to Governor King, Elephant Bay, 23 December 1802, in Helen Micco, *King Island and the Sealing Trade, 1802*, Roebuck Books, Fyshwick, ACT, 1971, pp. 42–3.

21. Cornell, p. 506.

22. Péron, *Voyage de découvertes*, vol. 2. pp. xxv–xxx.

23. Jacques Arago, *Narrative of a Voyage round the World* …, London, 1823, p. i.

24. Arago, *Narrative* …, vol. I, p. 169.

25. Quoted in *Two Voyages to the South Seas by Jules S-C Dumont d'Urville*, translated by Helen Rosenman, Melbourne University Press, 1987, 2 vols, vol. I, p. 284.

26. *The Governor's Noble Guest. Hyacinthe de Bougainville's account of Port Jackson*, 1825, translated and edited by Marc Serge Rivière, Melbourne University Press, 1999, pp. 16, 241–2 and 23.

27. *The Governor's Noble Guest*, pp. 108, 123, 126, 128 and 130–3.

28. *The Governor's Noble Guest*, p. 25.

29. Rosenman, vol. I, pp. xxxv and 193.

30. Rosenman, vol. I, pp. 8, 5–6 and 238.

31. Cyrille Laplace, *Voyage autour du monde par les mers de l'Inde et de Chine* …, Paris, 1833, 4 vols, vol. iv, pp. 51–2.

32. Laplace, vol. I, pp. xiii–xiv.

33. Rosenman, vol. II, pp. 392, 446 and 447.

34. Rosenman, vol. II, p. 495.

35. Rosenman, vol. II, p. 319.

36. A detailed account of D'Urville's death is presented in Olive White,

New Zealand, 1826–7 from the French by Dumont d'Urville, Wingfield Press, Wellington, 1950, p. 45.

37. John Kenny, *Before the First Fleet* ..., pp. 13–14. The spelling of 'Duyfken' is not fixed (one also sees 'Duyffken' and 'Duijffken').

38. J. E. Heeres, *The Part Borne by the Dutch in the Discovery of Australia, 1606–1775*, London, 1899, pp. 36–7, 40 and 21.

39. *Dampier's Voyages*, edited by John Masefield, London, 1906, 2 vols; vol. 1, p. 453 and vol. 2, p. 400.

40. Kenny, p. 112.

41. Heeres, pp. 94–7.

42. Joseph Banks, *The Endeavour Journal of Joseph Banks, 1768–1771*, ed. J. C. Bealgehole, 2 vols, Sydney 1962, vol. 2, p. 55.

43. James Cook, *The Journals of Captain James Cook*, ed. J. C. Bealgehole, 4 vols, Hakluyt Society, Cambridge, 1955–67, vol. 1, p. 312.

44. Banks, vol. 2, p. 134.

45. Banks, vol. 2, p. 122.

Chapter 1   Descriptions of the Aboriginal Australians

1. J. Kenny, pp. 103, 104 and 106.

2. Joseph Banks, vol. II, p. 123.

3. James Cook, vol. I, p. 399.

4. James Cook, vol. III, p. 55.

5. E. Duyker, *The Discovery of Tasmania*, pp. 20 and 85.

6. N. J. B. Plomley, *The General*, pp. 287 and 305.

7. Cornell, p. 330.

8. Duyker, p. 42.

9. Cornell, p. 303.

10. Pierre Bernard Milius, *Récit d'un voyage aux terres australes*, Société Havraise d'Etudes Diverses, 1987, p. 30 (translation by present author).

11. Cornell, p. 344.

12. Labillardière, *Voyage in Search of La Pérouse*, vol. II, p. 39.

13. Plomley, *The General*, p. 285.

14. Cook, vol. III, p. 785.

15. Cornell, p. 320.

16. N. J. B. Plomley, *The Baudin Expedition and the Tasmanian Aborigines, 1802*, Blubber Head Press, Hobart, 1983, p. 123.

17. Cornell, p. 173.
18. Péron, *Voyage de découvertes aux terres australes*, vol. I, p. 73.
19. Marc-Serge Rivière, *A Woman of Courage. Rose de Freycinet's Diary 1817–1820*, National Library of Australia, 1996, p. 51.
20. Labillardière, *Voyage in Search of La Pérouse*, vol. I, p. 471.
21. Extending approximately from Wilson's Promontory to Cape Adieu.
22. Péron, *Voyage de découvertes ...*, vol. I, p. 364.
23. Rosenman, vol. I, pp. 387 and 388.
24. Jacques Arago, *Souvenirs d'un aveugle, Voyage autour du monde*, Paris, 1839, tome 4, pp. 51 and 87.
25. Laplace, vol. III, p. 358.
26. Banks, vol. II, p. 93.
27. Duyker, p. 25.
28. Labillardière, *Voyage in Search of La Pérouse*, vol. II, p. 72.
29. Plomley, *The General*, p. 364.
30. Cornell, p. 344.
31. Milius, p. 48.
32. Milius, pp. 31 and 48 respectively.
33. Jacques Arago, *Narrative of a Voyage Round the World*, vol. I, p. 172.
34. Duyker, pp. 20, 24, 34 and 42.
35. Labillardière, vol. II, p. 34.
36. Plomley, *The General*, pp. 300 and 306.
37. Péron, *Voyage de découvertes ...* , vol. I, pp. 222–3 and 252.
38. Cornell, pp. 324 and 344.
39. Plomley, *The Baudin Expedition ...*, pp. 141 and 131.
40. Péron, *Voyage de découvertes ...*, vol. I, p. 81.
41. Inga Clendinnen, *True Stories*, ABC Books, 1999, p. 3. Clendinnen adds (p. 6): 'What I want to say is "take your hands off her, you Frenchmen". I see them as foreign intruders molesting my country-woman, someone from my territory'.
42. Plomley, *The General*, pp. 283, 300 and 310.
43. The Bible, Genesis, Chapter II, verses 22, 25, and III, 7, 8.
44. J-J. Rousseau, *Lettre à M. D'Alembert*, Flammarion, Paris, 1967, p. 173.
45. Plomley, *The General*, pp. 368 and 292.
46. Plomley, *The Baudin Expedition ...*, p. 107.
47. Rosenman, vol I, pp. 39 and 42.
48. Péron, *Voyage de découvertes*, vol. I, p. 364.

49. Duyker, pp. 34 and 26.

50. Labillardière, vol. II, p. 34.

51. Rosenman, vol. I, p. 170

52. Labillardière, vol. II, p. 49.

53. Labillardière, vol. II, p. 36.

54. Baudin's letter to the Minister of Marine and Colonies from Port Jackson, 11 November 1802 (quoted in Plomley, *The Baudin Expedition* ..., p. 107).

55. Kenny, *Before the First Fleet* ..., p. 106.

56. Rosenman, vol. I, pp. 28, 29, 49 and 48.

57. Rosenman, vol I, pp. 188–9.

58. Duyker, p. 22.

59. Plomley, *The General*, p. 122.

60. Cornell, p. 303. How his head was 'shaved' is not known.

61. Labillardière, vol. II, pp. 54–60.

62. Duyker, p. 25, and Plomley, *The General*, p. 338. The 'Kafirs' (an Arabic word meaning 'non-believer') are the people of southern Africa.

63. Milius, pp. 37 and 48.

64. Lesson, vol. II, p. 275.

65. Bougainville, *Journal de la Navigation autour du globe*, vol. I, p. 516.

66. Duyker, p. 33.

67. Plomley, *The General*, p. 362.

68. Plomley, *The Baudin Expedition* ..., p. 125.

69. Lesson, vol. II, pp. 275 and 279.

70. Rosenman, vol. II, p. 412.

71. Labillardière, vol. II, pp. 39 and 76.

72. Kenny, *Beyond the First Fleet* . . ., p. 108.

73. Freycinet, Louis, *Voyage de découvertes anx terres australes. Navigation et Géographie*, vol. II, Imprimerie Royale, Paris, 1815, p. 292 (translation by present author).

74. Lesson, vol. II, p. 279.

75. Bougainville, vol. I, p. 516.

76. Rosenman, vol II, p. 408.

77. Jacques Arago, *Souvenirs d'un aveugle*, tome 4, p. 93. David Collins, secretary to Governor Phillip until 1796, observed a similar operation — but on a boy — and suggests that the teeth were knocked out rather than broken off. 'When the gum was properly prepared,' he noted,

'the stick was applied as high upon the tooth as the gum would admit of.' Some ten minutes later, the tooth 'was at last forced out'. David Collins, *An Account of the English Colony in New South Wales,* London, 1798, p. 579.

78. Freycinet, *Voyage de découvertes … Navigation et Géographie,* vol. II, p. 292.

79. Bougainville, vol. I, p. 516.

80. As is suggested by the results of archeological excavations. (See Lyndall Ryan, *The Aboriginal Tasmanians,* Allen and Unwin, 2nd edition, 1996, p. xxi.)

81. Duyker, pp. 22 and 42.

82. Bougainville, vol. I, p. 516.

83. Milius, p. 48.

84. Plomley, *The Baudin Expedition,* p. 131.

85. Duyker, p. 26.

86. Rosenman, vol. I, p. 44.

87. A similar practice was observed in New South Wales by David Collins. 'Both sexes use the disgusting practice of rubbing fish oil into their skins,' he wrote, 'but they are compelled to as a guard against the … mosquitoes and flies.' (Collins, op. cit., p. 551).

88. Plomley, *The General,* p. 338, and Labillardière, vol. II, p. 38.

89. Cornell, p. 303.

90. Milius, p. 38.

91. Péron, *Voyage de découvertes …,* vol. I, pp. 226 and 227–8.

92. Plomley, *The Baudin Expedition,* p. 110.

93. Péron, *Voyage de découvertes …,* vol. I, pp. 253–4.

94. Labillardière, vol. II, p. 48.

95. Du Bartas, *Devine Weekes and Workes,* London, 1613, p. 158.

96. Plomley, *The General,* pp. 122–3, 362, 282 and 362 respectively.

97. Cornell, p. 321.

98. Duyker, pp. 94, 83, 80 and 78.

99. Arago, *Narrative …,* vol. II, p. 169.

100. Duyker, p. 25, and Lesson, vol. II, p. 275.

101. Plomley, *The General,* pp. 282, 362 and 122.

102. Duyker, p. 25; Plomley, *The General,* pp. 122 and 362; Milius, p. 48.

103. Plomley, *The General,* pp. 300, 328, 282, 122 and 362.

104. Banks, vol. II, p. 131.

105. Plomley, *The General*, pp. 362 and 300.
106. Freycinet, *Voyage de découvertes ... Navigation et Géographie*, vol. II, p. 292.
107. Péron, *Voyage de découvertes ...*, vol. I, p. 280.
108. J. E. Heeres, *The Part Borne by the Dutch in the Discovery of Australia, 1606–1765*, London, 1899, pp. 41–2, quoted in Kenny, p. 103.
109. Dampier, 1698, pp. 312–6, quoted in Kenny, pp. 107–8.
110. Duyker, p. 25.
111. Plomley, *The General*, p. 283.
112. Labillardière, vol. II, p. 76.
113. Plomley, *The General*, p. 300. A full account of this scarring in Tasmania may be found in N. J. B. Plomley's *The Tasmanian Tribes and Cicatrices as Tribal Indication among the Tasmanian Aborigines*, Queen Victoria Museum and Art Gallery, Tasmania, 1992, 71 pages.
114. Cornell, p. 344.
115. Banks, vol. II, p. 126.
116. Plomley, *The Baudin Expedition ...*, pp. 130–1.
117. Bougainville, vol. I, p. 515.
118. Rosenman, vol II, p. 408.
119. Duyker, p. 33.
120. Plomley, *The General*, p. 300.
121. Cornell, p. 344.
122. Péron, *Voyage de découvertes*, vol. II, p. 163.
123. Milius, p. 48.
124. Arago, *Narrative ...*, vol. II, p. 169.
125. Lesson, vol. II, p. 275.
126. Rosenman, vol II, p. 338.
127. Plomley, *The General*, p. 282.
128. Péron, *Voyage de découvertes*, vol. I, p. 280.
129. Cook, vol. III, pp. 784–5.
130. Plomley, *The General*, pp. 282, 300 and 363.
131. Péron, *Voyage de découvertes*, vol. II, p. 252.
132. Arago, *Souvenirs ...*, vol IV, p. 91.
133. Duyker, pp. 24, 42 and 33.
134. *Le Petit Larousse illustré 2001*, Paris, 2001, p. 780.
135. Plomley, *The General*, pp. 279–81.
136. Péron, *Voyage de découvertes*, vol. I, pp. 279–80.

137. Banks, vol. II, p. 92.

138. Matthew Flinders, *A Voyage to Terra Australis … in the years 1801, 1802 and 1803*, London, 1814, 3 vols, vol. I, pp. 65 and 68.

139. Quoted in G. Stocking, *French Anthropology in 1800*, in *Isis*, 1964, vol. 55, 2, no. 180, p. 142.

140. Robert Dawson, chief agent of the Australian Agricultural Company in Sydney from 1825 to 1829, wrote that 'the natives', if not disturbed, 'would remain for a day or two alternately eating and sleeping, such being their usual habit at a kangaroo feast'. They could also, however, 'fast a very long time' when obliged to do so, and 'tighten their opossum belts about the waist to alleviate the pains of hunger'. (R. Dawson, *The Present State of Australia*, London, 1830, pp. 193 and 203).

141. This presentation of Péron's experiments with the dynamometer is taken from Péron, *Voyage de découvertes …*, vol. I, chapter XX, pp. 446–71. (His complete results, too detailed to present here, are in his pp. 477–84).

142. Péron, *Voyage de découvertes …*, vol. I, p. 482.

143. Péron, *Voyage de découvertes …*, vol. I, p. 477.

144. L. de Freycinet, *Reflections on New South Wales, 1788–1839*, Hordern Press, 2001, pp. 115 and 108. Gaimard's figures for four native women were 32.7 and 5.9.

145. Duyker, pp. 78 and 87.

146. Milius, p. 35.

147. Péron, *Voyage de découvertes …*, vol. I, pp. 252 and 80.

148. Milius, p. 48.

149. Bougainville, vol. I, p. 485.

150. Arago, *Souvenirs*, vol. IV, p. 91.

151. See Rhys Jones, 'Why did the Tasmanians stop eating fish?', in R. Gould, *Explorations in Ethnoarchaeology*, University of New Mexico Press, Albuquerque, 1978, pp. 11–47.

152. Duyker, p. 26. Page 34 of Duyker's book says that Le Dez saw 'fishbones and many burnt shells' but the original French (p. 87) states that he saw '*des aretes de beaucoup de coquillages brulées*': the burnt bones of many shells (the feminine *brulées* referring to *aretes*).

153. Labillardière, vol. II, p. 57.

154. Plomley, *The General*, pp. 305, 341 and 367. On p. 305 Raoul says they

'have no other food than fish', but his context shows clearly that this is the result of 'fishing' exclusively for shellfish.

155. Cornell, pp. 318, 323, 324, 345 and 350.
156. Plomley, *The General*, pp. 116 and 341.
157. Rhys Jones, op.cit., p. 44.
158. Plomley, *The General*, pp. 280, 301, 308.
159. Plomley, *The Baudin Expedition ...*, p. 127.
160. Plomley, *The General*, p. 291.
161. Kenny, p. 142.
162. Plomley, *The General*, p. 282.
163. Péron, *Voyage de découvertes ...*, vol. II, p. 151.
164. Rosenman, vol. I, p. 45.
165. Arago, *Narrative ...*, vol. I, p. 179.
166. Collins, pp. 34 and 36.
167. Freycinet, *Voyage de découvertes ... Navigation et Géographie*, vol. II, pp. 292–3.
168. Rosenman, vol. I, p. 67.
169. Laplace, vol. III, p. 262.
170. Péron, *Voyage de découvertes ...*, vol. II, p. 155.
171. Rosenman, vol. I, p. 43.
172. Francis Barrallier, *Journal of the Expedition into the Interior of New South Wales, 1802*, Marsh Walsh Publishing, Melbourne, 1975, p. 2 (note 5).
173. Barrallier, p. 6.
174. Laplace, vol. III, p. 262.
175. *Bruny d'Entrecasteaux, Voyage to Australia and the South Pacific, 1791–1793*, edited and translated by E. and M. Duyker, Melbourne University Press, Melbourne, 2001, page 121.
176. Lesson, vol. II, pp. 289 and 290.
177. Arago, *Narrative ...*, vol. I, pp. 166 and 171.
178. Arago, *Narrative ...*, vol. II, p. 173.
179. Rosenman, vol. II, p. 387.
180. Quoted in Kenny, p. 103.
181. *Bruny d'Entrecasteaux*, pp. 46 and 147. Dawson (p. 336) says 'the natives of all parts of the colony speak of the distant tribes, or those with whom they are at enmity, as cannibals' because they feel 'they cannot, in any way, so much degrade their enemies in the eyes of the white people, as by calling them cannibals'.

182. Duyker, pp. 22 and 34.

183. Labillardière, vol. I, p. 171.

184. Quoted in Plomley, *The General*, p. 118.

185. Cornell, p. 345.

186. Freycinet, *Voyage de découvertes ... Navigation et Géographie*, vol. II, p. 49.

187. Plomley, *The General*, p. 119.

188. Labillardière, vol. I, p. 175.

189. Cook, *The Journals ...*, vol. III, pp. 786 and 55.

190. Péron, *Voyage de découvertes ...*, vol. II, p. 208.

191. Arago, *Narrative ...*, vol. I, p. 181.

192. Rosenman, vol. I, p. 49.

193. Péron, *Voyage de découvertes*, vol. II, p. 123.

194. Rosenman, vol. I, p. 67.

195. Dawson, p. 70.

196. Péron, *Voyage de découvertes*, vol. II, p. 214.

197. Arago, *Narrative ...*, vol. I, pp. 180–1.

198. Duyker, pp. 29 and 26.

199. Milius, p. 36.

200. Kenny, p. 106.

201. Labillardière, vol. I, pp. 433 and 441.

202. Cornell, p. 174.

203. Péron, *Voyage de découvertes*, vol. II, p. 152.

204. Duyker, pp. 24 and 34.

205. Cornell, p. 307.

206. Duyker, p. 34.

207. Milius, p. 7.

208. Banks, vol. II, p. 129.

209. Duyker, p. 34.

210. Labillardière, vol. II, p. 62.

211. Plomley, *The General*, p. 302.

212. Labillardière, vol. I, p. 222, and G. Mortimer, *Observations and Remarks made during a Voyage ... commanded by John Henry Cox, Esq.*, London, 1791, p. 20.

213. Banks, vol. II, p. 131.

214. Rosenman, vol I, p. 49.

215. Banks, vol. II, p. 134.

216. Freycinet, *Voyage de découvertes … Navigation et Géographie*, vol. II, pp. 293 and 45.
217. Bougainville, vol. I, p. 485.
218. Lesson, vol. II, p. 289.
219. Péron, *Voyage de découvertes*, vol. II, p. 122.
220. *Bruny d'Entrecasteaux …*, p. 125.
221. Plomley, *The General*, pp. 133 and 121.
222. Cornell, pp. 304, 312 and 334.
223. Freycinet, *Voyage de découvertes … Navigation et Géographie*, vol. II, p. 61.
224. Freycinet, *Voyage de découvertes … Navigation et Géographie*, vol. II, pp. 44–5.
225. Freycinet, *Voyage de découvertes … Navigation et Géographie*, vol. II, p. 293.
226. Banks, vol. II, p. 134.
227. Rosenman, vol. II, p. 413.
228. Duyker, p. 20.
229. Plomley, *The General*, pp. 282 and 305.
230. Cornell, p. 345.
231. Labillardière, vol. II, pp. 222 and 42.
232. Cornell, p. 345.
233. Labillardière, vol. II, p. 52.
234. Rosenman, vol. I, p. 45.
235. Laplace, vol. III, p. 257.
236. Kenny, p. 112.
237. Cornell, p. 345.

Chapter 2   Relations between the Aboriginal Australians and the French

1. Duyker, pp. 31–2, 20 and 41.
2. Duyker, p. 47. Captain Cook's first landing at Botany Bay in April 1770 had also met opposition, whereupon, wrote Banks, 'a Musquet loaded with small shot was fird [sic]', wounding one man in the legs. Banks thought, however, that this caused 'no material harm' (Joseph Banks, vol. II, p. 54).
3. Collins, pp. 4 and 17.

4. Collins, p. 18.

5. J. F. G. de Lapérouse, *A Voyage round the World in the Years 1785–8*, vol. III, p. 412.

6. *Bruny d'Entrecasteaux, Voyage to Australia and the South Pacific, 1791–1793*, pp. 32, 36 and 42.

7. Labillardière, vol. I, pp. 221–3, 230 and 233–4. Not all visitors here were met with such apprehension. In 1777 at Adventure Bay (some 20 kilometres away, on the east coast of Bruny Island) Cook had been 'agreeably surprised with a visit from some of the Natives: eight men and a boy' one day, and from no less than 'about twenty' the next, who expressed not 'the least fear or distrust' (*The Journals of Captain James Cook*, vol. III, p. 55).

8. *Bruny ...*, p. 114.

9. Labillardière, vol. II, pp. 32–4, 40–2 and 45.

10. *Bruny ...*, p. 142.

11. Labillardière, vol. II, p. 45.

12. Plomley, *The General*, pp. 224, 279 and 281.

13. Plomley, *The General*, p. 302.

14. Labillardière, vol. II, p. 45.

15. Plomley, *The General*, pp. 361 and 302. The Indigenous people were not of course acquainted with stringed instruments.

16. Plomley, *The General*, p. 300.

17. Labillardière, vol. II, pp. 51 and 61–2.

18. Plomley, *The General*, p. 362.

19. Plomley, *The General*, p. 284.

20. Labillardière, vol. II, pp. 54–5, 57, and 61–2.

21. Plomley, *The General*, pp. 306–7.

22. Labillardière, vol. II, p. 64.

23. *Bruny ...*, pp. 145 and 144. Kermadec's diary (Plomley, *The General*, p. 159) also shows Shrove Tuesday on this date.

24. *Bruny ...*, p. 45.

25. Plomley, *The General*, p. 284.

26. Labillardière, vol. II, pp. 66, 72 and 74.

27. Plomley, *The General*, p. 279.

28. Labillardière, vol. II, pp. 63, 33 and 63.

29. Plomley, *The General*, pp. 279, 285 and 284.

30. Labillardière, vol II, p. 65.

31. *Bruny ...*, p. 146.

32. Labillardière, vol. II, pp. 35–6.

33. *Bruny ...,* p. 147.

34. Plomley, *The General*, p. 302.

35. Cornell, p. 173.

36. Cornell, p. 174.

37. J. Bonnemains, *Mon Voyage aux Terres australes, journal personnel du commandant Baudin*, Imprimerie Nationale, 2001, p. 234.

38. Quoted in F. Horner, *The French Reconnaissance*, Melbourne University Press, 1987, p. 152.

39. F. Péron, *A Voyage of Discovery to the Southern Hemisphere*, London, 1809 (reprinted by Marsh Walsh Publishing, Melbourne, 1975), pp. 67–8 and p. 69.

40. Bonnemains, *Mon Voyage ...*, pp. 249–52. (Péron presents an abridged version of Depuch's account in his *Voyage de découvertes ...*, vol. I, pp. 24–40).

41. Milius, pp. 14–15.

42. Bonnemains, *Mon Voyage ...*, p. 243.

43. Bonnemains, *Mon Voyage ...*, p. 252.

44. Cornell, pp. 301–2.

45. Péron, *A Voyage ...*, pp. 172–4 (French original, vol. III, pp. 220–3).

46. Quoted in N. J. B. Plomley, *The Baudin Expedition and the Tasmanian Aborigines, 1802*, p. 113.

47. Péron, *A Voyage ...*, p. 177–8, and Plomley, *The Baudin Expedition*, p. 113.

48. Péron, *A Voyage ...*, pp. 180–1.

49. Plomley, *The Baudin Expedition*, p. 130.

50. Cornell, pp. 302–3.

51. Cornell, p. 304.

52. Milius, pp. 31–2.

53. Plomley, *The Baudin Expedition*, p. 142.

54. Cornell, pp. 305 and 304.

55. Plomley, *The Baudin Expedition*, p. 142. The Aboriginal historian Kaye McPherson, in her *Risdon Cove, from the Dreamtime to Now* (Manuta Tunapee Puggaluggalia Publishers, Lindisfarne, 2001), says 'the Tasmanian Aboriginal people used a form of Coo or challenge. It is a show of aggression that is never meant to lead to death. If you are not

quick enough to escape the spear thrown at you … it is not the spear-thrower's fault, but rather your lack of agility' (p. 24).

56. Plomley, *The Baudin Expedition*, pp. 122 and 142.
57. Cornell, p. 305.
58. Milius, p. 31.
59. Cornell, p. 305.
60. The phonetic resemblance to the English expression is remarkable. Could these Tasmanians have encountered earlier English explorers? But then, in what context could they have heard this expression? Milius (p. 33) spells this word 'Kaöé' and (p. 34) believed it 'probable that they [the native people] had already communicated with Europeans'. It is certain they knew the effect guns could have, and Baudin (Cornell, p. 321) had 'no doubt that at some other time some of them must have had an unpleasant experience of one'.
61. Cornell, pp. 319–21.
62. Cornell, p. 322.
63. He means 'two' days earlier.
64. Cornell, pp. 323–4.
65. Péron, *A Voyage …*, pp. 197–8. The London 1809 translator's words 'consequence of complete civilization' are a rendering of the French original 'produit heureux du perfectionnement de l'ordre social' (Péron, *Voyage de découvertes …*, vol. I, p. 253).
66. Péron, *A Voyage …*, pp. 198–99.
67. Cornell, p. 324.
68. Plomley, *The Baudin Expedition*, p. 125.
69. Péron, *A Voyage …*, p. 200.
70. Péron, *A Voyage …*, p. 202.
71. As spelled by Péron in the original French edition (vol. I, p. 263 etc.). The 1809 London translation spells this 'Boulanger'.
72. Cornell, p. 340.
73. Plomley, *The Baudin Expedition …*, p. 127. Hamelin says this occurred on '3/4 Ventôse' (thus approximately 22 February).
74. Péron, *Voyage de découvertes …*, vol. I, pp. 278–87 (found in pp. 216–23 of the London translation).
75. Péron, *A Voyage …*, pp. 218–19. 'Savage nations' is a rather free translation of the original *peuplades féroces et grossières* (vol. I, p. 282).
76. Péron, *A Voyage …*, pp. 220 and 223.

77. Cornell, p. 343.

78. Péron, *A Voyage* ..., p. 205.

79. Péron, *Voyage de découvertes* ..., vol. I, pp. 264, 274, 275 and 277.

80. Péron, *Voyage de découvertes* ..., vol. I, p. 305.

81. 'Farouche' can also mean 'wild', 'fierce' or 'savage'.

82. Péron, *Voyage de découvertes* ..., vol. II, pp. 155–6.

83. Cornell, p. 491.

84. Cornell, p. 506.

85. Cornell, pp. 509–10. 'Guichenot' is spelled thus by Baudin (in Cornell, and in the original French in Bonnemains, *Mon Voyage* ...). In Freycinet's list of 'savans et artistes' (*Voyage de découvertes ... Navigation et Géographie*, p. xij) we also see 'Guichenot' which, Freycinet notes, is spelled differently elsewhere 'in error'.

86. Péron, *Voyage de découvertes* ..., vol. II, pp. 216–23. Péron spells 'Guichenault' thus.

87. Arago, *Narrative* ..., vol. I, pp. 170–1 and 179.

88. Arago, *Narrative* ..., vol. I, pp. 171–3.

89. Arago, *Narrative* ..., vol. I, pp. 174–6.

90. During a brief stay in Jervis Bay in November, D'Urville also noted that 'not one of [the natives] attempted the slightest larceny' and spoke of their 'impeccable conduct' (Rosenman, vol. I, p. 67).

91. Rosenman, vol. I, pp. 28–31.

92. Rosenman, vol. I, pp. 35, 41, 42 and 45.

93. Rosenman, vol. I, pp. 39–42.

94. Rosenman, vol. II, pp. 387–8.

95. Rosenman, vol. II, pp. 412–3.

96. *Bruny* ..., pp. 140, 141, 142 and 147.

97. *Bruny* ..., pp. 174, 179 and 232.

98. Plomley, *The General*, pp. 279, 281, 283, 285, 299–300, 301 and 302. The 'immortal' Jean-Jacques Rousseau had died in 1778. His *Discours sur l'origine ... de l'inégalité parmi les hommes* was published in 1754.

99. Milius, p. 10.

100. Freycinet, *Voyage de découvertes* ..., vol II, pp. 162 and 204.

101. Bonnemains, p. 252.

102. Péron, *A Voyage* ..., p. 74. One may recall here, however, how D'Entrecasteaux had been disappointed with his reception among the people of the Pacific.

103. Cornell, p. 344.

104. Péron, *A Voyage …*, pp. 180 and 181.

105. L. Freycinet, *Voyage de découvertes … Navigation et Géographie*, vol. II, pp. 43–4.

106. Milius, p. 36.

107. Baudin, letter to Minister of Marine and Colonies, 11 November 1802, quoted in Plomley, *The Baudin Expedition …*, p. 103.

108. Plomley, *The Baudin Expedition …*, pp. 132 and 133.

109. Péron, *A Voyage …*, pp. 219, 221 and 222.

110. Arago, *Narrative …*, vol. I, pp. 172 and 182.

111. Rosenman, pp. 48 and 388.

112. Kaye McPherson (Tereetee Lore), pp. 32–3.

113. Degérando, p. 64.

114. Rossel, vol. I, p. 552 (translation by present author).

115. Duyker, pp. 41, 33 and 25.

116. Plomley, *The General*, pp. 363, 280, 290, 310–1, 339 and 363 respectively.

117. Péron, *A Voyage …*, pp. 177, 196, 216, 218–19 and 197 respectively. Péron's vocabularly list, published in the 1824 French edition of this work, may be consulted in Appendix 1.

118. Rossel, vol. I, p. 552. A more detailed list (some 140 words) may be found in Plomley, *The General*, pp. 312–17.

119. Labillardière, vol. II, Appendix, pp. 43–47.

120. Plomley, *The General*, p. 289.

121. Plomley, *The General*, pp. 295 and 296.

122. Cornell, p. 303.

123. Plomley, *The General*, p. 305.

124. Rosenman, vol. II, p. 416.

125. Arago, *Narrative …*, vol. I, pp. 171, 174 and 175. One recalls that in the D'Entrecasteaux Channel Baudin had noted similarly how ' "Kaoué, kaoué" kept recurring' (Cornell, p. 320).

126. Arago, *Narrative …*, vol. II, pp. 269 and 271.

127. Bonnemains, *Mon Voyage …*, pp. 250 and 251.

128. In January 1802 Flinders had noticed here too how in 'the difficulty of pronouncing the F and S, they resemble the Port Jackson natives. (Flinders, vol. I, 1814, p. 67).

129. Rosenman, vol. I, pp. 40–1 and 46.

130. Lesson, vol. II, p. 296.

131. Lesson, vol. II, pp. 296–7, and Collins, vol. I, pp. 611–12. Collins (p. 609) also said the native people's language 'certainly has no analogy with any other language', although he found it 'extremely grateful to the ear, being in many instances expressive and sonorous'.

132. Duyker, pp. 40 and 46.

133. Plomley, *The General*, p. 304.

134. Péron, *A Voyage ...*, pp. 173–4.

135. Péron, *Voyage de découvertes ...*, vol. I, p. 224.

136. Murray Upper tapes, Black Oral History Collection, History Department, James Cook University, quoted in Henry Reynolds, *The Other Side of the Frontier*, James Cook University, Townsville, 1981, p. 24.

137. *Bruny ...*, p. 146.

138. Plomley, *The General*, p. 340.

139. Plomley, *The General*, p. 377.

140. Cornell, pp. 320, 324 and 340.

141. Plomley, *The Baudin Expedition ...*, pp. 111 and 127. At Endeavour River in July 1770 three 'indians' had kept one of Cook's men for 'about half an hour, behaving most civilly to him, only satisfying their curiosity by examining his body' (Banks, II, p. 98).

142. Péron, *A Voyage ...*, p. 217.

143. Rosenman, vol. I, p. 41. When Matthew Flinders observed in 1802 that the native people of King George Sound kept their women 'out of sight with seeming jealousy', he felt that they 'appeared to suspect the same conduct in us', and thus believed 'that there must be women in the ship'. (Flinders, *A Voyage ...*, vol. I, p. 65).

Chapter 3   Relations between the Aboriginal Australians themselves

1. This was probably Henrietta Villa, built in 1822. John Piper (1773–1851) was an important landowner in Sydney, and in 1825 became chairman of directors of the Bank of New South Wales. Point Piper is named after him, and his portrait is today in the Mitchell Library.

2. Jacques Arago, *Narrative ...*, vol. 2, pp. 170–71. Some twenty years earlier here in Sydney David Collins had seen a woman a few hours after

giving birth, and had noted how, 'to my great surprise, she was walking about alone and picking up sticks to mend her fire' (Collins, p. 561).

3. Jacques Arago, *Souvenirs ...*, vol. IV, p. 96.

4. Labillardière, vol. II, pp. 46, 47, 55–6 and 48 respectively.

5. Arago, *Souvenirs ...*, vol. IV, pp. 97–8.

6. Rosenman, vol. I, pp. 44 and 40.

7. Laplace, vol. III, pp. 202 and 263. His source is doubtless David Collins who observed the burial of a woman with her baby. 'When the body was placed in the grave,' he wrote, 'the bye-standers were amazed to see the father himself place the living child in it with the mother. Having laid the child down, he threw upon it a large stone, and the grave was instantly filled in by the other natives' (Collins, op. cit, p. 607).

8. Duyker, p. 25.

9. Cornell, p. 491.

10. Péron, *A Voyage ...*, p. 181.

11. Plomley, *The General*, pp. 368 and 311.

12. Labillardière, vol. II, p. 61.

13. Péron, *A Voyage ...*, pp. 199–200.

14. Barrallier, pp. 22–4.

15. Milius, p 39. Collins thought the women were 'the mere slaves of the men', although he also believed that they could be 'the causes of their quarrels' (Collins, op. cit., p. 583).

16. Plomley, *The General*, pp. 341–2.

17. Laplace, vol. III, p. 262.

18. Plomley, *The General*, p. 364.

19. Barrallier, p. 22 (note 31). In 1826 Dawson had described how the women 'are made to do all the drudgery' and 'carry the wood for fires, make the nets for fishing, and carry every thing that they move about with' (Dawson, p. 67). Watkin Tench, who lived at Port Jackson from January 1788 until December 1791, considered that 'women are in all respects treated with savage barbarity' (Captain W. Tench, *A Complete Account of the Settlement at Port Jackson*, London, 1793, p. 199).

20. Arago, *Narrative ...*, vol. II, p. 170.

21. Laplace, vol. III, p. 263.

22. Rosenman, vol. 1, p. 45.

23. Milius, p. 48.

24. Lesson, vol. II, p. 291. Dawson (op. cit., p. 153) noted how 'the blacks generally take their wives from other tribes … and, in the event of her making resistance, which is frequently the case, her paramour silences her with a severe blow on the head with his waddy while he is carrying her off'. Collins (op. cit., p. 559) too had described how 'the poor wretch is stolen upon in the absence of her protectors, being first stupefied with blows, inflicted with clubs or wooden swords, on the head, back and shoulders, every one of which is followed by a stream of blood'.

25. Arago, *Souvenirs* …, p. 92.

26. Lesson, vol. II, p. 291.

27. Plomley, *The General*, pp. 309, 283, 302, 295, 363 and 365–7 respectively. The Englishmen Collins and Dawson also seem to have different views on this subject. Collins (p. 559) noted that 'many of the men with whom we were acquainted did not confine themselves to one woman' and observed that 'in general … the two women were always jealous of and quarrelling with each other'. Dawson (p. 154) believed that 'polygamy is not common amongst them, although it sometimes occurs'. 'I know,' he wrote, 'of only three instances of it, and the wives … lived, as far as I saw, in perfect harmony with each other.'

28. Louis Freycinet, *Voyage de découvertes aux terres australes. Navigation et Géographie*, vol. II, p. 293.

29. Rosenman, vol. I, p. 45.

30. Cornell, p. 506.

31. Duyker, p. 34.

32. Plomley, *The General*, p. 290.

33. Cornell, p. 350.

34. Milius, p. 48.

35. Lesson, vol. II, p. 286.

36. Duyker, p. 41.

37. Cornell, pp. 486–7.

38. Milius, p. 37.

39. Cornell, pp. 345 and 506.

40. Duyker, p. 32.

41. Milius, p. 37.

42. Rosenman, vol. I, p. 88.

43. Arago, *Souvenirs ...,* pp. 53–4.

44. 'bois de fer'.

45. Literally *casse-têtes,* or clubs.

46. About 66 centimetres.

47. About 262 grams.

48. Eugène Delessert, *Voyages dans les deux océans, Atlantique et Pacifique, 1844–1847,* Paris, 1848, pp. 132–5. Parts of Delessert's description of the boomerang indeed rather resemble that of Major Sir Thomas Mitchell in his *Three Expeditions to the Interior of Eastern Australia,* London, 1839, vol. 2, pp. 348–9.

49. Lesson, vol. 2, p. 286. Dawson felt similarly. 'They fall to with their waddys upon each other's heads, which are voluntarily held forward to receive alternately blows that would fell an ox, till one or more falls or is disabled' (pp. 65–6).

50. Arago, *Souvenirs ...,* pp. 87–8 and 99.

51. Arago, *Narrative ...* The text is from vol. II, p. 172, and the illustration is opposite this page.

52. Arago, *Souvenirs ...,* pp. 116–21.

53. Lesson's account may be consulted in his journal, vol. II, pp. 283–5.

54. Lesson (vol. II, 285–6) wrote that this woman was 'a sorceress! ... who was reproached for having caused the death by drowning of the tribe's most skilful fisherman. She was also accused of a second crime: a chief who fell out of a tree and was badly hurt had a dream ... in which this unfortunate woman was represented as having used her power to make him fall'.

55. Lesson (vol. II, p. 285) says 'the wounded savage was accused by Hati, chief of the Paramatta people, to be the cause of the death of his two nephews'. Lesson, however, thought it was 'obvious that the two children had died of a serious illness'.

56. Rosenman, pp. 85–8.

57. Milius, p. 48. The Englishmen Collins (pp. 586–92) and Dawson (pp. 63–5) report similar observations regarding Indigenous punishment.

58. Péron, *Voyage de découvertes ...,* vol. I, pp. 265 and 272.

59. Bonnemains, *Baudin in Australian Waters,* pp. 125 and 126.

60. Péron, *A Voyage ...,* pp. 208, 209 and 210.

61. Plomley, *The Baudin Expedition,* pp. 138 and 140–1.

62. Cornell, p. 341.

63. Arago, *Souvenirs ...,* pp. 99–100.

64. Lesson, vol. II, p. 292. Collins (op. cit., p. 601) wrote that 'the first peculiarity noticeable in their funeral ceremonies is the disposal of the dead: their young they consign to the grave; those who have passed the middle age are burnt'.

65. Arago, *Souvenirs ...,* pp. 100–101.

66. Lesson, vol. II, p. 292. Collins believed that, if every country in the world had a religion, he would 'safely pronounce them [the Aborigines] an exception' (op. cit., p. 547).

67. Delessert, p. 140.

Chapter 4   Relations between the Aboriginal Australians and the British

1. Péron, *A Voyage ...,* pp. 271–90. Péron claims here that it was he and his companions who 'succeeded in persuading governor King ... to order a new expedition to the Western Mountains, in October 1802, and the conducting of it was entrusted to M. Bareiller [sic], a French emigrant' (p. 290).

2. Sydney Town will in fact be incorporated as a city only in July 1842. King was governor from 1800 to 1806, and Macquarie from 1810 to 1821.

3. Arago, *Narrative ...,* vol. 2, pp. 161–7.

4. Lesson, vol. II, pp. 233 and 253. Lesson's figure for 1824 is clearly an estimate. In his *150 years of Sydney* (Shakespeare Head Press, 1933, p. 69) C. H. Bertie presents the following figures for the 'population of Sydney': 1030 persons in 1788, 2537 in 1800, 6158 in 1810 and 12 079 in 1820.

5. Arago, *Narrative ...,* vol. 2, p. 154.

6. Arago, *Souvenirs ...,* p. 52.

7. Laplace, vol. III, p. 361.

8. Lesson, vol. II, p. 291.

9. Bougainville, vol. I, p. 486.

10. Arago, *Souvenirs ...,* p. 121. It has been estimated that the number of Aborigines in New South Wales declined from approximately 53 400 in 1788 to 25 000 in 1861 (in *Australians: A Historical Atlas,* Fairfax,

Syme and Weldon Associates, 1987, p. 141). Justice Barron Field was Judge-Advocate in New South Wales from 1817 to 1828, and was one of the founders of the Society for promoting Christian knowledge among the Aborigines.

11. Arago, *Narrative* ..., vol. II, p. 168.

12. Lesson, vol. II, p. 277.

13. Delessert, pp. 150–1.

14. Lesson, vol. II, pp. 291 and 278. At one time Bungaree had five wives (named Askabout, Boatman, Broomstick, Onion and Pincher). Subsequently Gooseberry became his principal wife, with the title of Queen (*The Australian Dictionary of Biography*, Melbourne University Press, 1966, vol. I, p. 177).

15. *Memoirs of Madame la Marquise de Montespan*, London, 1895, vol. I, pp. 224–7.

16. *The Australian Dictionary of Biography*, Melbourne University Press, 1966, vol. I, p. 177.

17. Bougainville, vol. I, pp. 485–6.

18. Bougainville, vol. I, p. 487.

19. Marc Serge Rivière, *The Governor's Noble Guest*, p. 212.

20. Louis Freycinet, *Voyage de découvertes* ..., vol. II, p. 292.

21. Arago, *Souvenirs* ..., pp. 77–8.

22. Arago, *Narrative* ..., pp. 173–5.

23. Arago, *Souvenirs* ..., pp. 62–3.

24. Bougainville, vol. I, p. 485.

25. Arago, *Souvenirs* ..., p. 51.

26. Laplace, vol. III, pp. 358–9.

27. Delessert, pp. 149–50 and 148.

28. Louis de Freycinet, *Reflections on New South Wales, 1788–1839*, p. 308.

29. Milius, p. 49.

30. Arago, *Souvenirs* ..., pp. 105–6.

31. Lesson, vol. II, p. 277.

32. Freycinet, *Reflections* ..., p. 308.

33. Arago, *Souvenirs* ..., p. 106.

34. Lesson, vol. II, p. 276.

35. Bougainville, vol. I, p. 486.

36. Freycinet, *Reflections* ..., p. 308.

37. Arago, *Narrative* ..., vol. 2, pp. 168–9.

38. Lesson, vol. II, pp. 292 and 291.
39. Milius, p. 49.
40. Freycinet, *Voyage de découvertes* ..., p. 294.
41. Freycinet, *Reflections* ..., pp. 306, 309 and 310.
42. Arago, *Souvenirs* ..., p. 88.
43. Rosenman, vol. I, p. 90.
44. Lesson, vol. II, pp. 275–6.
45. Bougainville, vol. I, pp. 457–8. (In Rivière, p. 150, the translator translates 'formes de civilisation' as 'so-called civilisation'.)
46. Laplace, vol. III, p. 361.
47. Delessert, p. 150.
48. Delessert, pp. 177–8.
49. Delessert, p. 151.
50. Rosenman, vol. I, p. 189.
51. Rosenman, vol. II, p. 462.
52. Hobart was established in 1804, after a brief attempt at settlement at Risdon Cove. A detailed account of the circumstances surrounding this letter may be found in Frank Horner's *The French Reconnaissance*, pp. 266–75.
53. The full text of this letter may be seen in Helen Micco, *King Island and the Sealing Trade, 1802*, pp. 42–3.

Bibliography

Arago, Jacques, *Narrative of a Voyage Round the World*, London, 1823, 2 vols.

Arago, Jacques, *Souvenirs d'un aveugle: Voyage autour du monde*, Hortet et Ozanne, Paris, 1839, 4 vols.

Australians: A Historical Atlas, Fairfax, Syme and Weldon Associates, Sydney, 1987.

Banks, Joseph, *The Endeavour Journal of Joseph Banks, 1768-1771*, ed. J. C. Beaglehole, Trustees of the Public Library of New South Wales in association with Angus and Robertson, Sydney, 1962, 2 vols.

Barrallier, Francis, *Journal of the Expedition into the Interior of New South Wales, 1802*, Marsh Walsh Publishing, Melbourne, 1975.

Bertie, C. H., *150 Years of Sydney*, Shakespeare Head Press, Sydney, 1933.

Bonnemains, Jacqueline, *Baudin in Australian Waters. The Artwork of the French Voyage of Discovery to the Southern Lands, 1800-1804*, Oxford University Press, Australia, 1988.

Bonnemains, Jacqueline, *Mon Voyage aux terres australes, journal personnel du commandant Baudin*, Imprimerie Nationale, 2001.

Bougainville, Hyacinthe de, *Journal de la navigation autour du globe*, Paris, 1837, 2 vols.

Bruny d'Entrecasteaux, Voyage to Australia and the South Pacific,

1791-1793, translated by E. and M. Duyker, Melbourne University Press, Melbourne, 2001.

Clendinnen, Inga, *True Stories*, ABC Books, Sydney, 1993.

Collins, David, *An Account of the Colony of New South Wales*, London, 1798.

Cook, James, *The Journals of Captain James Cook*, ed. J. C. Beaglehole, Hakluyt Society, Cambridge, 1955–67, 4 vols.

Cornell, Christine, *The Journal of Post-Captain Nicolas Baudin*, Libraries Board of South Australia, Adelaide, 1974.

Dawson, Robert, *The Present State of Australia: A Description of the Country ... and of Its Aboriginal Inhabitants*, London, 1830.

Degérando, Joseph-Marie, *The Observation of Savage Peoples, 1800*, translated by F. C. T. Moore, Routledge and Kegan Paul, London, 1969.

Delessert, Eugène, *Voyages dans les deux océans, Atlantique et Pacifique, 1844-1847*, Paris, 1848.

Dictionnaire historique de la langue française, Paris, 1885.

Diderot, Denis, *Oeuvres complètes*, Paris, 1875.

Du Bartas, *Devine Weekes and Workes*, London, 1613.

Duyker, E., *The Discovery of Tasmania*, St David's Park Publishing, Hobart, 1992.

Flinders, Matthew, *A Voyage to Terra Australis ... in the Years 1801, 1802 and 1803*, London, 1814.

Freycinet, Louis de, *Reflections on New South Wales, 1788-1839*, Hordern Press, Potts Point, NSW, 2001. This is a translation by Thomas Cullity of Chapters XXIX to XL, 'Historique', vol. 2, parts 2 and 3, of Freycinet's *Voyage autour du monde ... pendant les années 1817-1820*, Paris, 1839.

Freycinet, Louis de, *Voyage autour du monde ... Historique*, vol. 2, part 2, Paris, 1939.

Freycinet, Louis, *Voyage de découvertes aux terres australes. Navigation et Géographie*, Imprimerie Royale, Paris, 1815.

Heeres, J. E., *The Part Borne by the Dutch in the Discovery of Australia, 1606-1765*, London, 1899.

Horner, Frank, *The French Reconnaissance*, Melbourne University Press, Melbourne, 1987.

Jasmin, J. 'Faibles sauvages … corps indigènes, corps indigents', in *Mers australes-terres australes, Baudin 1800-4*, Bibliothèque Municipale du Havre, 1988.

Jones, Rhys, 'Why did the Tasmanians stop eating fish?', in R. Gould, *Explorations in Ethnoarcheology*, University of New Mexico Press, Albuquerque, 1987, pp. 11-47.

Kenny, John, *Before the First Fleet. Europeans in Australia, 1606-1777*, Kangaroo Press, Sydney, 1995.

Kenny, John, *Bennelong, First Notable Aboriginal*, Royal Australian Historical Society, Sydney, 1973.

Labillardière, Jacques de, *Voyage in Search of La Pérouse*, Stockdale, London, 1800, 2 vols.

La Pérouse, J. F. G. de, *A Voyage Round the World in the Years 1785-8*, ed. M. L. A. Milet-Mureau, London, 1798, 3 vols.

Laplace, Cyrille, *Voyage autour du monde par les mers de l'Inde et de Chine*, Paris, 1833-5, 4 vols.

Lesson, René Primavère, *Voyage autour du monde sur la corvette 'La Coquille'*, Paris, 1838, 2 vols.

Masefield, John, *Dampier's Voyages*, London, 1906, 2 vols.

McPherson, Kaye (Tereetee Lore), *Risdon Cove, From the Dreamtime to Now. The Centenary of Federation, 2001*, Manuta Tunapee Puggaluggalia Publishers, Lindisfarne, Tasmania, 2001.

Memoirs of Madame la Marquise de Montespan, London, 1895, 2 vols.

Micco, Helen, *King Island and the Sealing Trade*, Roebuck Books, Fyshwick, ACT, 1971.

Milius, Pierre Bernard, *Récit d'un voyage aux terres australes*, Société Havraise d'Etudes Diverses, 1987.

Mitchell, Major Sir Thomas, *Three Expeditions to the Interior of Eastern Australia*, London, 1839, 2 vols.

Mortimer, G., *Observations and Remarks Made during a Voyage … Commanded by John Henry Cox, Esq.*, London, 1791.

Péron, François and Freycinet, Louis, *Voyage de découvertes aux terres australes. Historique,* 2 vols, Paris, 1807 and 1816.

Péron, François and Freycinet, Louis, *Voyage de découvertes ... Atlas (Historique) par MM. Lesueur et Petit,* Paris, 1807.

Péron, François, *A Voyage of Discovery to the Southern Hemisphere ...,* London, 1809. Reprinted by Marsh Walsh Publishing, Melbourne, 1975. (Translation of vol. 1 of *Voyage de ...*).

Plomley, N. J. B., *The Baudin Expedition and the Tasmanian Aborigines, 1802,* Blubber Head Press, Hobart, 1983.

Plomley, N. J. B., *The General,* Queen Victoria Museum, Launceston, 1993.

Plomley, N. J. B. *The Tasmanian Tribes and Cicatrices ...,* Queen Victoria Museum, Hobart, 1992.

Reynolds, Henry, *The Other Side of the Frontier,* History Department, James Cook University, Townsville, 1981.

Richard, Hélène, *Le Voyage de D'Entrecasteaux à la recherche de Lapérouse,* Paris, 1986.

Rivière, Marc Serge, *A Woman of Courage. Rose de Freycinet's Diary, 1817-20,* National Library of Australia, Canberra, 1996.

Rivière, Marc Serge, *The Governor's Noble Guest,* Melbourne University Press, Melbourne, 1999.

Rosenman, Helen, *Two Voyages to the South Seas by Jules S-C. Dumont d'Urville,* Melbourne University Press, Melbourne, 1987, 2 vols.

Rousseau, Jean-Jacques, *Emile for Today,* Heinemann, London, 1956.

Rousseau, Jean-Jacques, *Lettre à M. D'Alembert,* Flammarion, Paris, 1967.

Rousseau, Jean-Jacques, *Rousseau, Judge of Jean-Jacques,* University of New England Press, Hanover, NH, 1990.

Rousseau, Jean-Jacques, *The Social Contract and Discourses,* London, 1913.

Rossel, Paul de, *Voyage de Dentrecasteaux à la recherche de Lapérouse,* Paris, 1808, 2 vols.

Ryan, Lyndall, *The Aboriginal Tasmanians,* Allen and Unwin, St Leonards, NSW, 1996.

Scott, Ernest, *The Life of Matthew Flinders*, Angus and Robertson, Sydney, 1914.

Stocking, G., 'French Anthropology in 1800', in *Isis*, 1964, vol. 35, 2, no. 180.

Tench, Captain W., *A Complete Account of the Settlement at Port Jackson*, London, 1793.

The Australian Dictionary of Biography, Melbourne University Press, Melbourne, 1966.

Triebel, L. A., *The French Exploration of Australia*, Hobart, 1957.

White, Olive, *New Zealand 1826-7 from the French by Dumont d'Urville*, Wingfield Press, Wellington, 1950.

Index